REBELS & INFORMERS

Stirrings of Irish Independence

OLIVER KNOX

St. Martin's Press

New York

St. Martin's Press

REBELS AND INFORMERS

Copyright © 1997 by Oliver Knox

St. Martin's Press, Scholarly and Reference Division,
175 Fifth Avenue, New York, N.Y. 10010

First published in the United States of America in 1997

Printed in Great Britain by The University Press, Cambridge

ISBN 0-312-21097-3

Library of Congress Cataloging-in-Publication Data

Knox, Oliver
Rebels and informers : stirrings of Irish independence / Oliver Knox.
p.   cm.
Includes bibliographical references and index.
ISBN 0-312-21097-3
1. Ireland – History – Rebellion of 1798.   2. Ireland – History – 1760–1820.   I. Title.
DA949.K58   1997
941.507–dc21   97-39214   CIP

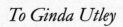

To Ginda Utley

Contents

Illustrations

The author and publisher would like to thank the following for permission to reproduce illustrations: Plates 1 and 4, National Portrait Gallery, London; 3, 6 and 7, National Library of Ireland; 5, Ulster Museum. Plate 2 is reproduced from R.R. Madden, *The United Irishmen, their Lives and Times* (London, 1857–60).

Acknowledgements

My hours have been mostly spent in the British Library, in the old round reading room, where I have never ceased to be grateful for the courtesy and expedition of the staff whom I have so often plagued with elementary questions. The same applies to the rather less frequent hours spent, in an atmosphere of even greater hushedness, in the Manuscript Rooms of the British Museum. I envy those who have spent very great parts of their life in the dedicated pursuit of their studies, and am sure that, whatever may be the differences between the old and the new Library, at least the staff and curators of the new library will be equally diligent and helpful.

The London Library in St James's Square provides the principal reason why many of my coevals have resisted the temptation to retreat into the countryside in their later years. It is impossible to express quite how much we members owe to all those who serve in this splendid institution; I hope I have not abused too many of the privileges of membership: I have sometimes telephoned at the end of the day with a trifling bibliographical enquiry, to be answered with unfailing courtesy.

Then there are my thanks to those who work in the Public Record Office in Kew (and in Belfast), and to public libraries in many other counties where I have pursued all too erratic lines of enquiry.

As for mentors and friends, I hope particularly I have not tired the patience and good will of that wonderful veteran of this period, Professor R.B. McDowell. Also it will be readily apparent how much I owe to the works of Professor Roy Foster, the late Professor J.C. Beckett and of Marianne Elliott, whose biography of Wolfe Tone can fairly be called definitive; I hope that some readers will be encouraged to pursue, in her work, their enquiries into the life and times of this most engaging and spirited (and doomed) of characters.

ix

Acknowledgements

I have had agreeable and useful conversation with Stella Tillyard, author of *Aristocrats*, which brought so vividly to life the characters of the four Lennox sisters, one of whom, Emily, was the mother of Lord Edward Fitzgerald.

I spent one happy day in the company of Guy Strutt, whose ancestors and many of the portraits in whose family house have so many Fitzgerald connections (Charlotte Strutt was one of Edward Fitzgerald's sisters, though very much on the other side).

Surfings over the Internet have led me to make enquiries in the States; Virginia Weathers in particular, of the University of South Carolina, has enabled me to find out a little more about the character of the scoundrel Digges, one of the probable early informers of my tale.

My friend Roger Lubbock ploughed nobly through an earlier version, and made perceptive comments which led me to considerable recasting. Ingrid Grimes was an extraordinarily sensitive, thorough and patient editor. At John Murray, Grant MacIntyre provided exactly the discreet, amused and highly intelligent help that most authors only dream about.

Next, I am enormously grateful to Virginia Utley; not only for her skilful interpretation of many difficult points, but her many suggestions and above all her gentle, persistent encouragement throughout. I could not have done without her skill and patience during the inevitable crises – computer crashes, disk losses, and simply loss of nerve.

Finally, I write this preface on the eve of my golden wedding; but I owe far, far more than fifty years of love and gratitude to Patty, my wife.

Chronology

1791 *August*   Wolfe Tone's pamphlet *An Argument on Behalf of the Catholics of Ireland* published in Dublin
14 October   Belfast Society of United Irishmen founded: Chairman, Samuel McTier
9 November   First meeting of Dublin Society of United Irishmen: Chairman, Simon Butler; Secretary, Napper Tandy
December   Catholic Committee split; 'old guard' of Lord Kenmare and 67 others leave; 'young turks', headed by Keogh, take over

Louis XVI tries to flee France (June), only to be brought back to Paris and forced to accept the constitution
Boswell's *Life of Johnson* published
Premiere of Mozart's *Die Zauberflöte* in Vienna

1792 *4 January*   First issue of *Northern Star*, organ of Belfast Society of United Irishmen (ed. Sam Neilson)
February   Burke writes 'A Letter to Sir Hercules Langrishe . . . on the Subject of Roman Catholics in Ireland'; Catholic Committee's petition for parliamentary franchise rejected by Irish House of Commons (though Catholic Relief Act allows Catholics to practise Law); William Drennan concerned in petition to boycott sugar in campaign to abolish slavery
25 July   Tone appointed Assistant Secretary to the Catholic Committee
18 November   At dinner at White's in Paris, Lord Edward Fitzgerald renounces his title; revolutionary toasts are drunk
December   Dublin Society of United Irishmen encourages Volunteers; 'Citizen Soldiers, to Arms'; Hamilton Rowan's and Drennan's prosecutions for sedition begin

18 December   Catholic delegates, accompanied by Tone, sail from Belfast to London to present petition to the King (their coach drawn through Belfast by sympathizers)

April   France declares war against Austria

August   The Jacobins gain the upper hand and King Louis' powers suspended; the royal family thrown into prison; Austria and Prussia attack France

September   Massacres, in which 12,000 prisoners, priests, aristocrats and counter-revolutionaries murdered; a Republic formally declared

French win great victory at Valmy, to the joy of republican sympathizers everywhere, especially in Belfast

December   King George III embodies the militia

Coleridge and Burke concerned with the abolition of slavery; the former writing a Greek Sapphic Ode, the latter proposing a plan for orderly abolition

Paine's *Rights of Man* cheaply distributed, then banned; Paine, charged with sedition, flees to Paris

Shelley born

Mary Wollstonecraft's *A Vindication of the Rights of Women* published

In Bonn, Haydn meets Beethoven and accepts him as a pupil

1793   *2 January*   Catholic delegates, Tone in attendance, present petition to George III

11 January   Committee of United Irishmen start planning parliamentary reform

16 February   Ulster convention of Volunteers meets at Dungannon

March   Ulster Volunteer Movement quashed by proclamation; movement of arms forbidden under the Gunpowder Act (Fitzgerald objects vigorously at Committee stage)

9 April   Catholic Relief Act extends parliamentary franchise to Catholics, allowing them to hold most civil and military offices

19 April   Militia Act fixes new strength at around 15,000

June   Colonel Oswald, agent of French revolutionary Government, secretly visits Ireland

16 August   Convention Act forbids popular assemblies claiming to represent the people under the pretext of preparing petitions to King or Parliament

November   Rowan travels to Edinburgh to support cause of Scottish radicals

January   Louis XVI executed

February   France declares war against Britain and Holland, and the Terror gains pace

April Civil War breaks out in the Vendée

July Marat murdered in his bath by Charlotte Corday; Robespierre
elected to the Committee of Public Safety

October Marie Antoinette executed

In Scotland, Muir and other radicals sentenced to be transported to
Botany Bay; Burns writes 'Scots wha hae' in protest

Kant's *Religion within the Limits of Reason Alone* published

Back from France, Wordsworth writes 'An Evening Walk' and
Descriptive Sketches

Haydn composes 6 string quartets, Beethoven his earliest piano trios

1794 *29 January* Rowan at last brought to trial for distributing 'Citizen
Soldiers, to Arms'; sentenced to two years' imprisonment and
£500 fine

15 February United Irish plan for parliamentary reform
published in *Dublin Evening Post*

1 March Catholics allowed to take degrees at Dublin University

1 April Revd William Jackson, French agent, arrives in Dublin
with John Cockaigne; meets Tone and Rowan; is arrested for
high treason, but not tried until April 1795

14 April Irish-born General Dillon executed in France

April–May Tone makes compact with Government: voluntary
exile, no prosecution

2 May Rowan escapes from prison; fishing-boat takes him to
Brittany; he stays for a year in Paris

23 May Dublin Society of United Irishmen raided and
suppressed

25 June Drennan tried for seditious libel and acquitted

11 July Coalition Government formed in London; Duke of
Portland becomes Home Secretary, responsible for Ireland

3 December Catholic Committee prepares fresh petitions in
Dublin for repeal of penal laws

End of year Fitzwilliam sails to take up brief Lord-Lieutenancy,
determined to topple old Ascendancy guard

Treason trials in Britain; continuing upheavals in France

July Robespierre (whom Rowan met briefly in Paris) executed: his
death the subject of a play by Coleridge and Southey

England captures several French West Indian islands, and assumes
protectorate of Corsica, the better to control the Mediterranean

1795 *4 January* Fitzwilliam sworn in as Lord-Lieutenant, and at once
tries to dismiss Beresford and other Ascendancy grandees

24 January Belfast Protestants petition Parliament for repeal of
all penal statutes against Catholics

23 February   Fitzwilliam dismissed

31 March   Camden sworn in as new Lord-Lieutenant

10 May   Ulster United Irishmen meet secretly in Belfast and adopt new constitution (including cells, oaths, etc.)

13 June   Tone embarks on *Cincinnatus* from Belfast, for USA

18 July   Rowan reaches Philadelphia from France

7 September   Lawrence O'Connor, schoolmaster and Defender, hanged for high treason at Naas

21 September   'Battle of the Diamond' in Co. Armagh between Peep O'Day Boys and Defenders leads to foundation of Orange Order: 30 dead on field

1 October   Catholic seminary opens at Maynooth

War against France goes badly for most of the year

Corresponding Societies – with many radical reform programmes, similar to those of the United Irishmen – hold mass meetings in London

1 October   In St James's Park, immense mob batters state coach taking the King to the House of Lords: cries of 'Bread! Peace! No Pitt!'

Keats and Carlyle born

Paine's *Age of Reason*, part 2, published

1796   *1 January*   Tone sails from New York to Le Havre; once in Paris, he soon establishes himself as envoy of United Irishmen, and continually presses for invasion of Ireland

24 March   Insurrection Act provides death penalty for administering illegal oaths: curfews and arms searches instigated

June–August   Fitzgerald and O'Connor set off to travel through Switzerland to discuss with General Hoche United Irishmen's support for French invasion

12 July   Orange parades in Lurgan and Portadown

16 September   Russell, Neilsen and many others suspected of French sympathies arrested in Belfast and charged with high treason

26 October   Habeas Corpus suspended

22–7 December   French fleet, Tone and some 14,000 troops aboard, arrive in Bantry Bay, Co. Cork; unable to land in wild storms over Christmas, the expedition disperses and returns to Brest

Triumphs in Italy for Napoleon

British recapture 'slave islands' from French

Proposals to abolish slavery defeated in the House of Commons

Coleridge, clad in black, gives political lectures ('Preaching spread a sort of sanctity over my sedition')

Washington retires from public life
Gibbon's *Memoirs of my Own Life* published

1797 *March*   General Lake starts 'pacification' of an Ulster in turmoil
May–June   Mutinies at Spithead and Nore, partly engineered by
Duckett (many Irishmen in fleet)
19 May   *Northern Star* presses broken up in Belfast by militia
28 September   *The Press* (ed. Arthur O'Connor) publishes its first
number
17 October   William Orr, Presbyterian United Irishman, hanged
for administering illegal oaths: Drennan writes elegy
November   Army in Ireland described by its new
Commander-in-Chief Sir Ralph Abercromby as 'in a state of
licentiousness'

Tentative peace overtures by England to France fail (but are
reopened in April)
February   Nelson wins great victory off Cape St Vincent
July   Burke dies
October   Admiral Duncan cripples Dutch fleet at Camperdown, thus
ending threat of French invasion of England from Holland
France and Austria sign peace treaty
George Reynolds's musical piece *Bantry Bay*, based on the failed
French invasion, is performed to great applause at Covent Garden
Edward Bunting's *A General Collection of Ancient Irish Music* is
published
Schubert born

1798 *12 March*   Leinster Directory of United Irishmen rounded up at
Oliver Bond's house; all but two members of the 'supreme
executive' executed
29 March   Castlereagh becomes Chief Secretary
30 March   Privy Council proclaims Ireland in state of rebellion;
imposes martial law
19–21 April   Lord Clare's visitation of Trinity College, Dublin,
and expulsion of 19 United Irishmen
25 April   Lake succeeds Abercromby as Commander-in-Chief in
Ireland
19 May   Fitzgerald arrested and fatally wounded
23 May   Rebellion proper starts in Leinster
26 May   Rebels defeated in Co. Meath
27 May   Great battle at Oulart Hill, Co. Wexford; local yeomanry
massacred and put to rout
29 May   350 rebels killed at Curragh, Co. Kildare
30 May   Martial law imposed

30 May – 21 June   Wexford town captured and administered by rebels

4 June   Edward Fitzgerald dies of wounds

5 June   Rebels routed at New Ross; Protestants massacred at nearby Scullabogue

6 June   Rebellion extends to Ulster

7 June   United Irishmen attack Antrim town, but repulsed, with heavy losses

9 June   Wexford rebels, making for Dublin, repulsed at Arklow

13 June   Battle of Ballynahinch in Co. Down; rebels defeated

14 June   John and Henry Sheares executed

20 June   Lord Cornwallis sworn in as Lord-Lieutenant

21 June   Bloodiest battle of Rebellion at Vinegar Hill in Wexford

4 August   Arthur O'Connor, Thomas Emmet and William Macnevin save their skins by delivering to the Government their 'Memoir, or detailed statement of the origin and progress of the Irish Union'

22 August   French force of about 1,000, under General Humbert, lands at Killala, Co. Mayo

8 September   Humbert surrenders to Cornwallis at Ballinamuck (but only after surprising Cornwallis and winning large part of Co. Mayo)

12–20 October   French invasion led by Admiral Bompard engages British squadron commanded by Sir John Borlase Warren; seven out of the ten French ships captured; Tone arrested after being brought to shore at Buncrana, Co. Donegal

19 November   Tone cuts his throat and dies in prison in Dublin: a slow death

House of Commons still rejects abolition of slavery

February   Rome falls to the French; Pope Pius VI is expelled and arrested

Napoleon campaigns in Egypt and the Middle East

Malthus's *Essay on the Population* published

Alexander Knox writes his *Essays on the Political Circumstances in Ireland*

Wordsworth writes *Tintern Abbey*

1799   *May*   The Union resolutions are approved by both Irish and English Parliaments

Summer   The Union Bills receive the Royal Assent

1800   *1 January*   The new Union flag flies throughout the British Isles

I

Introduction and some reflections

The islands in the west . . . are not misty, or not for long;
they have unusually clear outlines, though the outline,
because of the movement of light, does not appear
constant.

P.J. Kavanagh, *Finding Connections*

A recent Secretary of State for Northern Ireland asked, after six
months or so in office, that he be reminded which took place
first, the Rebellion or the Union? The former costing some 30,000
lives in 1798; the other still a cause of the greatest possible dissen-
sion. Another friend and political *engagé* thought that if I was writing
about Wolfe Tone, I would bury myself in stories about the 'Wild
Geese', the Irish soldiers who left Ireland after the siege of Limerick,
over a century earlier.

I mention these things because it seems strange, when it is commonplace to say that the Irish both north and south of the border
are so haunted by their sense of history – receiving their mandate
from ghosts, as Conor Cruise O'Brien has remarked – that so few
Englishmen this side of the water bother themselves at all with
modern Irish history.

Herbert Butterfield wrote in 1965, over thirty years ago:

there is in Ireland a peculiar relationship between past and present, utterly
different from that peculiar relationship which the Englishman has had
with his history. It involves a high consciousness of those events which
one wants to celebrate and those wrongs which are to be kept in mind –

things which, even if they had happened long ago, seem to be remembered as though they had taken place only last week.[1]

I would go even further. There are a hundred miles of bookshelves full of eighteenth-century Irish history. But perhaps, for all that, there is no such thing as Irish history at all – the past, present and future being the same thing, one and indistinguishable. History is today, yesterday, tomorrow all at once. The there and then merges into the here and now. Celtic giants loom and dwarves* diminish – and vice versa – into an indeterminate mist.

To elide past and present in this way is a convenient excuse. Scholars do fix dates. It is even possible for onlookers to agree, without too many shifty qualifications, on a time when something happened. Yet it seldom seems hard and fast. The words used are such that no inaccuracy altogether lacks some shadow of truth, no accuracy is altogether incontestable. Time in Ireland is not so much a non-existent dimension as a slippery element of its own; as elusive as a blob of mercury.

Once, standing on Galley Head in West Cork, I was looking out to sea, saw distant breakers and asked a chance passer-by, 'Is that where the *Lusitania* went down?'

'Oh, I'd say she'd be lying a little further out than that.'

That to me has a familiar flavour of the *contemporaneity* of Irish history. (In fact, I afterwards discovered that the *Lusitania* went down about thirty miles east of where I was standing.)

In the west of Ireland where my family have had a small property now for thirty years, I am not at all surprised when a stranger refers to it as 'O'Driscoll's land' – since, five or more centuries ago, the O'Driscolls were virtual kings of Baltimore and owned great stretches of land around these parts.

To own land which is not seen by neighbours to belong – really and truly to belong – to its foreign owner does not give the freeholder in Ireland the sense of unchallengeable security that his English equivalent believes he and his family can enjoy *in saecula saeculorum*. It is not that the former seriously believes that he may one

---

* A real dwarf does indeed enter Irish history in the 1790s; 'Count' Boruwlaski, 39 in. high, whose shoes were *almost* 6 in. long, was touring Ireland at the time of the French expedition to Bantry Bay; news of the attempted landing interrupted and ruined the concert planned for him in Athlone.

day have his land repossessed in turn; nor that he sees any *necessity* to acknowledge a debt of remorse for what his ancestors may have done during acts of plantation centuries ago. No; but there is, or was, a pinprick of inquietude that suggests he would do well to assert his rights by, for instance, the building of a great house, with walls round its domain: that he must create a tradition of his own as powerful and explicit as the tradition his ancestors narrowly failed to destroy. He never succeeds, of course. And very often the country is an accomplice in reclaiming the property: lands abandoned revert to overgrown wilderness in one generation.[2]

The neighbourly doubts lurking in those who are uneasy about their title-deeds – those who have half-acknowledged memories of their own forefathers' usurpation of title – lead to an unhappy seesaw of covert defensiveness or loud assertion. Secrecy and whispers flourish. A chain-reaction can be triggered at any time, without warning.

Many other familiar moods and concepts, like quicksands constant in their approximate whereabouts but treacherous in their sudden unpredicability, lurk on the shores of Irish history. Questions of character, for example. The four rebels upon whom I concentrate in this book seem on first introduction to be entirely recognizable to us today. So much seems familiar in their tone of voice, their marvellous gift for language. But I am aware that their beautifully written English conceals many attitudes very foreign to us – about the nature of cruelty, punishment, revenge, death and so on. Their accessibility is something of a mirage.

One might start with attempting to pin down the nature of Ascendancy, that collection of attitudes which formed the dominating background of the lives of so many Irishmen for so long. The term 'Ascendancy' is defined so succinctly by A.W.P. Malcolmson in his biography of Speaker Foster that I am happy to crib it whole:

Anglo-Irish Ascendancy requires definition. The Anglo-Irish were the descendants of people of English origin who had settled in Ireland during the fifteenth, sixteenth, seventeenth and eighteenth centuries, usually after receiving grants for military and other services to the British Crown. In religion they were not only Protestant, but Anglican, in distinction to the Protestant Dissenting families of Scottish origins who were planted in Ulster in the early seventeenth century, or who planted themselves in the

3

late seventeenth century. The Anglo-Irish were a social élite rather than a strictly ethnic group . . . for most of the eighteenth century [they] held a virtual monopoly, legal or practical, of political power: a legal monopoly in that Catholics were excluded by law from Parliament, the parliamentary franchise and the corporations; a practical monopoly in that Protestant dissenters, though never excluded by law from Parliament or the parliamentary franchise, numbered only a handful of members in any House of Commons.[3]

Roy Foster, in his *Modern Ireland*, has written of how he finds something gamy and colonial, reminding one of Kenya, say, in the 1930s, about Ascendancy attitudes in eighteenth-century Ireland. There is something of the same feeling about the impermanence of things, the necessity to catch the pleasures of life before they vanish, the same unease and hectic gaiety, drunkenness and adultery. It is hard to overestimate the insecurity of rulers in the face of subjects who have a subterranean language of response. All this led to a political and social life where over-reaction was the rule rather than the exception. Duels were fought over trivia; to tread by accident on a lady's train when ascending the stairs of the theatre was enough to be called out. Here is Wolfe Tone in March 1796, indulging in memories:

> I have not had spirits, since the news of poor Sweetman's death, to go on with my memorandums . . . it seems the quarrel arose about treading on a lady's gown, in coming out of the opera; – a worthy cause for two brave men to fight about! They fought at four yards' distance, which was Sweetman's choice, but Captain Watson (an Irishman also) is likely to recover; my poor friend is gone. When he received the shot, which went through his body, he cried out to Watson, 'Are you wounded?' – 'Yes,' replied the other, 'I believe mortally.' – 'And so am I,' replied Sweetman, instantly falling.[4]

Leaving aside the saving irony in 'the worthy cause', what is there in so much of Irish history which leads to rejection of compromise? Partly, I think, the feeling that each side's dragon will always recover, as it has in the past: a feeling not too hard to understand among a people which believes itself to have been oppressed for century after century, under the real or fancied heels of a close and more powerful neighbour.

The arrogance of some members of the Protestant Ascendancy who governed Ireland in the eighteenth century was enough to turn the stomach of anyone young and generous. I will quote just one example: extreme, but the tone will give the flavour of attitudes which may well often have been expressed with more delicacy, but must have always caused resentment. Here is a letter from that great pillar of the Ascendancy, John Beresford, the Commissioner of the Revenue, to Lord Auckland on 9 August 1798:

> The Ministers of England are extremely ignorant of the situation, nature and disposition of the people of Ireland. To enter properly into that subject, and minutely, would require a quarto volume; but be assured that the whole body of the lower orders of the Roman Catholics of this country are totally inimical to the English Government; that they are under the influence of the lowest and worst part of their priesthood; that all the extravagant and horrid tenets of their religion are as deeply engraved in their hearts as they were a century, or three centuries ago, and that they are as barbarous, ignorant and ferocious as they then were; and if ministers imagine that they can treat with such men just as they would with the people of Yorkshire if they rebelled, they will find themselves mistaken.[5]

The failure to shrug off memories of wrongs done either to oneself or by oneself in the ever-present past – the refusal to come to terms with the difficulties or sometimes the sheer impossibility of doing anything about it – is a handy stimulus to rage and despair with which to goad the depths of one's soul.

It is impossible to read the history of late eighteenth-century Ireland without brooding on the nature of suspicion. Its sources are easy to find – on the one side dispossession, the yoke of alien rule, the pro-scription of religion; and, on the other side, an uneasy awareness that once or twice a generation the arsenal of explosives may well ignite. Splendid fireworks, dozens slain, terrible beauty.

Two divergent paths lead away from these recurrent disasters: one towards ever deeper distrust and outright resentment, enmity and hatred, cloaked, as may from time to time seem advisable, in charm and subterfuge; the other towards silence, suppression, brooding, abandonment of principle. To meet the demons of suspicion in the latter manner may lead to an apparently flaccid, complaisant type of behaviour, to trimming or temporary surrender. But 'temporary' is the word. A chance phrase, interpreted (or misinterpreted), an askance look, a questionable intonation, may precipitate an over-reaction. Measures are taken; in no time at all, the pistons of mistrust and revenge acquire their perpetual motion.

What things lie at the heart of such endemic ruthlessness? It is not the hatred of the individual. To take my first rebel, Wolfe Tone was personally magnanimous and delightful. He did not hate this or that Englishman. One of his greatest friends was George Knox, with whom he had been at the Middle Temple in 1787 and who, despite being on different sides of the fence, became godfather to one of his children; sometimes his reference to individual opponents is playful and affectionate, or at least suggests that respect and liking was not abandoned. No, the hatred for *England*, which led to such frank ruthlessness, was hatred for a picture-book monster, but none the less rancorous for that. It seems far too scalding an emotion to be attributed only to the modesty of his social standing – his being only on the fringe of the magic circle of the Ascendancy – or to a perception of the undeserved 'inferiority' of his country. Did it derive from some hereditary sense of an ancient wrong or injury, done not to himself but to his father or father's father?

But in truth it is impossible to convey, let alone explain the starkness of his hatred. Tone had no direct, personal reason to hate England. He was a Protestant, a highly educated product of Trinity College, Dublin. He was popular with his contemporaries. He was a favourite with girls, and pursued them successfully. His character is in general blithe, free, adventurous, self-mocking – the catalogue of virtues is long and delightful. So the bilious hate which erupts too often for comfort gives the reader a taste of poison: 'The truth is, I hate the very name of England; I hated her before my exile; I hated her since, and I will hate her always.'[6] The charm and apparent disingenuousness of Tone's style should blind no one to his cunning – even when, as in his *Memoirs*, he claims to be talking aloud to himself: charm and cunning, disarmingly acknowledged.

Contemporary accounts, at the beginning of the 1790s, are *not* dark with premonitory shadows of rebellion: at least, less so than in many other periods of Irish history. The 1780s had, on the whole, been a decade of optimism. Religious toleration was far greater than it had been in living memory; many of the penal laws under which Catholics laboured were (almost) dead letters. Dublin was becoming for the fortunate a magnificent city, a jewel of the Age of Englightenment. The easy-going good humour, the wit and civility of everyday life was there for the growing middle classes to enjoy. Parliamentary independence, at least, had been gained for Ireland. Of course there were grave problems such as the inequities of trade, terrible poverty for those who had to endure it, the injustices of tithes, the casual corruption of places and pensions, the controlling grip of London on all executive power – a long list. But none of them seemed likely to end in blood.

Yet there were many reasons why the increasing tolerance and relative peacefulness of the mid-eighteenth century collapsed in the last decade or so of the century. The American War of Independence had shown how a people could refuse to be bound by laws in whose making they had no share; the French Revolution had shown how it was possible to throw out a corrupt ruling class; and the sham of the legislative independence, hard-won in 1782, became more and more obvious. All the executive power, all the places and pensions and privilege, remained in the hands of a Protestant Ascendancy and the Lord-Lieutenant's men, secure in Dublin Castle, and with a Lord-Lieutenant himself nominated by the Crown and its Ministers in London.

The declared thrust of the strategy of the United Irish movement which was founded in 1791 was to harness Presbyterian resentment against the corruption and sheer unrepresentativeness of Parliament, in tandem with Catholic resentment against their exclusion from all political and most professional life.

The politics of insecurity invariably includes over-reaction. On the whole, however, the leaders of both Catholics and Dissenters were careful to avoid saying anything in public which might smack of *lèse majesté*. This was prudent. Moderate Catholic rank and file were likely to be monarchical by instinct, by upbringing and by analogy with the hierarchy of the Church; and moderate Presbyterians were likely to think that the great cause of parliamentary reform might not be helped by streperous advocacy of revolution.

But more dangerous, resentful grievances smouldered, waiting to be fanned into flame. There was the gross inequity of paying tithes, for example, to maintain the clergy and Church to which one did not belong; and the memories of the loss of one's forefathers' land. Many such bitternesses were expressed in the explosion of newspapers, pamphlets and manifestos of the 1780s and 1790s. There was no shortage of ingredients favouring peasant revolt. And it was when the forces of ill-formulated mass, agrarian discontent merged with those of educated professionals and artisans that revolution began to stir: great houses were raided, pikes cut and stored in cabins everywhere.

Once uprisings began to break out, the behaviour of the armed forces in Ireland – which prompted General Abercromby's celebrated complaint that the army in the 1790s 'was in a state of licentiousness which must render it formidable to anyone but the enemy' – takes one into a thicket of terror. Perhaps sensibilities today are blunted by tales of the grand, unimaginable atrocities; sometimes the small, casual instances are more telling. (The snuffing out of the spark of human kindness among ordinary men, for example, seems almost as bad as tales about monsters of iniquity.) Here is an instance from a speech in 1797 in the English House of Lords by the civilized Lord Moira:*

> At 9 o'clock every man was called upon to extinguish his candle and his fire, and the military enforced the regulations with the most insulting expressions. The hardship of this regulation was frequently felt in the most cruel manner. An instance had occurred within his own knowledge in which a party of soldiers had come to the house by the roadside; they insisted that he should extinguish his candle; the man entreated that he might be permitted to retain a light because he was watching by the bedside of his child which was subject to convulsion fits. The party, however, rigorously insisted.[7]

If one had to choose a single decisive moment in the 1790s when the wheels started to move, irreversibly, towards rebellion, it would not,

---

* This Irish peer was a most distinguished soldier. He later became the first Marquess of Hastings, a Governor-General of Bengal and a Viceroy of India. He believed in the virtues of tolerance and saw a great deal of good in his fellow Irishmen. In the Rebellion, some of the tenants whose loyalty he had praised helped to burn down his demesne. The *Anti-Jacobin* mocked him with verses whose refrain was 'There is no town as loyal as Ballynahinch'.

I think, lie in the fiasco of Fitzwilliam's brief viceroyship in 1794 and the dashing of moderate hopes for reform and complete emancipation. Certainly that was important. But more ominous was the welding together of the United Irishmen and the Catholic, agrarian revolutionary movement of the Defenders. That meant the betrayal of the former's original *raison d'être*: the unity of the sects in the search for reform and independence from England. It meant the formation of a movement that was militant, populist, ruthless, conspiratorial.

It is an irony that those who, two hundred years ago, took the lead in working for the phantasmagoric unity of the sects and an independent Ireland were, almost to a man, members of Protestant churches – less inspired, however, by religion than by the Scottish Enlightenment, the American War of Independence and the ideals of the French Revolution. Soon, though, the old patterns of thought and memory reasserted themselves, and the militant resentment of the great Catholic majority gained the loudest (but still incoherent) voice.

This allows us a passing glance at the animosities which still flourish with such virulence in Northern Ireland. I have heard it asked how a civilized European country, on the verge of the second millennium, could possibly still be in the throes of antiquated religious passions. An English friend of mine confessed, in a conversation in Belfast, that he was not himself a Christian: more of an agnostic, possibly even an atheist. He simply could not comprehend the roots of sectarianism. But his Belfast companion would not let him off the religious hook as easily as that. He pursued him: 'Of course not, of course not. You're an unbeliever. But are you a Protestant unbeliever or a Catholic unbeliever?' The depth of the divide, now as then, has little to do with religious observances, nothing to do with theology, but everything to do with history, culture, family, injustice, perceived attitudes on every question under the sun (or in the mist).

An astonishing range of formal barriers still survived throughout most of the century against Catholics' entry into education, against their bequeathing land, erecting steeples on their churches, practising any profession, bearing arms, exercising the vote, or taking *any* part in local or national politics. The penal laws in theory prevented all these. In practice, desuetude and tolerance had made many fairly easy to circumvent. But the risk of their implementation remained in the background, rather as if a frontier, for long traversed on the nod, might suddenly be closed on an arbitrary diktat.

Voting for, and sitting in, Parliament was the hinge round which much of the agitation turned in the last years of the century. (The Catholic Relief Act of 1793 removed most hurdles save that of membership of Parliament or appointment to some of the highest posts in the land.) Though similar impediments remained in England, one must remember that being in a minority or majority of the population makes a vast deal of difference.

In Tone's famous pamphlet *An Argument on Behalf of the Catholics of Ireland* one can see his suspicions fermenting that England's policy towards Ireland was, and always had been, modelled on Caesar's toward Gaul – divide and rule. If this was England's devious conspiracy, then one could understand why she cherished the antagonisms of unrelenting Protestants against the barbarian Catholics. It explained the monopoly, the continued tyranny of the English Ascendancy. Conversely, on this particular reading of history, the best way to topple the alien tyranny, to become free, would be to forge a link between Catholics and Protestants. Ireland united could then, at last, shake off hated English rule.

Catholic emancipation, the granting of all civic and political rights to the vast majority of the Irish, was thus not just a matter of propriety and common justice. It was above all, to those who thought like Tone, the essential first step towards ousting Ireland's evil genius, England.

This was not, of course, how Pitt and his Ministers saw things. What appears in Irish eyes as English deviousness is, usually, more the consequence of English indolence: the ingrained habit of attending to Irish affairs only when time can be spared from more pressing matters, such as continental war. This was particularly true in the 1790s. Here is an entry from the diaries of Sylvester Douglas, Lord Glenbervie, describing his call at Downing Street on his appointment as Chief Secretary in early 1794. Pitt's cursory impatience is easy to read between the lines:

> We discussed the topics of the Catholics, the Volunteers, the militia, the supply of troops from Ireland, the measure of trying to procure some contribution of money from thence for the war, the idea of Union. He said that Ireland had hitherto been, and must yet continue, a government of expedients; but wished, rather than had any very specific hopes for, a general remodelling of the political frame of that country. He desires to

keep back if possible concessions which may at a convenient opportunity be purchased by some sort of union – which, however, he seems to despair of ever seeing accomplished. He holds very cheap the fears of the Protestants in Ireland, should the Catholics get into Parliament, of the recovery of the obsolete tithes to the landed property, and believes those fears are not real, but brought forward to induce government to protect them in the monopoly of power and emoluments. His plan seems to be to let the weight of the Catholics, from their numbers and their increasing property, carry them by imperceptible steps into the legislature and their share of office; but he seems to wish this plan not to be known to be his by the Irish Government.[8]

And again, after a second conference with Pitt before Douglas left for Ireland to take up his appointment, the same weary recognition of Ireland's troubles, the same reluctance to grasp the nettle, can be seen:

> The Catholics, being the great majority of the inhabitants, must in justice and in policy be admitted by degrees to a full participation of all the advantages now held exclusively by Protestants; but this must be done as it were insensibly to the Protestants . . . Mr Pitt truly thinks that such a monopoly cannot long be maintained, but that, on the other hand, it is natural that those who had it should be very unwilling to relinquish it, and that it would be impolitic, and also even in some degree unjust, to wrest it from them with violence.[9]

The words 'Parliamentary Reform' may be beginning to resound in our ears again, in 1997, but echoes of rotten boroughs are dim. It is worth recalling the size of the demand for reform. One must remember that in many other respects, Parliament in Dublin in the eighteenth century worked in ways which would be familiar to Clerks or secretaries in the House of Commons today – the Speaker and his mace, committees of ways and means, forms of debate and adjournment and so on. There were even fairly regular elections. But a speech by the great parliamentarian Henry Grattan in the Irish House of Commons on 9 February 1793 pulls the reader up short:

> constituents do now expect a reform of Parliament, and that is a measure not more necessary for their freedom than their felicity . . . I will advert to the state of your representation – it is short. Of three hundred members, above two hundred are returned by individuals; from forty to fifty are returned by ten persons; several of your boroughs have no resident

elector at all, some of them have but one; and, on the whole, *two-thirds of the representatives in the House of Commons are returned by less than one hundred persons!* [my italics] This is not that antient, that venerable constitution of King, Lords and Commons. It is not even an aristocracy. It is an oligarchy. It is not an oligarchy of property, but of accident . . .[10]

The clamour was loud for reform of every sort. There was understandable resentment of a system so alive with corruption. The sizes of pensions, the undisguised favouritism when it came to sinecures and places and privileges, were obvious scandals. Even leaving aside the inspiring examples of the American War of Independence and the dawn of the French Revolution, desire for reform spread among the heirs of the Scottish Enlightenment – the radical, Presbyterian Dissenters of the North. And the swell of resentment rose high among the emerging Catholic middle class throughout the island. It is easy to see why the English Government, perceiving the dark clouds of war with republican and expansionary France gathering, was alarmed to see the two currents, Catholic and Presbyterian, threatening to converge. This was what it correctly feared was behind the much repeated, blander phrase of 'parliamentary reform and Catholic emancipation'.

The English nowadays do not love uniforms as they once did. The Irish loved them even more, most of all when they were not the King's uniforms, but private ones such as those with the colours of their first General, the civilized and indecisive Whig grandee, Lord Charlemont.

Soon after the outbreak of the American war, 'a Mr Tottenham, who had served in the army and had an old attachment to red clothes' formed a company of light infantry in King's County.[11] We hear no more of Mr Tottenham. But of most companies of volunteer corps that drilled and marched and counter-marched in the late eighteenth century we hear a very great deal. Throughout the late 1770s and the 1780s, in all the provinces but especially in Ulster, Volunteers sprang up in their tens of thousands.

Their uniforms were gorgeous, varied, a matter for envy and emulation. For example, back in the summer of 1778, members of the Belfast First Volunteer Company, 'in smart new uniforms of scarlet turned up with black velvet, black hats, white waistcoats and breeches, paraded to church' . . . and listened to a very sensible sermon commending the spirit which had led to the company's formation.[12] And another Belfast Volunteer Company, the Blue Company, raised on the eve of the raid by Paul Jones (of the dance) 'adopted a blue uniform faced with blue, and blue hats adorned with gold lace'.

True, the Volunteers never faced a proper military test in all the years of their soldiering: they never 'took the tented field'. But they did exercise a formidable background pressure on the side of the landed gentry. They formed a core of 'patriots' determined to assert the constitutional and trading rights of Ireland. They were, in origin, a standing rebuke against a Government which in the American War of Independence had denuded their country of troops, in order that it could fight a colonial war, in which many Irishmen (particularly the rising merchant class of the Protestant North) sympathized with the rebels. Nor did the Volunteers wish to see their country laid open to piracy and the threat of invasion from France. They were ready to provide their own uniforms at their own expense, to elect their own officers, carry out their own drills, pay for everything except their arms, which, with some reluctance, were handed over to them by the Government.

Many saw the Volunteers as a political élite forwarding the cause of reform – as the true representation of the people. Others saw them as the embodiment of active public virtue, reminiscent of the better citizens of ancient Greece and Rome; others again regarded them as more dangerous: the nation in arms asserting its will. To witness a parade of Volunteers was to be reminded of one of the sacred principles of the Glorious Revolution of 1688, the right of every citizen to arm in the defence of his property.

From the movement's birth in the 1770s the Government had misgivings that it might spread out of control. It was seen as a species of nationalism, pro-American in spirit and tainted with republicanism. 'Presbyterians in the North in their hearts are Americans,' declared the Lord-Lieutenant, Lord Harcourt.[13] At one dinner, when glasses were raised to the Volunteers, 'Lord Hillsborough cried "fy, fy, fy" and each time knocked his hand on the table, "Do you know, Sir, there is not a toast could be more disagreeable to the Government?"'[14]

A few words on my selection of protagonists: I have simply selected those among the United Irishmen who interest me most. Wolfe Tone is an inevitable choice, not so much because of the heroic myths and near-idolatry that have grown up around his name, but far more because of his style, the disarming yet ultimately tragic thread of theatrical self-mockery which runs through his writings. As for Archibald Hamilton Rowan, it would be impossible for anyone *not* to have enjoyed being a friend of his – such transparent and quixotic honour, such passionate adherence to principle, such uncomplicated pleasure in simple things, such open-handedness to all, especially to those less well off than himself, such passion for amateur sailing and amateur watch-making, such endearing, fond obstinacy about taking opossums across the Atlantic. Then there is William Drennan, beneath whose layers of self-righteousness and pomposity and lack of humour there lurked a good and worthy man: a poet, too, redeemed by quite unexpected flashes of self-awareness, which show how foolish it is to judge character too harshly. Lastly, there is Lord Edward Fitzgerald whose dangerous charm – even more dangerous to himself than to others – sparkled with good-natured vanity, good looks, instinctive generosity and courage. His ingenuous high spirits, his lack of any meanness or malice, his unaffected delight in the obvious pleasures of life: none of these qualities made him particularly eligible to be a revolutionary. In military life, as when designing forts, he was a child playing soldiers; at other times he was little more than a privileged young man seeking adventure. It is easy to understand how engaging this careless and spoilt young aristocrat was to some; how tiresome his radical chic is, still, to others. He never troubled himself with reflection (except of himself in the mirror), or expressed thoughtful interest, other than of the fashionable and romantic kind, in political ideas. But he was brave. He attracted love and loyalty.

Chapter 2 looks very briefly at the lives of these principal characters up to the start of my story: that is, the foundation of the Societies of United Irishmen in the autumn of 1791 – when the Rebellion, still eight years in the future, begins to cast its shadows.

Four further characters play so important a part in the protagonists' backgrounds that they deserve introduction at this early stage. I have very briefly sketched here the greatest Irish parliamentarian of the century, a sacked Lord-Lieutenant and a couple of extra rebels whom I had at one time thought of elevating into protagonists. I hope this choice may (to use a phrase later applied to an English General whom we shall meet during the French non-landing at Bantry Bay at Christmas 1796) be considered 'eccentric rather than mad'. Others can wait their turn in the text, or in footnotes.

Somewhere in the middle distance behind my rebels stands the slight, wiry figure of eighteenth-century Ireland's greatest statesman and orator – and failure – Henry Grattan (1746–1820). In 1782, still in his thirties, he seemed to have brought home the political holy grail. He had won the independence of Ireland, or at least, the legislative independence of the Dublin Parliament. No longer was it now subservient to Westminster; no longer did Bills require the assent of the Privy Council in London. It looked as if there really were, at last, two sister kingdoms. A grateful nation voted that a splendid house be given to Grattan, much as a grateful England had given Blenheim to the Duke of Marlborough for his military victories.

Alas, the victory was soon seen to be cruelly hollow. The power of law-making might now reside in Dublin, in name. But three things made it a sham. The first was that executive power had not been transferred. It was formally vested in the Lord-Lieutenant and his Ministers. Second, the Lord-Lieutenant himself was by no means independent. He was appointed by the English Government – the Home Secretary or the Prime Minister. Third, the Lord-Lieutenant, for all the splendid ceremony and conviviality of his court, and for all the constitutional deference paid to him, by no means controlled all the levers. The *éminences* behind him were far more powerful. These were the great Ascendancy families who continued to hold, and job, all the offices of state, whose nominees and families exercised most of the patronage: in practice electing most of the Members of Parliament. Even more than in England, places and preferment and pensions constituted a jungle of privilege.

The great families who stalked through this jungle may have been, for the most part, well-educated, civilized men dutifully seeing to their vast estates. When one reads their diaries and letters, there is little that seems mean and grasping about them. To apply the whole-sale word 'corruption' to this system of patrician power seems like gutter abuse. The due processes of the law were generally observed. Bribery was well mannered. There was quite a lot of high-mindedness about. Concern that the vast majority of the population was still disenfranchised was, in everyday life, left to lie half-forgotten in the background. But Grattan remained the conscience of the reformers (even if not of the revolutionaries). He always refused to accept office.

Grattan adored Ireland, and the idea of Ireland. He loathed the monopoly of power with which it was accursed. He lacked political shrewdness and political luck; but from 1782 onwards he towered over the House of Commons in what came to be called 'Grattan's Parliament'. Here is a sketch of him taking part in a debate:

> Grattan is without exception the most singular speaker that ever with such a singular figure, voice and manner made an oration. His voice was totally lost at every third or fourth sentence and his action was violent to a degree of fury which is felt because it is genuine enthusiasm . . . [his] face is one of the finest and most expressive I ever saw, although this would seem joking to some, and there is a genteel awkwardness about him and all that he says and does which, I think, doubles the impression he makes.[15]

During the 1780s the Lord-Lieutenants of Ireland, appointed by the Home Secretary of the day, displayed tremendous grandness of style and splendour of hospitality. To appropriate a phrase of Professor McDowell, none of them was 'socially handicapped by their temperate habits'. But in the early 1790s Lord Westmorland was a dull dog, stuffy, cautious, believing that 'the business of the Government here is to keep everything as quiet as possible'.[16] Worse, he was seen by London to be too much under the thumb of such overweening figures of the Ascendancy as the Lord Chancellor Fitzgibbon and the Beresford family (who were called 'the Kings of Ireland', for the vast patronage they dispensed). Some of these men's doings in relation to my protagonists are set out in the text of my tale. Lord Camden makes a brief appearance at the very end, during the Rebellion for whose outbreak he must take a small portion of blame. The style of his dispatches suggests a timid, indecisive man with swings of mood.

It may then seem perverse to give apparent pride of place here to the name of William Wentworth Fitzwilliam (1748–1833), who was Lord-Lieutenant of Ireland for only two short months in the midwinter of 1795, before being ignominiously sacked and recalled.

Perverse, until one remembers that his viceroyship has often been seen as the hinge on which the history of the decade turned.

Fitzwilliam had been appointed following the arrival of the Whigs into a coalition government; his old friend and Home Secretary, the Duke of Portland, had prevailed on Pitt. Fitzwilliam had enormous estates in Ireland; his rent roll was said to be more than £20,000 a year. As he saw it, his job was to accelerate the relief of Catholics, even to complete their enfranchisement, allowing them to sit in Parliament. Reform was in the air; the old guard would be dismissed; Grattan would be his ally. All this and more was rumoured in the months before he arrived. Much of his programme appeared almost like a milder version of the stated aims of the United Irishmen.

But there was one fearful flaw. The terms of reference of his appointment were not clear enough: still are not clear enough. For example, he was instructed not to raise the matter of Catholic disenfranchisement, but not to oppose it too strenuously if it came to the point. And had he really been given the power unceremoniously to dismiss such great figures as Beresford and Fitzgibbon? Alas, Fitzwilliam was an impetuous man: a Hercules who tried to cleanse the Augean stable overnight. The Ascendancy brought its influence to bear with the Prime Minister Pitt, and Fitzwilliam was dismissed.

Dashed hopes are the most dangerous ones. When he left Dublin his carriage was detached from the horses and drawn by protesters. Black was worn. The mood was all disappointment, resentment, betrayal.

Napper Tandy (1740–1803) was embroiled in Dublin City politics and in street agitations for radical causes from the age of thirty onwards. He has about him that air of a petty grandee familiar to observers of small town-hall politicians everywhere – self important, impatient of those beneath him, obsequious to those above, choleric, pompous, ignorant. (Add 'sly' and 'cowardly' for good measure.) True, there are some things to set against that nightmare catalogue: a gift for oratory, an elemental forcefulness, an ability to catch the spirit of the times.

Tandy was outstandingly ugly. And it was his ugliness which led directly to the imbroglios recounted in the chapters on the winter and spring of 1793 and 1794. But far more damaging to his reputation was his 'shyness' – his shilly-shallying when it came to duels, his escaping from physical danger, his hiding in London. It is difficult to see how he could be taken very seriously, even if he had been the first Secretary of the United Irishmen, and was sometimes called the father of the movement. He was not a man of honour. That may be one reason why he survives only in footnotes of Ireland's late eighteenth century; perhaps would not survive at all were it not for the familiar ballad:

> Oh, I met with Napper Tandy and he took me by the hand
> And he says how's poor old Ireland and how does she stand?
> 'Tis the most distressful country that ever yet was seen
> For they're hanging men and women for the wearing of the green.

Brave efforts have recently been made to resuscitate him a little in the face of such denigration. And it can certainly be claimed that Tandy showed foresight of a kind in attempting an alliance between the United Irishmen and the peasant Catholic Defenders in County Louth. That dangerous alliance helped to precipitate the Rebellion. No matter that it was contrary to the fundamental rationale of the United Irishmen: the unity of the sects. Tandy even took the Defenders' oath. If discovered, that would have led to his prosecution. So he was capable of taking risks.

All the same, justifications falter when it comes to his later, quarrelsome life: his doubtful behaviour in Paris in the late 1790s, when he represented himself as the chief spokesman of the United Irishmen; his obstructive behaviour in the preparations for invasion in the city in 1798; his constant divisiveness. The picture of his old age is sad, alone in Bordeaux where he died in 1803; only the company of his housekeeper and his trappings as a French General to comfort him. He had never seen active service, and his abortive journey to Ireland in the *Anacreon* in 1798 (eventually putting in at Bergen in Norway) had been the last of his recorded fiascos.[17]

Arthur O'Connor (1763–1852) was a tall, dark, handsome man. He claimed descent from the ancient kings of Ireland, and had silver spoons specially made to match, if scarcely to prove, his claim. He could also boast (and did so, often) acquaintance with Fox and other leading Whigs. His family having intermarried with the local Cork aristocracy, he easily moved on to a larger stage: he had charm. As MP for Philipstown, he spoke at length in the Irish House of

Commons, mainly and not immoderately on trade, and wrote a three-volume book entitled *Monopoly: the Cause of All Evil*. It is not easy to read. He joined the United Irishmen in 1796, and became the editor and part proprietor of *The Press*.

His presence broods over my book chiefly because he was the evil genius of Lord Edward Fitzgerald, whom he called 'the twin of my soul', and whose sister Lucy he charmed and probably seduced.

Although he was appointed a General in the French army on the strength of his promises to help in the invasion of Ireland, his military experience was limited to one visit to Lafayette in Sedan in 1794. In later life he continually badgered Napoleon to increase his pension, and gave out that he was writing his memoirs. He suffered from severe megalomania. More fruitfully, he married Elisa, a 'fine, sprightly, young girl',[18] the daughter of Condorcet, and bought a château in the *département* of Loiret, near Orleans; his distant descendants live there still.[19]

His uncle Lord Longueville said of him: 'of all the bad men I ever was acquainted with he is the worst'.[20]

Finally, there are the informers. Here were the men who covertly served the interests of the Administration, carrying to the Castle and to such Under-Secretaries as the diligent Edward Cooke, the latest intelligence about the subversive activities of the United Irishmen and other rebels. Digges, Collins, McNally – it is easy, natural and correct to regard them as Judases, who betrayed their fellows for money. Two centuries, one may say, is not enough to erase their infamy (the usual phrase in this context). And the fact that they were mostly intelligent, cultivated men makes them all the more odious, whichever side one is on. It is easy to understand how the trade of informer is still the most despised and dangerous in Ireland today.

But say what one may about their honour or their character, the informers do seem to have provided most accurate and copious intelligence. No event occurred of which the Castle did not receive forewarning. The difficulty, however, lies in the word 'copious'. There was simply more than it was possible to digest. Everybody who has worked on even the furthest fringes of intelligence knows that information is only as good as those who sift and evaluate it. Although Cooke was the most perspicacious and balanced of servants of the Crown, he was simply overwhelmed. The impression one sometimes gets, that the Castle played a cat-and-mouse game with the United Irishmen, should not be exaggerated.

Nor should one forget the role of rumour. Often in hindsight, with access to papers and letters, this looks absurd, though at the time it is sometimes taken with deadly seriousness. Two examples here are the suspicion which once attached to the estimable Archbishop Troy of Dublin, as being 'up' – a secret member of the United Irishmen in the run-up to the Revolution. This rumour was taken seriously enough for McNally to report it; there is no likelihood whatsoever that it was true. The second were the wild reports about Rowan, one of my principal heroes, who was said to be on his way to lead a great invasion of Ireland, with something of the same romance as Bonnie Prince Charlie. At the time Rowan was, in fact, in disconsolate exile in America, sitting in a rowing boat on the marshy banks of the River Delaware.

2

Rebels and Informers

The motives that govern human action are so varied and
difficult to weigh, so easily misunderstood by observers,
and even by the actors themselves, that only a rash, or a
prejudiced, or a stupid man will pass an unqualified
judgement on the conduct of another.

J.C. Beckett, *The Making of Modern Ireland*[1]

As the son of a member of the guild of coachmakers, born in 1763
in a street just behind Dublin Castle, Wolfe Tone, although a
Protestant, was hardly a member of the Ascendancy. His upbringing
had its hardships. His mother, only five of whose sixteen children
survived to adulthood, was said to be stern. She had to be, since
Wolfe, her eldest son, writes of his life as a thirteen-year-old:

> my father, who for some years had entirely neglected his business and led
> a very dissipated and irregular life, meeting with an accident of a fall
> downstairs, by which he was dreadfully wounded in the head . . . found,
> on his recovery, his affairs so deranged in all aspects, that he determined
> on quitting business and retiring to the country.[2]

Perhaps because of their circumstances, none of the family was a
stay-at-home. All of them loved adventure, one brother running
away to sea at twelve, another enlisting in his teens in the East India
Company. But Wolfe helped, in some measure, to look after the
family. True, one of his temptations was to join the army:

> I trace to the splendid appearance of the troops, and the pomp and parade
> of military show [in Phoenix Park], the untamable desire which I ever

since have had to become a soldier, a desire which has never once quitted me, and which, after sixteen years of various adventures, I am at last at liberty to indulge. Being at this time approaching seventeen years of age, it will not be thought incredible that *woman* began to appear lovely in my eyes, and I very wisely imagined that a red coat and cockade, with a pair of gold epaulettes, would aid me considerably in my approaches to the objects of my adoration.[3]

He was all the same a very fair scholar. He learnt Greek and Latin well. He passed well into Trinity College, Dublin. The Age of Enlightenment had changed the balance, in all aspects of education, between the secular and the religious. Wolfe would, for example, have been familiar with the passages in Cicero which expounded the doctrines of public virtue, or those of Plato which might justify tyrannicide. He would probably have reflected more on the assassination of Caesar than on the crucifixion of Christ.

Wolfe's intelligence, the sparkle of his wit and a highly developed self-mockery made him popular. He was accepted by fellow students who, unlike himself, were born into the Ascendancy. One of them described his appearance:

> he was a very slender, angular, *rapid* moving man, a thin face, sallow and pock-marked, eyes small lively bright . . . laughed and talked fast with enthusiasm about music and other innocent things, so that one could not possibly suspect him of plots and treason . . . *wise* he could not be but he had not a foolish look – too lively and smart for that.[4]

By the early 1780s he was a leading light of the College's famous Historical Society, founded by Edmund Burke in 1745, debating such topics of resentment as *undue executive influence in parliament* and *aristocratic control of government*. Yet, quick to learn, he did not really apply himself. He was frank in his enjoyment of the glitter and raciness of the amazingly prosperous and lively middle-class Dublin of the latter half of the eighteenth century; perhaps the carriages which as a boy he had seen in his father's yard helped to give him a taste for display, colour and insignia, pageant. His love of adventure was constantly aroused.

The theatre also became part of the landscape of his life. At Trinity he voted for a medal to be struck in honour of Mrs Siddons. Still an undergraduate, he took leading parts in amateur theatricals in the Galway country house belonging to their Kildare neighbour and friend Richard Martin, MP, falling (with great physical yearning) in love with Eliza, Martin's 'neglected' wife. Night after night he swooned devotedly on the stage when he played Lord Randolf against her in *Douglas*.

His most recent biographer Marianne Elliott believes that it went no further. Women, I am sure, liked him because he was very quick, very lively, took himself with a proper levity and was good at transporting them into never-never land. He was a natural candidate for elopement; and at the age of twenty-one, saw a sixteen-year old* in the window of a well-to-do house in Grafton Street and soon carried her off. Forgiveness and family reconciliation followed; though the relationship with the Witherington in-laws was seldom easy.

The need for income and a profession became urgent. He went to London to study law at the Middle Temple. This was a well-trodden rung in the ladder for young men from Dublin with more brains than property. His learning was quick, but it has been said that although his interests were wide, they did not include law. His appetite for drama was unsatisfied. Once he went with his younger brother William to India House to enlist as a soldier; but no East Indiamen were due to sail at the time. And once he wrote a paper recommending that England should establish a military colony in the recently discovered Sandwich Islands (now Hawaii), as a valuable base from which privateers could harry Spanish trade. He took this essay to 10 Downing Street, to present it in person to the Prime Minister. But he was not received and no reply came:

> Mr Pitt took not the smallest notice of either memorial or letter . . . it was my first essay in what I may call politics . . . and my disappointment made an impression on me that is not yet quite obliterated. In my anger, I made something like a vow that, if I ever had an opportunity, I would make Mr Pitt sorry, and perhaps fortune may yet enable me to fulfil that resolution.[5]

Was the offence taken perhaps excessive, despite an undoubted propensity to see slights? Yet the idea of undertaking a South Seas adventure on behalf of England was one to which he returned again and again (one of his last diary entries before embarking on the

---

* Martha Witherington was the daughter of a woollen draper. Tone nicknamed her Matilda, the name of the character played by Eliza in *Douglas*. His biographer charitably calls this renaming 'rather heartless' of Tone. (Marianne Elliott, *Wolfe Tone*, p. 39), though Matilda she will stay throughout this book, too.

Bantry Bay expedition in 1796 referred, in a side-swipe against 'those abominable Spaniards', to 'Mr Pitt and my scheme for the Sandwich Islands').

Since he nurtured this exotic scheme for so many years after the first version had been dismissed (or rather neglected) by Pitt, one may ask how it can be reconciled with his often repeated expressions of hate for England. My own impression is that with Tone the hatred began as one of his effervescent, theatrical, quasi-fantastical emotions. But hate easily becomes addictive and enters the soul. What might have started as theatre became deadly and real. Had Pitt only been more polite . . . ?

In early 1789 Tone came back from London to Dublin with his brother William, to face both his own and his father's financial straits. Even then, he set about his legal career in a lacklustre way. He began to be attracted to journalism and politics, and for a while was flattered by the attentions of George Ponsonby, scion of one of the greatest Ascendancy families. But Ponsonby became too patronizing, and Tone's reputation was in danger of becoming merely that of a hack (with only a spoof novel *Belmont Castle* and a few pamphlets to his credit). He was unkindly called, by the beginning of the 1790s, 'the little counsellor who promised to write essays *gratis*'.

And then he fell into argument with a stranger in the gallery of the House of Commons in Dublin. This was Thomas Russell. Of the friendship that immediately sprang up Tone wrote later in his *Memoirs*:

> If I am ever inclined to murmur at the difficulties wherewith I have so long struggled, I think on the inestimable treasure I possess in the affection of my wife and the friendship of Russell, and acknowledge that all my labours and sufferings are overpaid. I may truly say that, even at this hour, when I am separated from both of them and uncertain whether I may ever be so happy as to see them again, there is no action of my life which has not a remote reference to their opinion, which I equally prize. When I think I have acted well . . . I say often to myself, My dearest love and my friend Russell will be glad of this.[6]

Russell was a young army ensign on half pay who had taken part in the attack on Tippoo Sahib in 1783. The friendship developed quickly into that curious brand of teasing intimacy familiar to everyone who has made a lifelong friend at boarding school. The formidable battery of private language, obscure nicknames, jokes and allusions greeted with laughter at every repetition; the exchange, at the outset of life, of views on God and all the other great abstractions: all this can be charted in the friendship between Tone and Russell. Some echoes of it can be found, not only in the *Memoirs*, but also in the hieroglyphics of Russell's notes which crawl over the pages in the Irish National Archives. (Russell's handwriting was so bad, his difficulty of expressing himself on paper so great, that he would nowadays attract all manner of sympathetic educational attention.)

They reinforced each other's views. Take the idyllic account of the sunny days spent on holidays with Matilda and his small family and his friend:

> I hired a little box of a house at the seaside, at Irishtown, where we spent the summer of 1790. Russell and I were inseparable, and, as our discussions were mostly political, and our sentiments agreed exactly, we extended our views, and fortified each other in the opinions, to the propagation and establishment of which we have ever since been devoted. I recall with transport the happy days we spent together during that period: the delicious dinners, in the preparation of which my wife, Russell and myself were all engaged; our afternoon walks, and the discussions we had as we lay stretched on the grass. It was delightful . . . every day produced a ballad, or political squib, which amused us after dinner.[7]

Both of them were becoming cynical about the milk-and-water ineffectualness of the Whigs and the sham of the independence which the Irish Parliament had won in 1782 ('a bumbling, imperfect business'). By the time he was twenty-six years old he was veering towards the conclusion, which sustained him through the rest of his life, that the influence of England was the 'radical vice of our Government . . . and that true independence was unattainable whilst the connection with England existed'. It was 'the root of the evil'.

How far, at this early stage, did he believe in complete separation? Certainly to express it openly would have been seditious, and he knew that. But one of the principal reasons why in the summer of 1791 he undertook the writing of his most famous pamphlet, *An Argument on Behalf of the Catholics of Ireland*, was not in fact sympathy for the handicaps under which the largest part of the population still laboured – their exclusion from all political and legal life including the vote, and subjection to the remnant of the penal laws – but rather, his growing belief that neither reform nor independence would come about unless Catholic and Dissenter joined hands. The 'union of the sects' was the first necessity.

In his *Argument*, then, he urged immediate emancipation. He rebutted Catholics' incapacity to be free, he denied their ignorance and refuted imputations against their allegiance. But the *Argument* is radical, not revolutionary; loyalty is protested to the King, and the 'bane' of the English connection is not mentioned. He wrote as a rational child of the Enlightenment, in an age when many thought that organized religion and its dogmas were soon to be thrown into the dustbin. Take the much-quoted passage:

> The emancipated and liberal Irishman, like the emancipated and liberal Frenchman, may go to Mass, may tell his beads, *or sprinkle his mistress with Holy Water;** but neither the one nor the other will attend to the rusty and extinguished thunderbolts of the Vatican or the idle anathemas which, indeed, His Holiness is now-a-days too prudent and cautious to issue.[8]

Tone's beliefs were neither implausible nor original. For example, in the spring of 1784 Thomas Carey, the editor of the *Volunteer Journal*, had written 'Let all ranks of oppressed Irishmen ask whence flow their wrongs. From the blasting connection with England.'[9] But Tone's talents were well suited to pamphleteering: a darting felicity of language, a simplicity and directness of argument, a dragonfly mind alighting just long enough to fix the attention. In any case, the paper had an instant success. Priced at one shilling, it sold 6,000 copies by the end of the year. (Compare this with the sales of today's political pamphlets which in England, even on the most burning issues of the day, seldom exceed 1,000.) By the autumn of 1791, Wolfe Tone was a name known well beyond the confines of the Irish Bar, Trinity College and the Castle's intelligence.

William Drennan, born in 1754, wins a rebel's place in the history of eighteenth-century Ireland, if only because he was the proud author of the 'Test' – that is, the words which were meant to be solemnly repeated by every new member of the Society of United Irishmen:

---

* It may be significant that this commonly quoted phrase, which I have italicized, was omitted in the April 1792 edition of the *Argument*. Did somebody point out to Tone that Catholic susceptibilities were not as muted as he thought, or hoped? Had he been pressed to make a tactful amendment?

I, A.B., in the presence of God, do pledge myself to my country, that I will use all my abilities and influence in the attainment of an impartial and adequate representation of the Irish nation in Parliament and as a means of an absolute and immediate necessity in accomplishing this chief good of Ireland, I shall do whatever lies in my power to form a brotherhood of affection, an identity of interests, a communion of all rights, and an union of power among Irishmen of all religious persuasions without which every reform must be partial, not national, inadequate to the wants, delusive to the wishes and insufficient for the freedom and happiness of this country.[10]

Drennan had brooded on the idea of some such body as the Society for fifteen years or more before the actual day of its formation, expressing, for example, in one of the earliest of his many hundreds of letters to his sister Martha McTier (in the summer of 1785) the simple wish which underlay all his hope for the reform of the Irish Parliament, and for the (gradual) emancipation of Catholics – in fact, the sum of his political desire: 'If I could think of politics it should be to persuade the people to a separation from England.'[11]

He was born a 'son of the manse', with all the associations that phrase calls to mind. He 'might have passed, in appearance, for the demure minister of some remote village-congregation of the Scotch Kirk'.[12] He was 5 ft 6 in. tall, said to be 'perfectly formed, with eyes of a fine hazel hue'. In character he was serious, powdered with sanctimoniousness, had a great sense of his own rectitude, and *almost* no sense of absurdity.

Drennan was the youngest of nine, five of whose brothers were stillborn. Like many sons of Ulster Presbyterian ministers, he went to Scotland to study medicine. He was homesick, confessing that he 'was the joke of the lads here for making Belfast the eternal subject of my conversation. I dream of Belfast.'[13] This is of a piece with his sentimentality. It is hard to judge a sentimental man with any hope of fairness: one does not know at what levels of his being the yearning, the soft doubts, the elegiac platitudes operate. Drennan is a particularly difficult example because, just occasionally, he does look at himself with a measure of self-awareness; his confession of ridiculousness seems more ironical than one might expect. Thus in Edinburgh, in his early twenties, on the last page of his doctoral dissertation, written in faultless Latin (about the cutting of veins), he signed off with a self-accusation, 'I said, *while blushing*', before he went on to quote from the famous ode of Catullus on the happiness of longed-for rest after toil.[14]*

The vanity which in the character of Tone is laced with make-believe and self-mockery, is with Drennan served almost neat. Both had a passion for uniforms (whose colour and trimmings were so bound up in the politics of the Volunteers in Belfast), and a keen interest in their own appearance. It is impossible, however, to imagine Tone writing, as Drennan did when only thirty-one years old: 'I now wear spectacles in streets and in company and find them both pleasant and useful'[15] – to which his admirable sister Mrs McTier replied simply, at the foot of her letter, 'Damn your spectacles'. She endured uncomplainingly a great many of her younger brother's earnest reflections. By 1783, his degree in medicine at Edinburgh well behind him, he was beginning to become established as a doctor in Newry; one of the letters runs soberly:

> I am not very fond of clubs, and were it not for a desire of making acquaintance (though club acquaintances are not generally very lucrative ones) I would wish to avoid these meetings and rather cultivate the domestic parties . . . there are many who think that I should join frequently in the bacchanalian roar [in the taverns] particularly as my competitor lays claim to the title of a jolly fellow. Neither my health of body or mind will enable me to comply with this, and I must rest upon that *secret* esteem which men of this turn involuntarily pay to temperance and *unaffected* regularity of life to operate in their minds to any advantage, in place of that frail and fleeting friendship which is founded only on the companionship of the bottle. 13 guineas I have received in fees and spent 18 in two months.[16]

Oddly, it is in his care for money, his parsimony indeed, that his streak of humorous self-criticism surfaces again; after listening to a 'patriotic' sermon by the popular preacher Dean Kirwan one early summer in Dublin, he describes how

> One lady took her purse and not thinking it enough threw a watch with trinkets into the plate which was handed round by Lord Clonmell, etc.

---

* Dixie rubescens:
  'O quid solutis beatius curis
  Cum mens onus reponit, ac peregrino
  Labore fessi, veniamo Larem ad nostrum
  Desideratoque requiescimus lecto.'

You may conceive what a sermon it was when I felt the strongest desire to give a guinea, but somehow or other it was in falling transformed into a shilling – I doubt much if St Paul could have preached better.[17]*

Drennan's growing republicanism did not prevent his showing a frank and proper deference, as a young doctor beginning practice in Newry, to his grander patients. One of his early letters describes an impressive visit in summer 1785 to Lord Clanbrassil's mother at Dundalk:

I came to the great house at about six o'clock – a great room, great company, and great formality. I felt myself a very little discomposed, because I knew none but his Lordship who particularly addressed me . . . dinner was over, so I said I had taken some cold meat before I left Newry. We chatted a little and I belorded the only Lord I knew in proper place and time. In a short time . . . I was called into another great room where Lady Clanbrassil with a candle in her hand wafted me along through many passages till at last we came to the Lady Dowager's apartment – a fine spirited old woman of 82 – I made all proper questions and I was seemingly much approved by Her Ladyship with the candle. I felt her pulse with all due decorum . . . in the course of conversation I collected the degrees and titles of the nobility above and therefore was pretty right in my addresses.[18]

This disarming letter continues over three pages.

All the same, Drennan's sister was, understandably, not very kind in her comments on William's love life. For in 1785 he had told her of his rejected proposal of marriage: 'I received by post a peremptory denial, so peremptory indeed that, by awakening my pride a little it has not a little contributed to quiet my other feelings.' The lady of his fancy, Miss Jones, had written to tell him bluntly that she 'was sorry to find myself the ignorant cause of any uneasiness to you . . . I am not conscious of acting otherwise than natural civility and politeness dictate to every acquaintance.' So far, nothing very remarkable. But unfortunately, Drennan liked to versify. Only a few more months had passed before Martha rebuked him for a most elementary mistake in these matters. She told him that he was being widely

---

* Perhaps one might add that, in *The Sham Squire*, reference is made to Dean Kirwan's 'irresistible powers of persuasion' which 'even in times of public calamity and distress repeatedly produced contributions exceeding twelve hundred pounds at a sermon'. Drennan did well to contain himself.

ridiculed as the 'gentle, tender, votary of Hope, the love-breathing Edwin'. Somehow, curious in one so secretive, he had been found out reusing one of his love-poems:

> your [poem] 'Lottery of Love' was shown the other day to Miss Jones as lines addressed to Miss D. Ogle – this must be impossible, but how can it be contradicted? You were strangely imprudent, nay worse, indelicate, ever to shew those lines, to address them to another lady – I can't believe it.[19]

But the damage was done.

Perhaps some of his insensitivity can be put down to political pursuits taking precedence over the cultivation of social niceties: not unusual in any century. Throughout the 1780s, he continued to summon the Irish people to recover their pride and independence. He wrote letters to *The Belfast Newsletter* urging a second National Convention of Volunteers. Then in 1785, his pamphlet, curiously titled *Letters of Orellana: An Irish Helot*, was published after it had first appeared in *The Belfast Newsletter*.* This was Drennan's passionate exhortation to his fellow countrymen – his *fellow slaves*, as he calls them in the opening to each of the seven letters to the seven Northern counties – to fight for 'a more equal representation of people in the Parliament of Ireland'. Much of the argument and rhetoric is familiar, echoing manifestos of the American War of Independence:

> Our own wills, or what ought to be the same thing, the will of our representatives, either possesses an adequate share in the supreme legislative power, or it does not. If it does not, we are slaves. *We are so.*[20]

> If I be asked to name one of these constitutional rights, I cover my face with my hand, and I mention the right of being taxed by ourselves, or by our representatives in parliament, without the absolute enjoyment of which prerogative, what is the distance between an Irishmen and a Freeman? Not less than three thousand miles. Until you obtain the *practical* enjoyment of this primary, necessary, self-evident, uncontrovertible right, you can have no *constitution* and your just title – compliment yourselves as you please – is slaves.[21]

---

* A.T.Q. Stewart suggests the title may derive from Aphra Behn's *Oronooko, or the Royal Slave*, remarkable as the first expression in English literature of sympathy for the oppressed negroes (*A Deeper Silence*, p. 134). Drennan later regretted his choice of title. Orellana had failed, and had committed mass suicide with his followers (Larkin, *The Trial of William Drennan*, p. 7).

Reform must be gained by the exertions of all the people, must not simply be accepted as a series of concessions:

> Did the concession of the ministry at this moment present the nation with a reform bill in a gold box, I should accept it, as an Irishman, with a reluctance bordering upon disgust: when I reflected that my countrymen might only divert themselves for a little time with the blessing as children with a toy. I declare that I should be sorry that any minister brought about the redemption of a nation which ought to redeem itself . . .[22]

But although the Helot calls on all churchmen, Presbyterians and Catholics alike, to 'embrace each other in the mild spirit of Christianity, and to unite as a sacred compact in the cause of your sinking country', in one letter he reveals a characteristic ambivalence (which, later, he regrets having voiced):

> The Catholics are at this day absolutely INCAPABLE of making a good use of political liberty . . . I speak the sentiments of the most enlightened among them, and I assert it as a fact, that the most able men in that body are too wise to wish for a *complete* extention of civil franchise to those of their own persuasion . . .[23]

Thus, although Drennan was one of the earliest to preach that the one hope of independence from England lay in 'the unity of all the sects', and was altogether sincere in all his beliefs, driven by his strong Presbyterian conscience, I do not think it can be said that the brotherhood he so fervently advocated came naturally to him. Apart from the passage in *Orellana*, unguarded references to 'popery', trespassing on some pages of his letters, betray his less than ecumenical instincts. Describing a funeral, while still at Newry, he writes:

> I walked before the rest in a very disagreeable procession, preceded only by a beggar-looking fellow who kept constantly jingling a little bell in his hand as if to apprise the whole time that the deceased and the doctor were just a-coming. This is a constant ceremonial in funeral solemnities at this place, and not satisfied with this, there is always one of these bell-ringers that go through the town, informing everyone by their papistical bell who has died, at what hour . . .[24]

This contrariness of outward preaching and inner mood – for one can hardly maintain that the tone of voice is very brotherly – runs through many of the writings of members of the Society of United Irishmen, and remained a fatal flaw in achieving any real unity of Irishmen.* Drennan's feelings of 'brotherhood' rested more on what he thought he should believe, rather than what he really did believe. He slipped naturally into his prejudices. Of one Catholic leader he wrote:

> McKenna [a poplin merchant who became a leading member of the Dublin United Irishmen, admired by Tone if not by Drennan] is sensible, but very irregular in his life, and what most of his persuasion has in too great a degree, a slatternliness and often slovenliness of mind.[25]

On the other hand, Drennan's ambition to put his declared beliefs into practice was serious. One cannot deny his claim to be a founding father of the Society, even though he may sometimes have teetered on the brink of absurdity.

Drennan was very susceptible to the seduction of emblems, ceremonies, oaths, secrecy, and the ritual language of Freemasonry. A paper in the appendices of the House of Commons Committee of Secrecy's Report on the United Irish conspiracy, said to have been circulating in Dublin even before the foundation of the Belfast Society, is headed with Drennan's own design and the Masonic-like title of 'The Irish Brotherhood'. Its goal was the promotion of 'the Rights of Man' in Ireland and 'the Greatest Happiness of the Greatest Number'. Every member was to wear, day and night, an amulet around his neck

> containing the great principle which unites the Brotherhood, in letters of gold, and a ribbon, striped with all the original colours and enclosed in a sheath of white silk, to represent the pure union of all the mingled rays, and the abolition of all superficial distinctions, all colours and shades of difference, for the sake of one illustrious end.[26]

To many in this age, Freemasonry filled some of the spiritual void which had been left by the questioning of the truth and value of old-established religion; some of the human need for ceremony, secrecy, 'belonging'. A.T.Q. Stewart has written apropos of Drennan:

---

* Drennan in his letters made odd references to Catholics as 'savages' and once wrote after a meeting with the Catholic Committee: 'Catholics are to a man very suspicious and apt to take dislikes'.

[Freemasonry] is frequently an element in the many challenges to the status quo in State and Church. Montesquieu and Voltaire were Masons, as were Goethe and Mozart, Franklin and Washington . . . In Irish terms Freemasonry was important because it was almost the only sphere in which Catholics and Protestants could meet on equal terms. For Catholics it was a refuge from the penal laws . . . [this] explains what has always been something of a mystery about Irish politics in the 1780s, why the old asperities between Protestants and Catholics seemed suddenly to melt, and both persuasions, especially in the North of Ireland, seemed eager to create a new Irish nationality, one more liberal than the 'Protestant nation' or a hypothetical theocracy dominated by the Catholic Church . . .

But in general the old asperities had not softened . . . Far from being smothered in 1791, the sectarian flame was just about to break out with a renewed ferocity, which has hardly abated since . . . when all is said and done, the radicals and republicans were a small segment of the population, susceptible to the Enlightenment influences specific to the eighteenth century.[27]

When in late 1789 Drennan moved from Newry to Dublin, hoping to advance his medical career, he wrote to Samuel McTier, his brother-in-law, fellow United Irishman and ballast-master of the port of Belfast, asking him to furnish him with as many recommendatory letters as possible, and in particular 'from ladies to ladies, as it is in the accoucheur line my first aims are chiefly directed'. He also wrote to his sister:

I believe I shall take [a lodging] . . . in No 27 New Buildings, Dame Street, but tell not the price in the streets of Belfast, 50 guineas. The fact is, no genteel one and central one can be got cheaper and this one is most genteel. A good lodging is a hobby-horse of mine and I must crib in other things. A member of Parliament, Pennefeather, has the floor *above* me . . . I have not received the introduction to Lord Londonderry.[28]

He now began to launch himself seriously into the swim of things and was very soon meeting John Keogh, rich merchant and leading member of the Catholic Committee, listening to Grattan in the House of Commons, growing disillusioned with the Whig club 'which literally does nothing more than eat and drink', watching processions to the hustings of the General Election of 1790 in Dublin, and, above all, brooding on the possibility of 'instituting a Society'. On these latter two activities he wrote long and vivid letters to his brother-in-law in Belfast:

1790, May 3. I have just seen Grattan and [Edward's brother, Henry] Fitzgerald proceeding to the hustings at the head of more than 1400 men, 18 of the Corporations' bands of music playing, etc., Grattan advancing on his light fantastic toe, hope elevating and joy brightening his crest, his eyes rolling with that fine enthusiasm without which it is impossible to be a great man . . . while at some distance behind walks Napper Tandy, in all the surliness of republicanism, grinning most ghastly smiles, and as he lifts his hat from his head the human-headed monster raises a shout that reverberates through every corner of the castle. I see suitable devices and mottos on the standards – *The Men of the People* – *The Men that dare be Honest in the Worst of Times* – *A Place Bill* – *A Responsibility* – and in particular I distinguish a negro boy well dressed and holding on high the Cap of Liberty [was this Edward Fitzgerald's faithful servant Tony?], but I look in vain for a *Bill for Amended Representation*.[29]

1791, May 21. I should very much desire that a Society were instituted in this City having much of the secrecy and somewhat of the ceremonial of Freemasonry, so much secrecy as might communicate curiosity, uncertainty, expectation to the minds of surrounding men, so much impressive and affecting ceremony in its internal economy as without impeding real business might strike the soul through its senses. A benevolent conspiracy – a plot for the people – no *Whig* club – no party title – the Brotherhood its name – the Rights of Men and the Greatest Happiness of the Greatest Number its end – its general end Real Independence to Ireland, and Republicanism its particular purpose . . . Communication with the leading men in France, in England and in America so as to cement the scattered and shifting sand of republicanism into a body . . . and when thus cemented it to sink it like a caisson in the dark and troubled waters, a stable unseen power.[30]

From this day in May 1791 Drennan's letters become more and more intense, as his self-styled 'impregnable heart in politics' grows stronger.

Hamilton Rowan was a giant, born in London in 1751, who strode through the last quarter of the century casting after him shadows of eccentric behaviour, quarrels, duels, escapes. Throughout his long life his behaviour was a mixture of benevolence, generosity, indignation and wayward impetuosity. His descendants still own the family's battlemented castle at Killyleagh, County Down. His father's fortune, however, 'like that of many Irish gentlemen, had need of nursing, and so he [had] retired to England with his wife', the year before his only son was born.[31]

He was sent to Westminster School. By his own confession he was 'giddy and negligent', but acquired many passions which recur as leitmotifs on every page of his *Autobiography*. One was mechanical: he loved to tinker with watches, and became very good at it. 'Though he never made a *pocket watch*, and probably might mar many, yet all the interior machinery he knew and could name: the whole movement he took to pieces and replaced.'[32] Another passion was for water and boating; he was constantly jumping into rivers, leaping 'from unusual heights into the Thames', throwing his tutor at Cambridge into the Cam, swimming for a bet in uniform from Gosport to Portsmouth (with two gold watches in his pocket).

Always an inquisitive traveller, on his first vacation as a Cambridge undergraduate he made a trip to Holland 'to partake of the amusements of the ice in that country'. In Rotterdam, he found time to observe:

> we were at a loss to account for the frequent salutations of our companions, when we could see no persons in the street for whom, as we thought, they were likely to be intended; but upon inquiry, we found that most of the houses had small mirrors suspended outside them, in such a manner as to reflect the passengers in the street to other mirrors in the interior of the room, where the family resided, and it was to those their passing friends made their obeisances.[33]

A little later, having arranged a commission in the Huntingdon militia for his friend, and about to return to his governorship of South Carolina, Lord Charles Montague offered Rowan a passage as his secretary aboard the frigate *Tartar* from Falmouth. They put in at the Azores. Rowan records his first experience of falling in love. In a convent:

> I was shown into the parlour . . . in a short time a young person in the costume of the order entered on the other side of the grating: the customary salutations passed in French, in which tongue neither of us was a great proficient; but we soon discoursed as familiarly as if we had been old acquaintances. She told me her father had been a merchant at Fayal, but had died suddenly, leaving her but a small provision, which she had thrown into the funds of the convent, where she found herself extremely happy. On my taking leave of her, she presented me with a small bag of her own making, composed of stained fibres of the leaf of the aloes, and desired me to remember her as sister Celestine, in a tone which I thought told another tale. At the age I then was, few females who had youth and

good manners could displease; but a nun was a particularly interesting object, and of course I was desperately in love for the rest of the voyage, and until I became acquainted with the more languid but fairer faces of the Carolinians.[34]

Rowan also loved animals. He took his 'little [*sic*] dog' (generally a Newfoundland) with him everywhere, even in rowing boats on the Seine. Later in his life he was heard talking, and occasionally barking, to it in the streets of Dublin. On returning to England after nearly three months in Charleston, he sadly recalls, 'taking with me a racoon, an opossum and a young bear. After a very rough passage I landed at Portsmouth – my racoon dead, my bear washed overboard, and my opossum lost in the cable tier.'[35]

Half-way through his next few years, which he chose to spend in France – boating, duelling, mingling with Irish immigrants in the French service – Lord Charles reappeared in his life with a scheme to go to Lisbon; he himself had been promised the command of a Portuguese regiment by the Marquis of Pombal, and Rowan was to be given an instant appointment as a Lieutenant-Colonel; the regiment would then at once be dispatched to South America. The plan, though he confesses that it was 'most agreeable to my wandering turn of mind', came to nothing, but at least Rowan was delighted at some of the curious animals to be seen in an estate on the banks of the Tagus, including 'an elephant, the largest I had ever seen, but very tame; and a stable containing sixteen zebras in beautiful order'.

Once back in Paris, his 'wandering turn of mind' was temporarily stilled. There were no more military excursions. But he needed to be active:

Being always fond of boating, I had brought to Paris a small Thames-wherry, which I bought from Roberts of Lambeth, from whom the Westminster boys hired their boats. I fancied that I possessed superior dexterity in its management, and this led me to accompany the Queen when she went by water to Fontainebleau . . . I saw the Queen speaking to the Duke of Lauzun, and pointing it out; but alas! the only remark she had made was '*que cela peut être amusement pour un Seigneur Anglais!*'[36]

At the age of thirty, he married a young, forthright and sensible Irish girl who had often stayed with his mother at her house in Pinner. There was general approval of Miss Sarah Dawson. As much

as anyone could, she kept him in order. In their absences from one
another his letters strike a surprisingly subdued and domestic note
(or perhaps not surprising; enormous men are often very tender to
their wives, treating them with eggshell delicacy). Describing his
temporary lodgings in Paris he writes of his salon 'hung with
crimson damask, a large marble slab upon a gold frame . . . and a
handsome pier glass over the chimney, so well placed I wish my
Dawson were here to look at herself'.[37]

After their marriage, they led a busy social life in Paris, in the last
days of the *ancien régime*. The Duke of Manchester (the British
Ambassador and Lord Charles's brother) appointed Rowan 'to
attend the Duchess on her first presentation to the unfortunate
Queen, Marie Antoinette, then in high glory'. He found time to pay
visits to his sister Sydney in a convent in St Cyr – where she was
completing her education. He tells how once:

> We were ushered with great ceremony to the quarters of the lady abbess,
> by whom we were invited to dinner. During the dessert [she] said to me
> 'We know that the ecclesiastics in your country are permitted to marry.' It
> then appeared that having had occasion in the mean time to pay my sis-
> ter's pension, I had signed my order on the banker, 'ARCHD. HAMILTON
> ROWAN' and the Christian name of Archibald being little known to the
> abbess as a saint . . . she had supposed me to be an archbishop, and
> received me with a degree of civility (due to my supposed character); a
> civility, I fancy, well worthy of imitation elsewhere.[38]

Harold Nicolson, in the biography of his great-great-grandfather,
is unable to establish to his own satisfaction why his engaging bear of
an ancestor, whose interests were in his youth clearly not at all political, should have led him into such deep, revolutionary thickets when
he eventually returned to settle in Ireland:

> He was not a deep reader, nor was his temperament attuned to the
> nervous sensibility of Jean Jacques Rousseau. There is small trace in his
> letters and comments at the time . . . of the philosophic jargon of the Paris
> salons . . . Unquestionably he convinced himself that the faults of society
> could be directly attributed to the oppression of the governing class and
> that with the removal of privilege these faults, as if by magic, would melt
> away.[39]

This may tell us more about Harold Nicolson than Rowan. For
Rowan was a quintessential Don Quixote, tilting at windmills every-

where. Injustice made him reach at once for his sword and his purse, so that he could immediately both challenge the perpetrator and compensate the victim. He was no reader of books, certainly; but as a passionately indignant enemy of everything he saw to be arrogant, unjust, corrupt, he imbibed (although does not seem to have reflected much upon) contradictory draughts of equality and liberty.

On his return to his Ireland in 1784, he bought a small house in County Kildare. He stayed often in Dublin, and soon found causes and people to champion. His most celebrated protégée was the four-teen-year-old daughter of a hairdresser, who had been decoyed into a brothel, the madame of which extricated herself from trouble through her powerful connections (the plot is very contemporary). The dubious but readable Sir Jonah Barrington[40] tells the tale:

> the humour of Hamilton Rowan, which had a sort of quixotic tendency to resist all oppression and to redress every species of wrong, led him to take up the cause of Mary Neil with a zeal and enthusiastic perseverance which nobody but the knight of La Mancha could have exceeded. Day and night the ill-treatment of this girl was the subject his thoughts, his actions, his dreams . . . he vowed personal vengeance against all her calumniators, high and low.
>
> At about this time about twenty young barristers, including myself, had formed a dinner club in Dublin; we had taken large apartments for the purpose; and, as we were not yet troubled with *too much* business, were in the habit of faring luxuriously every day, and taking a bottle of the best claret which could be obtained . . . One day, whilst dining with our usual hilarity, the servant informed us that a gentleman below stairs desired to be admitted *for a moment.* We considered it to be some brother-barrister who requested permission to join our party, and desired him to be shown up. What was our surprise, however, on perceiving the figure that pre-sented itself! – a man, who might have served as a model for a Hercules, his gigantic limbs conveying the idea of almost supernatural strength: his shoulders, arms, and broad chest, were the very emblems of muscular energy; and his flat, rough countenance, overshadowed by enormous dark eyebrows, and deeply furrowed by strong lines of vigour and fortitude, completed one of the finest, yet most formidable figures I had ever beheld: close by his side stalked in a shaggy Newfoundland dog of cor-responding magnitude, with hair a foot long, and who, if he should be voraciously inclined, seemed well able to devour a barrister or two without overcharging his stomach: – as he entered, indeed, he alternately looked at us and then up at his master, as if only awaiting the order of the latter to commence the onslaught. His master held in his hand a large,

yellow, knotted club, slung by a leathern thong round his great wrist: he
also had a long small-sword by his side.

This apparition walked deliberately up to the table; and having made
his obeisance with seeming courtesy, a short pause ensued, during
which he looked round on all the company with an aspect, if not stern, yet
ill-calculated to set our minds at ease either as to his or to his dog's ulterior
intentions.

'Gentlemen' at length he said, in a tone and with an air at once so mild
and courteous, nay so polished, as fairly to give the lie, as it were, to his
gigantic and threatening figure: 'Gentlemen! I have heard with very great
regret that some members of this club have been so indiscreet as to
calumniate the character of Mary Neil, which, from the part I have taken,
I feel I have identified with my own: if any present hath done so, I doubt
not he will now have the courage and candour to avow it. – *Who* avows it?'
The dog looked up at him again; he returned the glance; but contented
himself, for the present, with patting the animal's head, and was silent: so
were we . . . never did I see the old axiom that 'what is everybody's business is nobody's business' more thoroughly exemplified. A few of the
company whispered each his neighbour, and I perceived one or two steal
a fruit-knife under the table-cloth, in case of extremities; but no one made
any reply. We were eighteen in number . . .

He repeated his demand (elevating his tone each time) thrice 'Does any
gentleman avow it?' A faint buzz now circulated round the room, but
there was no *answer* whatsoever . . . at length our visitor said, with a loud
voice, that he must suppose, if any gentleman had made any assertions
against Mary Neil's character, he would have had the courage and spirit to
aver it: 'therefore,' continued he, 'I shall take it for granted that my
information was erroneous; and, in that point of view, I regret having
alarmed your society.' And, without another word, he bowed three times
very low, and retired backwards toward the door (his dog also backing out
with equal politeness), where with a salaam doubly ceremonious Mr
Rowan ended this extraordinary interview. On the first of his departing
bows, by a simultaneous impulse, we all rose and returned his salute,
almost touching the table with our noses, but still in profound silence;
which bowing was repeated till he was fairly out of the room. Three or
four of the company then ran hastily to the window to be sure that he and
the dog were clear off into the street . . . then a general roar of laughter
ensued, and we talked it over in a hundred different ways: the whole of our
arguments, however, turned upon the question 'which had behaved the
politest upon the occasion?' but not one word was uttered as to which had
behaved the *stoutest*.

This spirit of false chivalry, which took such entire possession of
Hamilton Rowan's understanding, was soon diverted into the channels of
political theory; and from the discussion of general politics, he advanced
to the contemplation of sedition.[41]

The causes which Rowan took up were, at least until he entered the lists of United Irishmen, odd and unpredictable. A Sheriff, in helping to put an end to a session of bull-baiting on a field outside Dublin, had instructed some soldiers to fire on the crowd. In impugning the Sheriff, Rowan found himself defending the bull-baiting. Agreeing with the Solicitor-General who had pronounced that 'with truth there is no other country in Europe where the lower orders of the people are allowed so little amusement as in this kingdom', he wrote a pamphlet in which he maintained that bull-baiting was *not* like

> that barbarous, that cowardly practice of throwing at cocks upon Shrove Tuesday, an inhuman, an unmanly sport. At Cambridge there were constant bull-baitings, under the very eye of the Vice-Chancellor and all the doctors of law and divinity; and Paris, that seat of elegance, had her *combats du taureau avec de dogues Anglois* – bull-baitings, which were attended by the first nobility of that kingdom.[42]

His courage – pretty reckless – and his readiness at all times to spring, or lurch, to the help of those less fortunate than himself, led him to become an expert duellist.

It is not clear at what moment or why, during the late 1780s, his championship of odd causes developed into the politics of sedition. Perhaps it was only natural that the shameless corruption of the times – the contemptuous use of places, peerages and pensions, the sham of the independence of Parliament, the arbitrary use of power, should have rendered his large frame incandescent. Fiery instinct governed him. He was an *immediate* man.

The last sentence of one of the summings-up of his character by his cool, rational great-great-grandson can, however, be challenged:

> The incantations of Paris rationalism, the intoxicating phrases of the American Declaration of Independence, had bemused his mind; his loathing of unfairness, his detestation of privileged corruption, were so blinding and intense that in the hurry of his exasperation he never paused to consider what particular form of anarchy would supplant the order which he sought to destroy. At that stage at least his hatred of the oppressor was deeper and more impatient than his love, or his consideration, for the oppressed.[43]

I can detect in Rowan plenty of outrage, but not hatred: not that secret and suspicious hatred which corroded so many of the other

United Irishmen. Here, just before the curtain rises on the narrative of the years leading up to the Rebellion, is the sketch of a scene remembered by an old man in the next century – somebody whose sympathies were clearly not on the side of the United Irishmen, but who (like everyone who ever met Rowan) was happy to pay tribute to his gentlemanliness:

I entered college in the year 1791, a year rendered memorable by the institution of the Society of the United Irishmen. They held their meetings in an obscure passage called Back-Lane . . . The very aspect of the place seemed to render it adapted for cherishing a conspiracy. It was in the locality where the tailors, skinners and curriers held their guilds, and was the region of operative democracy . . . I walked in without hesitation – no one forbidding me – and found the society in full debate, the Hon. Simon Butler in the chair. I saw there, for the first time, the men with the three names, which were now become so familiar to the people of Dublin – Theobald Wolfe Tone, James Napper Tandy, and Archibald Hamilton Rowan.

The first was a slight, effeminate-looking man, with a hatchet face, a long, aquiline nose, rather handsome and genteel-looking, with lank, straight hair combed down on his sickly red cheek, exhibiting a face the most insignificant and mindless that could be imagined. His mode of speaking was in correspondence with face and person. It was polite and gentlemanly, but totally devoid of anything like energy or vigour. I set him down as a worthy, good-natured, flimsy man, in whom there was no harm, and as the least likely person in the world to do mischief to the state.

Tandy was the very opposite looking character. He was the ugliest man I ever gazed on. He had a dark, yellow, truculent-looking countenance, a long, drooping nose, rather sharpened at the point, and the muscles of his face formed two cords at each side of it. He had a remarkable hanging-down look, and an occasional twitching or convulsive motion of his nose and mouth, as if he was snapping on the side of him while he was speaking.

Not so Hamilton Rowan. I thought him not only the most handsome, but the largest man I had ever seen. Tone and Tandy looked like pygmies beside him. His ample and capacious forehead seemed the seat of thought and energy; while with such an external to make him feared, he had a courtesy of manner that excited love and confidence. He held in his hand a large stick, and was accompanied by a large dog.[44]

In the summer of 1766, on the shores of the new artificial lake in the great grounds of Carton House (some four hours by coach from Dublin), the three-year-old Lord Edward Fitzgerald and his brothers carried oyster shells to help his adored and adoring mother Emily, Duchess of Leinster, to ornament the ceiling of their new shell house, Waterstone. This cottage was intended to echo the grotto in the gardens of Goodwood, principal home of her father the Duke of Richmond. 'Darling Eddy' was the favourite of Emily's vast brood – her eldest son had just died at the age of sixteen: shells, as she may have been aware, are symbols of resurrection.

Whether such infant foretaste of the delights of gilded simplicity helped to shape Edward's aspirations and beliefs in the benignity of Nature one cannot tell. I am inclined to believe that it did; and his early schooldays would have confirmed it. Here is a description of a typical summer's day at the family 'school' on the sea coast south of Dublin, romantically named Frescati. It was spent under the eye of their devoted Scottish tutor Ogilvie, who later became the incongruous lover and, after the Duke of Leinster's death, the second husband of Emily (and father to at least three of her twenty-two children). School does not sound arduous:[45]

> In the morning after ten o'clock . . . they settled down to their school work until about one o'clock. Then they played croquet, bowls and other games or dug in the garden until dinner time. On dull days they played chess while the little ones ran about. After dinner they played and splashed in the sea until about five o'clock when the older ones did a last hour or so of school work.

Ogilvie wrote to Emily from Frescati, evening after evening, reporting his charges' more or less endearing habits:

> Eddy is just eating a crust as long and as thick as his arm. I stole a piece from him as he was drawing a square so he has laid down his pencil and says it is better to eat his bread first . . . He has begun his square again with a 'now square, nobody'll eat your bread'. Eddy is crying out, 'O Monstrous O Monstrous; indeed I'll never draw, there's an end of it. Indeed Mr Warren [their drawing master], I cannot draw, there's the truth of the matter. I must try again, I must try again . . .'[46]

Ogilvie took the boys fishing in the bay and to Dublin for the theatre. They all dug their gardens with him, in obedience to Rousseau's injunction to teach children the value of property by giving them land to till and make their own through cultivation. In summer they sickled and stacked hay together.

Such fond and doting attention, such schooldays spent in the innocence of Arcadia, must have contributed to Edward's lifelong hankering for the idyllic, encouraged by his mother. (A suitable education for a revolutionary, perhaps. One wonders what different channels this might have taken, had he come under the tuition of Rousseau himself – which he well might have done, since Emily had written to him in 1767, offering the now nearly mad philosopher an elegant retreat if he would educate her children.)

Throughout his short life, in a profusion of fond letters to his mother, Lord Edward rhapsodized on the pleasures of cottage gardening, describing, for example:

> a bay window, looking out into the garden, which is a small green plot, surrounded by good trees, and in it three of the finest thorns I ever saw, and all the trees so placed that you may shade yourself from the sun all hours of the day; the bay window covered with honeysuckle, and up to the window some roses . . . on the side of the house opposite the grass plot, there is ground enough for a flower-garden, communicating with the front garden by a little walk.[47]

Twice in his youth he travelled to North America and enjoyed huge and hopelessly intoxicating draughts of 'liberty'. The first was in 1781 as an eighteen-year-old Lieutenant in the 96th and 19th Regiments of Foot; he is said to have recalled these days as he lay on his deathbed nineteen years later: 'Ah! I was wounded then in a very different cause; that was in fighting *against* liberty – this, in fighting *for* it.'[48]

But the future revolutionary seems to have been a much-loved as well as a fearless soldier. Once, at Eutah Springs, he was found, badly wounded, by 'a poor negro, who carried him off on his back to his hut, and there nursed him most tenderly, till he was well enough of his wound to bear removing to Charleston'. In gratitude, he took the man into his service, and, his biographer Thomas Moore tells us, 'faithful Tony continued devotedly attached to his noble master to the end of his life',[49] a familiar and universally recognized phenomenon of the streets of Dublin in the 1790s. And one of his Commanding Officers, after Lord Edward's death, wrote to Moore of his 'frank and open manner, his universal benevolence, his *gaieté de coeur*, his valour almost chivalrous, his unassuming tone . . . his great animal spirits, which bore him up against all fatigue'.[50]

Yet however great his aristocratic charm and dash and courage, it is impossible to escape, in everything that Lord Edward did, the impression of extreme ingenuousness. Long letters to his mother spoke of the ideal life enjoyed by the old settlers in New Brunswick, 'They supply all their wants by their contrivances, so that they seldom buy anything. They ought to be the happiest people in the world, but they do not seem to know it . . . the equality of everybody and of their manner of life I like very much.' And again, after sleeping rough in the woods up-country he was equally enthusiastic about the agreeable life of noble savages, 'one of the nights we cooked our victuals, and did everything ourselves . . . Savages have all the real happiness of life, without any of those inconveniences, or ridiculous obstacles to it, which custom has introduced to us.'[51] He was forever expanding his paean to the joys of savage life, comparing it favourably to that enjoyed by the Holland House set in London:

> no cases of looking forward to the fortune for children – of thinking how you are to live: no separations in families, one in Ireland, one in England: no devilish politics, no fashions, customs, duties or appearances in the world to interfere with one's happiness. Instead of being served and supported by servants, everything is here done by one's relations – by the people one loves; and the mutual obligations you must be under increase your love for each other. To be sure, the poor ladies are obliged to cut a little wood and bring a little water. Now . . . [his sisters] Lucy and Sophia [would be] cooking and drying fish. As for you, dear mother, you would be smoking your pipe. Ogilvie and us boys, after having brought in our game, would be lying about the fire, while our squaws were helping the ladies to cook, or taking care of our papouses: all this in a fine wood, beside some beautiful lake, which when you are tired of, you would in ten minutes, without any baggage, get into your canoes and off with you elsewhere.[52]

However charmed the Fitzgerald family circle, few would disagree that this shows, even for someone aged only twenty-five, a rather optimistic view of human nature. Fewer still, perhaps, would choose to locate Utopia among the natives of Nova Scotia – apt though Utopians are to choose unlikely sites. But, to judge from his letters, Lord Edward seems to have reflected not at all on the ocean of difference between days and nights spent as an honoured guest, moving on and eventually back to civilization, and the hardness, exigencies and diseases of a native life from which his hosts could not escape.

There were parties up-country, too: 'I have had two parties with the savages which are still pleasanter – you may guess the reason –

there are *des dames*, who are the most comical creatures in the world.'[53] Lord Edward was amazingly open with his mother about sexual adventure. After a brief stay in Martinique under a flag of truce in 1793 he wrote, 'The women are pretty; dance and dress very well; and are, as the French officers say *vastly good-natured*'. But he always took care to reassure her that she was the one upon whom he doted. And indeed his mother does seem to have looked on her son's amours as 'a compliment rather than a betrayal, an indication that no serious attachment had displaced her in their hearts'.[54]

By the mid 1780s Lord Edward was on leave and half-pay. Much of his time he spent in high society in London, staying at Holland House and listening to the conversation of Fox and Sheridan. Not unnaturally he preferred this life to the amusements he found in Dublin, where he was also too often absent from his beloved mother. Desultorily, back in Ireland, he continued to study the art of military fortifications – in 1788 he had drawn plans of the fortifications of Cadiz – desultorily he toyed with the idea of becoming a lawyer. Apart from a few continuing reflections on the pleasures of primitive life and some doubts as to the propriety of the American War in which he had so bravely fought he gave no sign of revolutionary indications: he was happy to be given one of the family seats in the House of Commons in Dublin, becoming one of the 'Leinster squadron', at first subscribing to the moderate Whig and patriot opposition of Grattan. That was, at first, as far as he wished actively to go. Indeed, he was not far out in his estimation of his own character when he wrote, 'I never think of going to anything pleasant myself; I am led to it by somebody. I depend entirely upon other people, and then insensibly *je m'amuse*.'[55]

Were it not for Rebellion and his young death, should he then be taken altogether seriously? Heroic myth has exalted him (but then, it exalted the sulky Achilles). He was spoilt. His good looks, courage, gaiety, money, charm, connections were all presents from a fairy godfather of the most dangerous kind. Politically speaking, it is not altogether surprising that the Fitzgerald family – the sons of the Earl of Kildare and the first Duke of Leinster, that is – were sometimes treated with less seriousness than their wealth and splendid houses, their ancient lineage, their connections on both sides of the water might have been expected to command. Lord Edward's brother, the second Duke of Leinster, was once described as 'the most noble and puissant Patriot. His Grace Cromeboo of Leinster . . . a very high and very variable weathercock, whose face turns the City of Dublin, and some other interesting parts of this Kingdom, almost to peace or war.'[56] He was also called *this blockhead of a Duke*. 'His own ambition was a vice-treasureship for Ireland, of which he observed modestly . . . I confess I do not think it quite so honourable an employment as my rank ought to expect.'[57]

The end of the 1780s, with all the excitement of the 'events in France', saw Lord Edward beginning to 'give way without reserve to his judgement and feelings, and take part with the oppressed and against the oppressor to the full length that his own natural sense of justice and benevolence dictated'.[58] Perhaps he was not yet a fully-fledged republican. But the early days of the French Revolution were a paradise for anyone whose susceptibility to Utopianism was, like Lord Edward Fitzgerald's, well above the average.

There must be few, if any, secret societies which have not had a Judas or two in their midst. Reasonably alert authorities who become aware that, somewhere in their purview, a body is administering a ceremonial oath of secrecy, will scent danger, and take steps to infiltrate it. The Society of United Irishmen was no exception. Its history is riddled with informers from beginning to end. Especially after 1794, when it began to spread its tentacles wider, it never solved the insoluble problem of how to be both a closed society and a mass movement.

In the nature of things, informers are seldom if ever seen plain. Their exits and entrances are shadowy, their trails misleading. I have chosen to sketch only one informer at present, Leonard McNally: a consummate example of the genre, who made one of his closest colleagues at the Bar weep when he thought of his conspicuous loyalty to his clients.

The son of a Dublin merchant who had died when he was under ten years old, McNally had been somehow educated abroad, in Bordeaux. When he was nineteen he enterprisingly opened a grocery shop in Capel Street, Dublin, and also began to study Law. In his mid-twenties he was called to the Irish Bar, but decided – like Tone and so many other young Dubliners with more ambition than fortune – to go to London.

Nobody in his life accused him of any lack of physical courage. In his late twenties he was called to the English Bar at the Middle Temple. But briefs were few and in some poverty he turned to journalism and the theatre. He wrote well, and was for many years the editor of *The Public Ledger*. He was the author of 'Sweet Lass of Richmond Hill', and married a Miss Janson who lived there (and was, presumably, the lass). His talent for mixing the romantic and the cynical led him to write comedies and farces with fair success.

In some of these plays an Irish bitterness can be glimpsed. He shows the relish he takes in mistaken identities, in social deceits, in trickery. He nudges his audience into collusion.

It is part of the nature of the spy, or spy-to-be, to enjoy sailing close to the wind. When in his play *Fashionable Levities* (produced in 1785) Lady Flippant Savage conspires with her friend about liaisons, she advises 'you salute your acquaintance – giggle behind your fan, assume a perfect indifference, whisper your handsome husband to mortify them – and laugh out to shew your inward satisfaction and ineffable contempt'.

Here is an account of how McNally enjoyed dissimulation, even when no money was involved:

> McNally's political views were considered even more democratic than Curran's.* He made a bet that he would dine at the mess at the Fermanagh Militia, an ultra-Orange body. He joined them unasked, and made himself so agreeable, and every man there so pleasant, that he received a general invitation to their mess from that day . . . Mr McNally must at least have had a rare amount of what is familiarly termed 'cheek'. In his defence of Watty Cox [a gunsmith turned writer and bookseller, who also advised Edward Fitzgerald on military matters] he says 'Few men become informers until they have forfeited public character'.[59]

A glimpse of the murky springs of his character may perhaps be seen, still as it were behind the theatre-goer's fan, in his prologue to *Retaliation, A Farce*. The title-page announces this to have been performed 'with universal applause' at the Theatre Royal, Covent Garden, in 1782:

> Trite seems our Author's Task, when all Creation
> Obey the Maxims of *Retaliation*.
> The old, the young, the rich, poor, great, and small,
> Are governed by *retorting* one and all.

---

* Charles Curran, described as being of 'grotesquely simian appearance' and 'an imp of pandemonium', was universaly acknowledged to be the most formidable cross-examiner and advocate, and played the leading part in Drennan's defence against seditious libel.

Lord Dangle would intrigue to cut a Figure,
For Treach'ry makes your folks of rank look bigger –
My Lady's stung, and so, twixt Vice and Whim
Intrigues . . . and thus *retaliates* on him.

Jane was a Draper's Wife, and Jane within her
Felt strong Temptation to become a Sinner;
Not from Caprice or Whim – but mark – th'event is
She lik'd, and scarce knew why . . . the elder 'Prentice.

The Husband hears, and cursing at the Slur,
Resolves to break his vow as well as her . . .
So lifts his Maid to fill his Spouse's Station,
A blessed Instance of *Retaliation*.

Nor yet to private Life confine this Notion,
It spreads expansive as the boundless Ocean;
RETALIATE, speaks the hostile Cannon's roar –
RETALIATE, echoes from the British Shore –

The Genius of the Isle is now awake,
Speaks like brave Russell, frowns like noble Blake . . .

Retaliation is, alas, a familiar practice among those who believe that their families have suffered from centuries of alien rule of their country, of having land taken from them. It may be significant that McNally's father conformed to Protestantism to avoid the effect of the penal laws; resentment of the necessity of such acts of conformity contributing to endless guilt, unease and tergiversation among their descendants.

McNally enrolled in the Dublin Society of United Irishmen very soon after its foundation in 1792, defended many of its principal members, interviewed them in their cells and appeared very capably for them in Court.

To some extent, it seems that McNally regarded all his life as a series of dares. This may help to explain his courage. (Successful informers have to be brave in their fashion.) As a young man in London caught in the Gordon Riots in 1780, he rescued the Lord Chancellor's brother from a coach surrounded by the mob. Much later, he fought a duel with Sir Jonah Barrington, then still a judge in the Admiralty, with a reputation of being the most dangerous dueller in Ireland. The wound to his hip which led to a pronounced limp (and to his being subject to a lot of teasing) was probably the result of yet another duel; apart from the limp, he was thought handsome, with 'fine, dark, expressive eyes'.

What was there in his early years that bred in him the sniggering taste for some form of secret revenge, for hugging himself, for 'spitting on others from a great height': characteristics common in traitors? Apart from the money (which may well have been his main motive), how much did he really relish his double role? Certainly he became, in due course, a very eloquent and greatly respected lawyer, constantly retained by the principal members of the Society, visiting them in their cells, defending them in the courts with eloquence and fire – after having confirmed details of their guilt and revealed their lines of defence to the Government, in letters written in a very clear hand.

And he survived (with his pension) until 1820. Fitzpatrick writes:

> with such consummate hypocrisy was his turpitude veiled, that men who could read the inmost soul of others never for a moment suspected him . . . Charles Phillips, who practised for many years at the same bar with McNally, refused to believe that McNally had a pension from the Government. 'If I was asked to point out, next to Curran, the man most obnoxious to the Government – who most hated them; and was most hated by them – it would have been Leonard McNally, who stood by Curran's side while he denounced oppression, defied power, and dared every danger!'
>
> After the death of McNally, his representative claimed a continuance of the secret pension of £300 a year, which he had been enjoying since the calamitous period of the rebellion . . .
>
> The masterly manner in which McNally fortified his duplicity is worthy of attention. Persons usually the most clear-sighted regarded him as a paragon of purity and worth. Defending Finney, in conjunction with Philpot Curran, the latter, giving way to the impulse of his generous feelings, threw his arm over the shoulder of McNally, and, with emotion, said, 'My old and excellent friend, I have long known and respected the honesty of your heart, but never until this occasion was I acquainted with the extent of your abilities. I am not in the habit of paying compliments where they are undeserved.' Tears fell from Mr Curran as he hung over his friend. Nineteen years later, Curran died with the illusion undispelled.[60]

During the 1790s, in each of the chapters leading up to the Rebellion, McNally will make a number of entrances and exits, giving comfort and counsel to his fellow United Irishmen; and writing with clarity, contempt and gusto, secret reports to his paymasters in the

Castle which led many of these same Irishmen to the gallows. Many of his fellow informers will also appear; for example, Thomas Collins, the linen merchant who 'indulged in jeering facetiousness at the expense of men whose private proceedings he was reporting',[61] and sometimes John Pollock, the most deadly, insinuatingly effective of *agents provocateurs*, principal controller of McNally and of so many contributors to government intelligence, who at one time attempted to seduce Drennan.[62]

3

Founding of the Society

Hereditary bondsmen, know you not –
Who would be free themselves must strike the blow?
                    Byron, *Childe Harold's Pilgrimage*, Canto 2

I was invited to spend a few days in Belfast, in order to assist in framing
the first club of United Irishmen . . . about the beginning of October I
went down with my friend Russell who had by this time quitted the army
and was in Dublin, on his private affairs. The incidents of that journey
which was by far the most agreeable and interesting one I had ever made,
I recorded in a kind of diary.[1]

Wolfe Tone was writing this version of his visit to Belfast, some
five years later in Paris, as he sat and endured the frustration of
waiting and waiting to embark on the expedition to Ireland – the
doomed expedition which at last set out to Bantry Bay in the dead of
winter 1796. Nostalgia for Ireland perhaps coloured his recollections
of the pleasanter autumn of 1791, during the months of which he
had been acclaimed by both Catholic and Dissenter for his pamphlet
An Argument on Behalf of the Catholics of Ireland. He had been fêted,
given splendid dinners by friends in and out of Parliament, been
invited to write a declaration on the State of Ireland, and been
elected to the first or Green Company of Volunteers of Belfast, 'a
favour which they were very delicate in bestowing, as I believe I was
the only person, except the great Henry Flood, who was ever honoured with that mark of their approbation'. A few contemporary
jottings of that visit survive (forming the back pages of his edited
Memoirs), giving staccato impressions of the evening of 18 October

when the Society of United Irishmen of Belfast may be considered to have been formally founded:

> P.P.* and I made several orations on the state of the Roman Catholics, and the readiness of the citizens of Dublin to co-operate with the United Irishmen. The Intelligence received with great applause. Broke up at eleven; came home, resolved to go the coterie; dressed; went with P.P. P.P. changed his mind; after a quarter of an hour's fluctation in the lobby, and calling a council of waiters, at which the chamber-maid assisted; *pleasant, but wrong* [a recurring phrase – does it mean the same as it would nowadays, I wonder?]; came back again in something very like an ill humour. At the door P.P. changed his mind again, and proposed to return to the coterie; refused him plump. P.P. severe thereupon; taxed me with many faults, one of which was giving advice; told P.P. I would do so no more. P.P. frightened; submitted. Went to bed with a resolution to attack him in my turn next morning. Could not sleep; a cat in the room; got up and turned her out; fell asleep at last.[2]

Dawn seemed bright. Embracing the enlightened rationalism – proper to an alumnus of Trinity College, Dublin – of the late eighteenth-century Enlightenment, Tone had convinced himself, especially in the light of the early promise of events in France, that it should not be impossible, with one bound, to free the Irish people of the deadly trinity of tyranny, corruption and superstition. These hopes were challenged and nourished by arguments late into the night, rather than by any very deep study of Locke, Montesquieu and Molyneux (it is not so much *their* names but brief quotations from Shakespeare, Fielding and Richardson which pepper the pages of his diaries). When writing his *Memoirs* in his Paris room, he recollected the glad confident morning of the United Irishmen, crediting them with much more revolutionary vehemence than had been practical, or indeed imagined, at the time:

> To subvert the tyranny of our execrable government, to break the connection with England, the never-failing source of all our political evils and to assert the independence of my country – these were my objects. To unite the whole people of Ireland; to abolish the memory of all past dis-

---

* Tone was addicted to nicknames. This was his invention for his greatest friend Russell, and signifies 'Clerk of the Parish'. Russell could have a clerical, lugubrious air. For Tone, Russell invented 'Mr Hutton'. Hutton was the name of a Dublin coachmaker, so the nickname teased Tone for his father's (in fact quite grand) trade.

sensions; and to substitute the common name of Ireland in place of the denominations of Protestant, Catholic and Dissenter – these were my means . . .[3]

One of the chief practical arguments, which kept Tone, Russell and the 'men of the most distinguished public virtue' with whom he talked so late into those Belfast nights, turned on whether it was better to press on with parliamentary reform ahead of Catholic emancipation – or vice versa – or to take the two great questions together. If, say, the struggle for parliamentary reform took precedence, then the campaign for emancipation might flag. Tone himself was sure that the two struggles should be simultaneous. This was the development that pillars of the Ascendancy came to fear most, referring for example to the 'artful perversion of minds – reform and republicanism for the dissenter, emancipation and the ascendancy of the papacy for the papists'.[4]

Here is Tone's account, a week after that inaugural meeting, of a dinner at the McTier's (Sam, it will be remembered, was Drennan's brother-in-law, first ballast-master of the port of Belfast):

> A furious battle, which lasted two hours, on the Catholic question; as usual, neither party convinced. Teazed with the liberality of people agreeing in the principle, but doubting as to the expediency. Bruce* [was] brought at last to state his definite objection to the immediate emancipation of the Roman Catholics. His ideas are, 1st. Danger to true religion, inasmuch as the Roman Catholics would, if emancipated, establish an *inquisition*. 2nd. Danger of property by reviving the Court of Claims, and admitting any evidence to substantiate Catholic titles. 3rd. Danger, generally, of throwing the power into their hands, which would make this a Catholic Government, incapable of enjoying or extending liberty! Many other wild notions, which he afterwards gave up, but these three he repeated again and again, as his creed. Almost all the company of his opinion, excepting P.P. who made desperate battle, McTier, Getty and me.[5]

Tone, in those early days, showed little support for republicanism in today's sense (he had no objections, so it seemed, to the monarchy as one of the elements of a worthy, Aristotelian constitution comprising the one, the few, and the many). But a visit to a prosperous

---

* Bruce was the minister of the First Presbyterian church in Belfast, 'a man of fine bearing, proud of his descent from the royal blood of Scotland'.

bleach-green near Belfast – 'a noble concern: extensive machinery' – did prompt him to make a simultaneous dig at both monarchy and the inequities of English–Irish trade:

> German linens preferred, out of spite, by some families in England, particularly by the royal family. All the King's and Queen's linen, German, and, of course, all their retainers. Sinclair, for experiment, made up linen after the German mode; and sent it to the house in London which served the King, etc; worn for two years and much admired; ten per cent cheaper, and 20 per cent better, than the German linen. Great orders for *Irish German* linen, which he refused to execute. All but the royal family content to take it as mere Irish. *God save great George our King!*[6]

Thomas Attwood Digges was probably born in Maryland in 1742. I write 'probably' because Digges is a shadowy adventurer who liked secrecy, laid false trails and gave himself and his correspondents many changes of alias. He claims to have spent much of his early life in England where until the American War of Independence he acted as agent for various shipping companies. In 1778 he started a correspondence with Benjamin Franklin;[7] using language that reads like a scoundrel's: he professed his allegiance to the American cause, and offered to perform ill-defined services ('it is not prudent for me to be further explicit'), protesting his zeal, punctuality, secrecy and honour.

Suspected of treasonable correspondence, at some times he adopted the subterfuge of a pro-English attitude; at others, he showed what may have been his true colours, or at least the truest he had:

> The mode of war has certainly been ordered . . . to be altered to a more vigorous, I may say a more infamous one. Fire, devastation and plunder is to be expected – it is now the interest and intention of all England to render the American accession of as little avail as possible to France, you must destroy them or she will destroy you.[8]

It is fairly certain that Digges was up to no good in Belfast thirteen years after this correspondence. Obviously boasting of his experience and services in the cause of American independence, he gained the confidence of Tone and Russell. He saw them for breakfast or dinner almost every day during those last two weeks of October. Once, Tone says:

> Digges took me out to ask me my opinion of the United Irishmen. I told him I thought them men of spirit and decision, who seemed thoroughly

in earnest. He said he thought so too. I asked him whether they any-way resembled the Committees of America in 1775 and afterwards? He said 'Precisely'. In Digges' opinion, one Southern, when moved, equals twenty Northerns, but *very hard to move them*.[9]

Years later, in France, Tone came to remember this North–South comparison of Digges's, as he lamented the slowness of Ulster to show any spirit in the Rebellion – 'what mortification to me, who have so long looked up with admiration to the North, and especially to Belfast!' – a rather far-fetched comparison, surely, since it sounds as if Digges had referred to the American Northerners and Southerners, not to the Irish. But it shows how the conversation remained green in Tone's memory.

On another morning walk in Belfast, Digges egged on the ambitions for Ireland's separation from England, which Tone was continually nursing:

> Walked in the mall with Digges and P.P. . . . Put the plump question to Digges, relative to the possibility of Ireland's existence, independent of England. His opinion decidedly for independence. England would not risk a contest, the immediate consequence of which would be the destruction of her funds. Ireland supplies her with what, in case of a war, she could not possibly do without – as seamen and provisions. France would most probably assist, from the pride of giving freedom to one kingdom more. So would all the enemies of England. Nothing to be done, until the religious sects here are united, and England engaged in a foreign war. If Ireland were free, and well-governed, being that she is unencumbered with debt, she would, in arts, commerce, and manufactures, spring up like an air balloon, and leave England behind her, at an immense distance. There is no computing the rapidity with which she would rise.[10]

The radicals often met in taverns off the High Street. One was named the Dr Franklin Tavern, and Benjamin's portrait, 'awful and pompous, stood in a swinging frame over the door'.[11] It is easy to imagine Digges using the portrait to boast of his connections with Franklin, and of the services which he had been able to offer the cause of American independence.

Russell had, at some stage, showed Digges a postscript to Tone's Founding Resolutions;[12] and had even let him copy it, though he did not intend it for publication. This covering note of Tone's, it cannot be denied, was both separatist and conspiratorial in nature:

My unalterable opinion is that the bane of Irish prosperity is in the influence of England. I believe that influence will ever be extended while the connexion between the countries continues. Nevertheless, I know that opinion is for the present too hardy . . . I have not said [in my Resolutions] one word that looks like a wish for separation, though I give it to you and your friends as my most decided opinion that such an event would be a regeneration for this country.

The mystery was how this note fell into the hands of the Government. Although Russell could not at first believe Digges such a villain as to betray them, both he and Tone came to guess that he was in the business of selling information.

Was he then an *agent provocateur* when he encouraged the two young men in their dreams of independence, pointing to the Mexican uprising and suggesting that adventures mounted in support of liberty and freedom might enjoy the support of the US? Some of those with whom Digges had talked certainly suspected him. A year and a half later, after the House of Lords had discussed an Unlawful Meeting Bill, Drennan wrote to Sam McTier that 'Digges sent a private letter of Tone's to the Secret Committee on which the Chancellor expatiated much in the House to prove a plot for separating the countries'.[13] Tone subsequently referred to Digges as a 'rascal', and 'unfortunate'. These seem rather mild reprobations.

In a letter to Archbishop Troy of Dublin* dated 16 April 1792, John Carroll, Catholic Bishop of Baltimore, wrote:

I understand . . . that a principal owner in the business of the North, and in coalising Catholics with presbyterians, is a person from this country of the name of Digges . . . I am induced, by a solicitous regard for the Catholics of Ireland, and for your Lordship in particular, to mention some circumstances relating to Mr Digges . . . He is of respectable family and connections in this country, no one more so; in his early youth he was guilty of misdemeanours here, indicating rooted depravity, but amazing address, but even this could not screen him, and his friends, to rescue him from the hands of justice, and themselves from dishonour, [which] sent him out of the country . . . He arrived in England at the beginning of the American War, and with his wonted address and insinuating manners, engaged himself deeply into the familiarity of all the Americans in England, and the lords and commons who combated the ministry on the

---

* Archbishop Troy was no friend to the new, radicalized Catholic Committee, and tried to refuse a chapel in his parish for a meeting. When he was told a sledge [-hammer] would remove that difficulty, it was left open for them (D.A. Chart (ed.), *The Drennan Letters*, p. 64).

subject of the American War. He even wrote such good accounts of the designs of England to the American negotiators at Paris, that they conceived the highest confidence in his zeal for their cause, and entrusted him with the disposal of large sums of money for the relief of American prisoners languishing in England; but all this time, as it was afterwards known, he was a spy for Lord North . . . He never applied the money sent him. After the war he continued his malpractices, but [he] has sufficient dexterity, by shifting his scenes of action, and displaying extraordinary abilities, to gain confidence for a time. You may easily conceive how dangerous it would be for such a man to obtain any degree of trust in the management of your concerns, which require such sound heads and hearts.[14]

Too late! It is, however, fair to add that there is no firm proof of Digges's having been the informer. There are difficulties of timing. No reference to Castle payments to Digges has come to light.

One certainty, though, is that throughout the years to come the purloined or copied covering note became a principal piece of 'evidence in [the Government's] contention that Tone and the United Irishmen had been militant separatists since 1791 – a charge which Tone totally denied'.[15] Fortunately for him, as will be seen, both Tone and the Government preferred to negotiate an exile than to lay a capital charge.

The differences between Tone and Drennan lay not so much in content and policy, as in style and claims of precedence. Drennan had good reason to hope that history would see him as the true begetter of the United Irishmen. A month after those first meetings of the Belfast Society of United Irishmen he was writing to Sam McTier: 'Perhaps my little paper was the first seed of the Brotherhood, and, if so, I shall ever deem myself very happy – it appeared in June, and the address to the French, 14 July . . . and was promoted by the establishment of the United Irishmen of Belfast and Dublin.'[16]

And it is perfectly true that Drennan had been brooding on the idea of an 'Irish Brotherhood' for many months. It is equally certain that Tone suggested that the Society be called 'The United Irishmen'. His letter to Russell in Belfast, enclosing the draft of his Resolutions (which Digges came to copy), says: 'I have left, as you see, a blank for the name, which, I am clearly of the opinion, should be "The Society of United Irishmen".'[17]

There *is* something in a name. The difference between Drennan's and Tone's choice is typical of the difference between their style and approach: the former suggesting 'much of the secrecy and somewhat of the ceremonial of Freemasonry', the other immediate, to the point. There is something condescending about Drennan's comments on Tone's style; for example, when he suggested to Sam McTier that Tone should be approached to write the address for the 14 July celebrations he had written, 'Tone will probably be able to throw off some address to the people or to mould his resolutions to that shape. He has a ready and an excellent pen.'[18]

For his part, Drennan was certainly put out when criticized for his rhetorical flourishes. I quoted the solemn Declaration, or Test, administered at the first meeting of the Dublin Society in November, at my first discussion of Drennan (p. 27) because it is probably the prose composition of which he was proudest, the one which had earned him his place in Irish history. All the more irksome, then, for him to have had it opposed by Tone at his first attendance at the Dublin Society. Drennan wrote to McTier at Belfast – the voice of the injured author clearly audible in the letter:

[The Test] was carried unanimously in the committee, chiefly on account of its being a means of impressing more deeply on the mind the principles of the Society . . . subscription of name merely is often neglected and forgotten. It will not be so easily forgotten – the repetition of such a test before a large Society. The civic oath of France was a test found very useful, and it was not thought sufficient for the members of the new assembly to take it generally, but every individual member repeated the words from the tribune. It was opposed by Russell, Tone and Stokes,* as being too rhetorical, though I can't see a figure of rhetoric in it; as being too argumentative, though this seems not very consistent with the former objection; as being indeterminate, though I think the end and the means pretty plainly expressed. In short, after a good deal of conversation they, I think injudiciously and rashly on the first night of admission, occasioned a division in the Society, and on the question being put, they were the three negatives. Stokes retired before the Test was administered, which was first taken by Mr Butler [the barrister whom Drennan called 'the only man of fashion amongst us'], all standing, and afterwards by everyone present, repeating the words after the president. I fancy Tone and Russell wish everything to

---

* Whitley Stokes was a Fellow of Trinity College, Dublin, Professor of Medicine, and a founder of the Dublin Zoological Society; he wrote replies to Paine on religion and Malthus on population, and advocated the translation of the Bible into Irish (see McDowell, *Ireland in the Age of Imperialism*, p. 387).

follow your [Belfast] society, but it seems very proper that the society in the capital should originate any matter which they think useful . . .[19]

In a following letter to McTier, Drennan, with that nuance of menace characteristic of those who jib when they are teased, writes: 'Stokes will, I hope, be brought to attest'.

He went on complaining throughout that autumn. Setting up a determined, secret, oath-ridden society is not always an amicable affair, even at the worst of times, and Drennan's intensity cannot have made him an easy member at all. In December:

> Opposition was again made to the Test by Tone and Russell, chiefly on the ground of it being dangerous to exclude many who would, but for this, desire to become members . . . [but] better to have a society knit together and braced by a strong obligation than to admit those scrupulous, hesitating half-way men, who would soon damp the zeal . . . With regard to any squeamishness about the solemnity of the Test, it was not an oath of any sort of religious obligation, but an agreement and pledge between man and man . . . It was said that any change in the Test would render our Society liable abroad to the charge of levity and inconsistency . . .[20]

Levity was next to sinfulness. Drennan observed that the Catholics were the most zealous for the Test, 'I observed that the solemnity is the thing they like, perhaps from their religion'. Tone and Russell were again criticized as 'imprudent in making themselves unpopular', and although both sincere and able and zealous, 'don't know men as well as they will do'.

By the end of the year some sixty members of the Dublin Society of United Irishmen had taken the Test, out of an eventual roll-call of about four hundred. Not all of these were undeterred by its awful solemnity. At least five of them sold copious information to the Government, including lists of those attending each meetings, the verbatim accounts of the resolutions and so on. Alas for Drennan's hopes of a secrecy which was, in his words, 'to have given greater energy within, and greater influence without', and to have protected the identity of members until 'the moment came'.

In that summer of 1791, the Bastille Day celebrations had been particularly splendid and heady in Belfast. The undercurrent, long evident, of republicanism in the Presbyterian North began to flow more strongly than ever. The marching and the uniforms of the

Volunteer regiments (see p. 13) had been cheered wildly from every window, in every street:

> The French Revolution acted as a spell on the minds of Irishmen . . . their sympathy was roused to a state of excitement almost painful, and that longed to find relief and indulgence, in re-enacting such spirit-stirring scenes . . . they dedicated that day to the commemoration of the greatest event in human annals. Twenty-six millions of our fellow-creatures (nearly one-sixth of the inhabitants of Europe) breaking their chains, and throwing off almost in an instant the degrading yoke of slavery, is a scene so new, so interesting, and sublime . . .
>
> The Volunteer Societies, horse, foot, and artillery, with a dense multi-tude of spectators, assembled at the Exchange, and thence paraded the principal streets in all the pomp and pride of military array . . . such was the demonstration of public feeling in the liberal and enlightened town of Belfast, the Athens of Ireland . . .[21]

The Castle in Dublin was growing uneasy. But it would be a mistake to suppose that this was yet causing any agitation to Government in London. It was still possible for Burke to write: 'I have never known any of the successive Governments in my time, influenced by any [other] passion relative to Ireland than the wish that they should hear of it and of its concerns as little as possible.'[22]

For his part, Rowan had been an enthusiastic Volunteer ever since his return to live in Ireland. He had accepted the honour of the command of the Killinchy Volunteers, and written to their Secretary as far back as May, talking of his duty to put new energy into the movement, and to the 'universal obligation of bearing arms for the public defence':

> Are the Volunteers to be contented to meet annually in silent mock parade? Are they, with the arms of peace in their hands, to permit that constitution . . . to be mouldered down by the corrupt practices of a few? Or are they to stand forth as the guardians of the rights of mankind, and the determined opposers of every kind of tyranny? When I was proposed and admitted into the Killinchy company of Volunteers, it was not for the parade of a red coat, nor the merriment of a review day: it was to assist in defeating the insidious policy of corrupt courtiers . . .[23]

This is very much in the style, as we have already seen, of the stal-wart creature, half-Hercules, half-Quixote. We have seen that what drew him towards any allegiance, including his membership of the United Irishmen, was a hatred of injustice, corruption, betrayal of principle, scorn for 'fixing' – the persiflage of Ascendancy rule, the buying of parliamentary influence with places and pensions. Action, preferably colourful and dramatic action, was needed in every circumstance. Generous protest lay at the root of his soul, little consideration given to likely consequences.

Although Rowan kept in touch with his friends and family tenants in the North, he was now living in Kildare and spending his days in Dublin, and before the end of the year he became one of the first hundred members to join the Dublin Society of United Irishmen, and take Drennan's famous Test. Nor was he the only landed gentleman to do so. Both Drennan and Martha McTier looked on him with favour, the latter remarking that 'Tandy, Dowling etc., are not gentlemen. Rowan *is*, every inch of him . . . Tandy is not well. He lives an irregular life.'[24]

Tandy had just become the first Secretary of the new Dublin Society. It was not a wise choice (see p. 17); in large part, this was because of his nose. Tandy's notorious nose – as ugly as Cleopatra's was (presumably) beautiful – sparked a row in which Rowan played his customary, impetuous role as champion of victims, deserving and not-so-deserving. The episode brought the Dublin Society of United Irishmen into ridicule and farcical quarrel with the Castle, within a few weeks of its foundation.

The words which started the row, referring to the Society, were spoken by the Solicitor-General, John Toler,* in the House of Commons in February 1792:

> We are not at this day to be taught by political quacks, who tell us that radical reformations are necessary in parliament. I have seen papers signed by Tobias M'Kenna, with Simon Butler in the chair, and Napper Tandy lending his countenance. *It was rather odd that they could not contrive to put a better* face *on the matter* . . . (Laughter).[25]

The 'matter' was a petition' on behalf of the Roman Catholics of Ireland'. (We shall see in the next chapter, how Tone's work for the Catholic Committee was becoming his closest concern; before long he was appointed its Assistant Secretary – a misleadingly modest title.)

---

* John Toler enjoyed a long life (1739–1831). Serving nine years as Solicitor-General until 1798, ten years as Attorney-General until 1800, and finally Chief Justice of the Court of Common Pleas from 1800, his longevity may all the same have been his most remarkable achievement. Ball, the chronicler of Irish judges, describes him as 'inherently a jovial fox-hunting Tipperary gentleman, with strong Protestant and Tory predilections' (*Judges of Ireland*, p. 237).

The joke was feeble enough, better ignored. But in a burst of bravado Tandy 'asked for an explanation' on being told it. The Solicitor-General declined this request, tantamount to a challenge to a duel, 'such is my sense of my own honour, and the dignity of the House of Commons, that I cannot think of violating either by any way of explanation'. More exchanges followed. The Speaker issued a warrant for the appearance of Tandy at the Bar of the House, to answer his alleged breach of privilege. When the messenger found him, Tandy went into a parlour, as if for his hat, escaped through a window and disappeared into hiding.

Tone thought such behaviour reflected no credit on the Society. He persuaded Rowan to take the Chair at an early meeting and pass a resolution that it was the Solicitor-General who had committed the offence: Parliament was threatening liberty by the 'exercise of undefined privilege'.

A reward for the apprehension of 'said Tandy' was issued 'as practised in the English House of Commons'. One or two MPs protested that there appeared to be 'an unusual warmth in the proceedings'. But standing on dignity often creates a whirlpool. In the spring the Attorney-General declaimed:

> The crime with which Mr Tandy was charged was one of the most dangerous kind, and such as every man in the Kingdom should contribute to bring to justice. It was a violation of the most valuable privileges of that House – and the privileges of that House were the privileges of the people – and the law of the land; when those privileges were gone, and the freedom of debate was no longer held sacred, the constitution itself must soon follow.[26]

Tandy was at last brought to the Bar of the House. Proceedings were witnessed from the gallery by Tone and Rowan, both dressed up in their gaudy Whig club uniforms, in provocative demonstration of support. Speeches 'expatiated for some time on the enormity of Mr Tandy's offence'. Tandy was committed to Newgate.

Parliament, however, was prorogued the same day, which meant that Tandy was instantly freed, to laughter and hurrahs. Also, as it was not sitting, he could now challenge the Solicitor-General without any breach of privilege. Rowan had offered to be his second. The Solicitor-General walked round the streets of Dublin with a 'great stick', expecting to be affronted. But Tandy backed down, pleading domestic difficulties. Very 'shy', very discreditable. Drennan, distressed by elements of farce in the imbroglio, and irritated with Tandy for involving the Society so deeply in a personal quarrel, wrote: 'Poor Tandy, after eighteen years' struggle against his own interest in the public cause, has nearly lost his reputation as a gentleman in a quarter of an hour.'[27] Unperturbed, Rowan soon found even more challenging outlets for the exercise of his audacious chivalry.

As for Lord Edward Fitzgerald, very little is known of his movements in the latter half of 1791. There are no letters surviving to and from his mother, no Rousseauesque eulogies of native life, no reflections on the future of his military career, no confessions of revolutionary tendencies, no gardening at Frescati. His biographer Thomas Moore is silent (it is thought he may well have destroyed some scraps of evidence).

There is an easy solution to this problem of silence: Lord Edward Fitzgerald was conducting a serious affair in London with an older, married woman. The enchanting wife of his friend, the playwright/politician Richard Brinsley Sheridan, Elizabeth (née Linley), had become his mistress.

Elizabeth came of a famous musical and stage family. When nineteen years old she herself had sung before the King and Queen at Buckingham Palace, and King George had told her father that he had 'never in his life heard so fine a voice'.[28] She was a great beauty, too, John Wilkes saying that 'she was the most modest, pleasing and delicate flower I have seen for a long time'. She sat for Reynolds as his 'St Cecilia', and the Virgin in his 'Nativity'. Later, Horace Walpole, with his connoisseur's eye, placed her 'above all living beauties'. The Bishop of Meath, erring on the side of charity, pronounced her to be 'the connecting link between woman and angel'.

She had, understandably, been pursued by elderly bachelors and 'married majors'; and was later rumoured to have been the only person to have resisted the advances of the Duke of Clarence.* It was in order to escape from too many unwelcome attentions (it is

---

* Her Victorian biographer, Fraser Rae, who seems himself to have fallen a little under her spell, writes, 'She passed unscathed through terrible temptations. The Duke of Clarence "persecuted" her, to use the word which she wrote to Mrs Canning, with his attentions, and she was perhaps the only lady for whom he sighed in vain. Her devotion to her husband was not the least admirable of her traits' (*DNB*). If Sheridan knew of her affair with Fitzgerald, he drew a veil over it.

said) that she was eventually escorted by Sheridan to a convent in Lille, before marrying him within the year. Sheridan was afterwards referred to by some of her friends as 'her drag of a husband'.

She cut a much-admired figure at the parties and balls that were held after the theatre; it may have been here that she met Fitzgerald, who was about ten years younger than she was. She also moved in high Whig circles, canvassing and appearing on the hustings for Fox when he stood for Parliament in 1790. So she was a political, as well as a social and theatrical animal. It is quite likely that, among their other exchanges, Fitzgerald and his wordly, beautiful, theatrical, silver-voiced mistress confirmed each other in their opinions on the benefits to mankind of the Revolution in France. Indeed, did Elizabeth play some part in encouraging her young lover to become something more than a dilettante Utopian enthusiast: a rebel proper? He was, as one friend said, 'a perfect madman about her'.

There are one or two curious facts about the Sheridan–Fitzgerald connection, a whiff of complaisance in the air. Soon after giving birth to their child, and in the last stages of consumption, Elizabeth is said to have told her lover, referring to Pamela, adopted daughter of Madame Genlis: 'I should like you when I am dead to marry that girl.' But it was Sheridan who proposed marriage to Pamela within months of his wife's death. And she accepted. Yet in the event she became Fitzgerald's wife.[29]

Elizabeth's daughter died soon after her own death. In the recorded life of Fitzgerald the waters seem to have covered her memory as if she had never been. No direct reference to the affair was published until this century.

4

Tandy's nose

Un grand nez est proprement l'indice
D'un homme affable, bon, courtois, spirituel,
Libéral, courageux, tel que je suis.
　　　　Rostand, *Cyrano de Bergerac*, Act 1, scene 1

The affair of Tandy's nose continued to rumble on through all the
early months of 1792, erupting in parliamentary sittings on the
same days as much weightier contributions to political life (such as
the speeches of Edmund Burke's friend, the 'acute, artful and insidi-
ous'[1] Sir Hercules Langrishe, on the most important Bill for further
Catholic relief).

The significance of the episode is that it brought the Dublin
Society of United Irishmen into great prominence much earlier than
would otherwise have been the case. It also provided evidence, farcical as it may be, that the United Irishmen were not afraid to challenge
the power of Government: an overture to the years of turmoil ahead.

The parts played by Wolfe Tone, Hamilton Rowan and the Hon.
Simon Butler, Chairman of the Dublin Society of United Irishmen,
had incurred the displeasure of the Lord Chancellor; in particular,
their signing and printing the Society's Resolutions that claimed it
was not the Society, but the Solicitor-General himself, who had been
in breach of parliamentary privilege over the Tandy insult.

Lord Chancellor Fitzgibbon looms large in the government of late
eighteenth-century Ireland. The force of his personality matched the
powers of his office. He enjoyed speaking his mind with savage
clarity and absolutely no fear of exaggeration, hurling thunderbolts

65

with a large disregard of consequences. He once referred to 'the blundering stupidity of that old Balderdash bitch, Lord Sydney' (when Sydney was British Home Secretary). He vowed to 'make Catholics as tame as cats' – a remark in memory of which dead cats were said to have been pelted at his funeral cortège. (True or false? In any case, it shows how the principal architect of the Union was execrated.)

Fitzgibbon was a kinsman of Matilda, Tone's wife. In some ways he was a mirror image of his much younger relation. To Fitzgibbon the English connection was God, transcending all other loyalties; to Tone it was the Devil. To Fitzgibbon the maintenance of the Protestant Ascendancy, of which the only possible guarantor was British power, was the highest purpose of state. To Tone the alliance of Catholic and Dissenter was the only possible means of subverting that same power. Both men were passionate in their ideological detestations, yet could be hearteningly generous to political enemies.

Fitzgibbon, it has been suggested, may even have been responsible for concealing the signature on the seditious letter accompanying the Founding Resolutions, sent by Tone to Russell (the one Digges was suspected of having leaked).[2] But if so, by the time of the Tandy affair, he was in no mood to overlook his 'wayward kinsman's' behaviour.

In one foray, he inveighed against Simon Butler, saying that as a barrister his association with the United Irishmen and Tandy was a disgrace to his profession; and then turned his fire on Tone 'in the harshest and most contemptuous terms of disapprobation'. Later, he appears to have backed down a little, claiming that he meant no disrespect to either man and that 'he entertained a very high opinion of Tone'.[3] Such behaviour surely arose from contrasting facets of his strong character: political wrath and personal kindness. Then again, as the son of a father who had conformed to the Protestant religion for the sake of his career, he may have been subject to 'turmoils and tumults' of spirit. His undoubted rectitude would have made tugs of loyalty no easier. Perhaps bursts of rage were only to be expected.

There were to be other occasions in Tone's life when the Lord Chancellor – 'the most potent of the Catholics' adversaries' – and he were in conflict, although one often detects that awkward, almost affectionate respect which declared enemies may keep for each other until their graves.

The Tandy débâcle may have been one reason why Tone showed

ever greater reluctance to pursue his unsuccessful career at the Bar. His fees were sporadic at best. Another judge, much less respectable than Fitzgibbon, wrote:

> I thought it a pity, as he was really a good-hearted person, that he should not be fairly tried, and, if possible, pushed forward; and, being myself high on the circuit, I took him round in my carriage three times, and thought well of him; but he was too light and visionary, and as for law, was quite incapable of imbibing that species of science. His person was unfavourable, his countenance thin and sallow, and he had in his speech a harsh and gutteral pronunciation of the letter *R* . . . It is my belief that Tone could not have succeeded in any steady civil profession. He was not worldly enough, nor had he sufficient common-sense for his guidance.[4]

More than ever, Tone now needed a decent and steady income. Their second child was a year old in April. His father was totally improvident. The Witherington in-laws kept their distance from him after a family row. Only his 'ready pen' offered financial hope. He left his family at the home in Bodenstown, County Kildare, and moved into lodgings north of the Liffey, taking with him an astonishing amount of belongings packed by his patient Matilda, to equip him for living the life of a gentleman about town – snuff, toupee, fashionable short white waistcoats, tight white breeches, white silk stockings and an 'array of other waistcoats from ribbed cotton to striped or patterned silk for special occasions'.[5]

Fortunately, his authorship of *The Argument*, which ran into five editions, opened up to him prospects of a career. He became a frequent guest at the dinners of leading Catholics in both Dublin and Belfast. He developed a friendship with John Keogh, the most powerful member of the 'new' Catholic Committee – now rid of an aristocratic leadership that had been, in emancipationist eyes, far too accommodating in its relations with the Castle. Since Keogh was a man whose name he often invoked in times to come, this hard, shrewd, sly, successful merchant, some fifty years old, must be introduced.

To begin with, Sir Boyle Roche, MP,* had this to say about Keogh

---

*Sir Boyle Roche was called the greatest of all the *Brogueneers*. He delivered his speeches quaintly and with difficulty, 'richly ornamented with that flower of rhetoric called a BULL',
  'His matters now to sense, now to nonsense leaning
  means not, but blunders round *about a meaning*.'
(*Sketches of Irish Political Characters*, p. 145)

and others of the Committee (that 'turbulent, disorderly set of people' who should not, in his view, be allowed to present their petition for Catholic relief), in a debate on 20 February 1792:

> Who were they who affected to be the representatives of the Roman Catholics of Ireland? Were there amongst them any of the ancient nobility, or the gentry of Ireland? Was there a single man of respectability or character? There was indeed, Mr Edward Byrne, a sugar baker, a seller of wines and other commodities, and he was the first name, and put in the front of the battle. There was another, John Keogh; and who was he? Why, he was a retailer of poplines in Dame Street. These men met over their porter to consider of commanding the government – they met at a chop-house, at Derham's chop-house in particular, where the former of them in his cups happened to dream that he was the nabob of Ireland.[6]

Sir Boyle Roche used such words even although he must have known perfectly well that John Keogh owned a magnificent *palazzo* at Mount Jerome, and that Edward Byrne was said by some to be the richest man in Ireland from his sugar and distilling, and that the wonderful collection of John Sweetman, another member of the Catholic Committee, included works by Vermeer, Rubens and Holbein. Half the 'disorderly set' joined the Dublin Society of United Irishmen.

Tone's future was bound up in this new, insistent Catholic Committee far more closely (in these days before his exile) than with the United Irishmen. His salaried work for it was to begin in July. Later he was to write that in the society of Mount Jerome he 'spent many happy days, and some of them serviceable to the country. It was there that he [Keogh] and I used to frame our papers and manifestos. It was there that we drew up the Petition and Vindication of the Catholics, which produced such powerful effects both in England and Ireland.'[7] In his diaries (but, one imagines, not to his face) he nicknamed the older, wealthy businessman 'Gog'.*

Duelling in the eighteenth century was even more common in Ireland than in England. The habit was of some service to a people

---

* Gog was a good nickname for Keogh, both in onomatopoeia and in reference to the legendary City monster, son of a demon, whose effigy is still carried in the annual Lord Mayor's procession in London. Tough, shrewd, ambitious, overbearing, Gog was the model of the successful businessman down the ages. Tone looked on him with respect for his money and success, combined with some scorn for his vanity and cultural poverty.

accustomed to hard drinking, frequent insults, unwillingness to compromise, slowness to forgive, refusal to forget. It seemed

> so closely connected with the rules of good behaviour accepted and
> observed by Irish society that a sensible man of the world could only
> insist that men who quarrelled over the dinner table should not be
> allowed to fight when still in their cups, that seconds should always try
> and effect a reconciliation . . .[8]

All the same, it takes a very highly developed foolhardiness, especially for a man himself under threat of criminal prosecution, to
invite a Lord Chancellor to a duel.

In the early months of 1792 much of Rowan's life was devoted
to affairs of honour. The question of who had committed that parliamentary breach of privilege – all the business of Tandy's ugly
countenance, his challenge, his escape through the window from the
Sergeant-at-Arms, the Society's counter resolutions and so on –
would not go away. Some of the proceedings in the courts verged
on the farcical. For example, in June Tandy attempted to bring
personally to court not only the Attorney-General and the Lord
Chancellor but the Lord-Lieutenant himself.

Simon Butler was one of Tandy's counsel. (Another was McNally.)
Butler's arguments in the later proceedings were seen as vexatious.
Who was the Viceroy? Was there a 'Viceroy'? In what capacity was
the 'Viceroy' acting? Had the great seal of England on his patent any
more authority in Ireland than 'a new cake of wax or the seal of the
Great Mogul'? This farrago has a pre-Kafkaesque quality.*

In the following year Butler claimed that a House of Lords
investigation was acting *ultra vires* in its treatment of witnesses. Lord
Fitzgibbon again exclaimed that Butler was a disgrace to the gown he
wore. By this time Rowan was himself awaiting trial for his involve-
ment in the affair. 'Disgrace' was a word bound to bring Rowan into

---

* *Mr Butler*: 'It was necessary that the Earl of Westmorland should appear, and on being
declared against, plead that he *is* the Lord Lieutenant, and shew his letters patent in proof of
the fact, before it can be considered judicially before the Court.'
The Court: '. . . it would be ridiculous . . . they saw him attended with the usual state and
received in all the official dignities of the Lord Lieutenant . . . they had too full a knowledge
of the British Constitution to suppose there were two Earls of Westmorland of the
Kingdom of Great Britain, two peers titled of the same place etc., etc., etc.' (*Tandy v.
Westmorland*, Dublin, 1792). It is hard to believe that the Society supposed it could win this
argument.

the lists on behalf of a colleague. He offered to take a challenge direct to the Lord Chancellor on Butler's behalf.

Hamilton Rowan writes in his *Autobiography*:

> Fitzgibbon said that [Simon Butler] could not plead ignorance; that his noble birth and professional rank at the Bar, to both of which he was a disgrace, had aggravated his crime . . . I wrote to his Lordship requesting an appointment to wait on him on behalf of my friend Mr Butler . . . calling to his recollection the expressions he had made use of directed to Mr Butler, which I hoped to be permitted to say it was not his Lordship's intention to be taken personally, and had been made use of unreflectingly. Lord Fitzgibbon said that he thought the circumstances of the case called for the expressions he had used, that he never spoke unreflectingly in that situation, and under similar circumstances he would again use similar words. I then said that, in mine and Mr Butler's opinion the sentence of the Lords did not authorise the words he had made use of, and that if it had occurred between two private gentlemen, my conduct would be plain and easy; but his Lordship's situation of Chancellor embarrassed me. Here I paused. After some further conversation his Lordship said I knew his situation, and he wished me to recollect it.

Subsequently the Lord Chancellor returned the account Rowan had written of this conversation, which Mr Butler threatened to publish in the newspapers. The Lord Chancellor commented (coolly, one imagines) that 'it was not for him to advise Mr Butler'. The *Autobiography* proceeds:

> The next morning I received a visit from a very old friend, Colonel Murray, who accosted me with, 'So a pretty piece of work you have made, Hamilton, taking a challenge to the Chancellor'. 'How the deuce do you know that?' 'Why, to cut the matter short, I breakfasted this morning with Fitzgibbon, and he told me the whole affair'.[9]

Rowan, knowing that he was in danger, told his 'very old friend' that he now regretted having come to Ireland when party feeling ran so high. He hoped to be able to return to England if no prosecution was mounted against him. The Government, pleased to be rid of a nuisance, said that he could by all means leave the country, and stay outside it for a few years. This row might possibly have subsided had not a condition been made that Rowan should also strike his name out of the United Irishmen's Society. His sense of honour made it impossible to accept this.

Farce or not, trials related to Tandy occupied the forefront of the stage in Dublin through much of 1792, and were the backdrop against which Rowan played his role of willing duellist. They also brought the Dublin branch of the Society of United Irishmen ever more to the unfavourable notice of the Castle. And they formed the prelude to the far more serious trials in which both Drennan and Rowan were to face charges of distributing treasonable material – which might well have led to their deaths.

In these months we hear little or nothing of Rowan's private life. His wife Sarah, at home in their Kildare home (not far from Tone's family at Bodenstown) always regarded her husband's behaviour with disquiet, his friendships with distrust. We know that their son William, who became a distinguished Captain in the Royal Navy, was now nine years old, and that their daughter Jane had 'a mind and heart of the first order'. Otherwise public ferocity, not domestic tenderness, shaped all the foreground and horizons of this Ajax.

A letter Sarah sent him many years later, when he was in exile in America, suggests that his home life may not have been tranquil at any time:

> The truth is, all your faults originated from your connecting yourself with wicked and artful men, who cared not for you nor for any body else; and did I not think you had been misled this way, I should most certainly have a very different opinion of you from that which it is my sincere wish ever to retain; and now, for mercy's sake, give up all ideas of reforming the state in any way, however peaceable it may be . . .

He could have been left in no doubt of the strength of Sarah's feelings, when she added, even more damningly:

> The arch-deceiver, T—, has quit the country, and it is to be feared he may go where you are [in America]. I think it my duty to say that, if this should be the case, you ought to avoid all connection with him; and it is as well to say at once what is the fact – *his friend cannot be mine*; his wicked principles and artful manners have destroyed us.[10]

Does T— stand for Tone or Tandy? It isn't clear. But one clue is that Henry McDougall, the contemporary author of *Sketches of Irish Political Characters*, writes in his notice of Rowan:

> The great misfortune of his life was to get acquainted with Napper Tandy, by whom he was seduced into those politics which have ruined

and disgraced him. This unfortunate gentleman started in life with every advantage – a good understanding, a finished education, an independent fortune and a fine person; in manners no man is more engaging; in accomplishments, natural and acquired, few men are more gifted; and in amiability of temper and disposition, not surpassed by any one.

One has to admit that Rowan's sometimes indiscriminate friendship, generosity and sense of honour would not have made for domestic tranquillity, even in the calmest of weather: a man stalwart to his friends, awkward to his wife.

Drennan's letters in early 1792 show how irritated he had become with the ramifications of the Toler affair. He had no time for its absurdities. They were unbecoming. Many more important things were happening, notably the Catholics' campaign for parliamentary franchise.

Like Tone, he disliked seeing the Society drawn into disrepute over a personal quarrel. Private matters were best settled privately, especially when one of the participants was, like Tandy, so 'poltroon-ish'. He tried to elevate the considerations at stake:

> having associated for great national objects and to promote union among Irishmen of all national persuasions, this Society is entitled to the respect which such objects naturally claim . . . we are anxious to meet any constitutional enquiry into our conduct, reserving for that occasion the justification of our actions.[11]

That was more the note to be struck. It was important above all to settle relations with the Catholics. Over this, however, he evinced continual unease, reflecting the split in his own character between solemn aspiration and prudent calculation. There was a need to reconcile his prejudices and his principles:

> I am said to accuse the Catholics of duplicity of conduct. I do not recollect ever having said so – that they acted as a double part as a body is matter of fact, but that any individuals among them are acting with duplicity I deny, and firmly believe that the part, of which I know the most, acts with great zeal and integrity . . . My toast should be – *The Sovereignty of the People* – not of any party; the *Ascendancy of Christianity* – not of any church . . .[12]

On a more immediate, practical level, however, he was ready to complain that he saw little hope of their using his professional services; there is a tartness about his comment that '[Catholics] have the virtue of a persecuted sect to be closely attached to each other and to favour their own doctors exclusively'.[13]

Despite his captiousness and his prickly pride in being the author of the famous Test, Drennan was always thoughtful, genuinely interested in political ideas. He was well-read, more so than most of his colleagues in the Society. He verges towards recognizably democratic ideas, even though he certainly did not wish to rush into universal suffrage. One feels the friendly spectre of his much loved and revered father is always by his side, encouraging him to serious studies and reflection. In his young days (when he thought of writing a history of the Volunteers and read Tacitus, writing down sentences that made a deep impression on him) he noted 'how beautifully Gibbon has fitted them in the similar situations of his own history'.[14]

Later in the year he wrote to his brother-in-law in response to a request to draw up a declaration for a Belfast Whig club, copying out long passages from Locke, Blackstone and Mirabeau. Disarmingly, he said that he did not know what to say; thought it would be better to adopt others' words.

> In every state where the citizens do not participate in the power of the legislature by the delegation of a body *freely chosen by the majority of the nation*, wisely restrained by their instructions, particularly in the nature of their taxes and the collection of them, and *subject to their control*, there is not nor can there be public liberty (Mirabeau).[15]

It is tempting to draw a few comparisons between Rowan and Drennan. In their young days they shared much the same political views and ideals. But one was a man of honour, of instinct, had an absolute sense of what was due to others (and from himself), heedless of danger; dishonour for him encompassed such things as betrayal, the letting-down of friends and companions. The other was a man of morality, whose behaviour was more considered and codified, whose conscience was sterner and tested by reference to books, and who set store by his prudence.

One example of Drennan's worthiness, his readiness to join in the moral crusades of the day, comes in a letter which he wrote at this time to his brother-in-law about sugar and slavery (this was a year in which many mass petitions for abolition were mounted).

We have drawn up a subscription paper about abstinence from sugar . . . in this form: 'We, the undernamed, will engage that we will abstain from the use of sugar and rum, until the West India planters themselves have prohibited the importation of additional slaves, and commenced as speedy and effectual a subversion of slavery in their islands, or till we can obtain the produce of the sugar cane in some other mode, unconnected with slavery and unpolluted with blood'. This would be a touchstone to the Belfast traders in rum.[16]

There was nothing insincere or opportunist about his taking-up of moral crusades. About slavery, again, he was to quote, some years later, a friend's exclamation on hearing that subscriptions were being solicited for an association for carrying on the trade: 'May God eternally damn the soul of the man who subscribes the first guinea!' But the expression of his concerns sometimes sounds sanctimonious to a reader's ear. Perhaps he found it easier and more natural to be more generous about causes than towards people.

But in terms of the politics of the day rather than of eternal verities, Drennan – like Tone, and probably more so than Rowan – was clear about the nature of the four-handed game being played. His fellow Presbyterians of the North were pressing for radical parliamentary reform, and an end to all manner of abuses and corruption; beneath the surface, ambitions grew for republicanism and for real independence from England. The Catholics were bidding for the restoration of ever more of their lost rights, including the great prize of the right to the franchise. When Irish problems had to be addressed, England was above all anxious to see quiet, to appease the Catholic multitude, and to avert the threat of insurrection and invasion, all the more menacing now that clouds of war with France grew darker. And the Protestant Ascendancy, the effective kings of Ireland like Beresford and Fitzgibbon, saw clearly that their salvation lay in the maintenance of the English connection, and in the upholding of the Protestant Ascendancy. This was a recently coined phrase which Drennan himself, in his loftier moments, scorned.*

No wonder that the alliance of the first two parties, of the Catholics and the Presbyterians, looked such a fearsome thing to government eyes. Yet had Pitt been able to study the wording of the

---

* 'I don't understand the term *ascendancy*; it is really an astrological term denoting the star which had *uncontrolled dominion* over our nativity; and is the language of the soothsayer rather than that of the politician.' As often with Drennan, the superior tone is a little *too* audible.

private letters between Drennan and Sam McTier, he would have known, better than he did, how fragile a chain was being forged: how suspicion between the Catholic and Dissenter was never stilled, old rancour and fears never overcome.

In the early months of the Dublin Society of United Irishmen, no informer was of greater use to the Castle than the linen merchant Thomas Collins, one of the Society's first members. He had already been bankrupt once, and had to sell some hundreds of acres of land in King's County, not far from Dublin. He was reduced to selling cloth on commission. As with Digges, as with McNally (whom Collins cryptically described in a report in March 1792 as 'one of *us*'), the lure of gold was irresistible in the face of poverty. He does not seem to have been driven by any other motives, nor even to have pretended to himself, or to his paymasters, that he was. He approached the Government almost immediately he joined the Society, offering to report on its proceedings.

His reports, written in a round hand with few crossings-out, almost weekly over two years, have been described as 'models of their kind – clear, regular, well-arranged – and as Collins's sense of humour was more highly developed than his sense of honour, occasionally amusing . . . undoubtedly he performed his rather undignified duties for the Irish administration with intelligent zeal . . . he had both convivial and political contacts with Dublin radicalism.'[17]

Sometimes Collins's reports were written on the back of invitations to the meetings, most of the early ones in Music Hall, Fishamble Street (where the first performance of Handel's *Messiah* had been given). Summonses were sent out to every member under the name of the Secretary, Napper Tandy, whom Collins refers to disobligingly as 'Nappy'. There are often lists of all those present, names of those who took Drennan's Test, proposers and seconders of new members. Altogether there are many hundred reports in the 'Rebellion Papers' in Dublin's Irish National Archives.

Collins liked to stress the seditious nature of the proceedings which he attended. It was in his interests to do so, as it increased his value in the eyes of the Castle. (This is an occupational failing.) In fact the reports of what was said seem to lend themselves more to a rhetorical than to an out-and-out treasonable interpretation. One such report gives advance warning of a letter approved for circulation through the kingdom 'extremely well wrote takes up 4 pages of letter paper very closely wrote'. This seems to have been the document in which the Society's aims and resolutions were set out with fine flourishes. Collins quotes from it:

> Is it reasonable to govern & bind the natives of a country by strangers and slaves – we are not raised from being prostrate to our knees. We must stand upright & walk – there is a great deal of mass must be diffused into spirit and much spirit must be comprised into mass.
> We shall no longer walk over fields stained with the blood of our ancestors, we are not accountable for their faults . . .[18]

One can perhaps detect here the metaphorical pen of Drennan, one of whose couplets in 'Erin' runs:

> Alas for poor Erin! That some still are seen
> Who would dye the grass red, in their hatred for green.[19]

Many of Collins's reports in early 1792 were inevitably concerned with the Tandy affair ('poor Napper's sun is set, his declining to fight they say out-herods Herod but you and I know him of old'). Across the water, however, the English Government were probably more exercised by some of Collins's other information about links with potential trouble-makers in England. In connection with a meeting on 7 February 1792 Collins reported:

> Another letter from the Revolution Society in the city of Norwich England, highly approving of the conduct of our society and of the union of the *Irish* of all denominations, and declaring that they are determined to be free, as the oppression of the people of England from an infamous and corrupt administration is unsupportable.[20]

Collins's calls for payment for his services were frequent and whining, writing, for example, to the go-between Alderman Giffard, 'I called at your house last night but you was not at home . . . I am sure if convenient you will send me what I mentioned in my letter of Thursday morning, and have only to observe that I hope if I live until the end of next week that I shall be rather in a habit of paying rather than borrowing.' The ultimate recipient of his demands, as well as of his reports, was Edward Cooke, the Under-Secretary in the Castle (effectively the most powerful executive of the Government). He considered Collins a sensible man, 'thoroughly capable of business'. In a letter in 1794 when the Society was broken up, Cooke wrote charitably to Evan Nepean, the Secretary of State for War in London, that 'Mr Collins made a very satisfactory information . . . his residence here [in Dublin] will not be very pleasant'.[21] At last, after the Rebellion, he was found a post as naval officer in Dominica, well away from fears of vengeance. This was not a bad position at all: it was worth £600 a year, which he drew for fourteen years until his death in 1814.

Informers and secret agents throw no light on this period of Lord Edward Fitzgerald's life. Nor does his biographer Thomas Moore have much to say, except that he spent most of his time in Ireland, occasionally attending the House of Commons in Dublin. He does, however, mention that Fitzgerald was 'most heartily weary of the society he was living with, and [wished] himself in London, whither all his desires called him – not only from the delight he always felt in the converse of his own family, but from certain other less legitimate attractions on which it is not necessary to dwell, but to which his extreme readiness to love, and his power to make himself loved in return, rendered him constantly liable'.[22] This is surely a broad hint at Fitzgerald's affair with Mrs Sheridan, who was now bearing his child. Moore also quotes (without, however, any disapproval of its jarring conceit) a letter to his mother dating from this time:

> Dublin has been very lively this week, and promises as much for the next, but I think it is all the same thing – *La ***, *La ***, and a few young competitors for their places. I have been a great deal with these two. They want to console me for London, but it won't do, though I own they are very pleasant. Henry and I have been living at Leinster House quite alone. We generally ride to Black Rock . . . I have dined by myself, and intended to give up the evening to writing to you, but have had such a pressing invitation from Mrs ** to sup that I cannot refuse. I hope it is to make up a quarrel which she began the other night, because I said I thought she was cold. I find it is the worst thing one can say of a Dublin woman – you cannot conceive what an affront it is reckoned.[23]

In the intervals of these amorous worries and delights, Fitzgerald is likely to have given some time to reading Paine's recently published

Rights of Man. He could hardly have avoided doing so: four Irish newspapers carried long extracts. By the end of the following year he was referring to 'my old friend Paine'.* And the latest news of the French Revolution – a term by now common in the newspaper headlines – would have confirmed him (as so many others) in his generous objections to the privileges of his own class. Notions of republicanism and revolution were certainly losing no ground.

But whatever private designs he was hatching in early 1792, his public expressions cannot yet be called fiery. In Parliament where he sat as one of two members for Kildare County, alongside his brothers Charles and Henry who were members, respectively, for the Borough of Cavan and the City of Dublin, he made no stir at all, gave no hint of rebelliousness to come. He toed the moderate Whig line – and the Whig clubs did not even include in their plans for parliamentary reform any extension of the franchise. However, he was later in the year to make up for his outward show of polite moderation, and abandon all counsels of caution, all discretion.

---

* Thomas Paine was elected as an honorary member of the Dublin Society of United Irishmen in May; at one meeting, chaired by Rowan, when his admission was discussed Simon Butler moved that from his singular exertions in the cause of freedom Paine deserved the 'utmost veneration' of the Society. (But there is no record that Fitzgerald met Paine before the autumn of 1792.)

5

Dinner at White's

These are the times that try men's souls. The summer
soldier and the sunshine patriot will, in this crisis, shrink
from the service of their country; but he that stands it
now, deserves the love and thanks of men and women.
Thomas Paine, *The Crisis*, Introduction

In October 1792, without even telling his mother, Lord Edward
Fitzgerald left Dublin for Paris, via London and Boulogne. On his
way he dined with his cousin Charles Fox, finding him 'quite right
about all the good French news' and, once in Paris, called on Paine,
who was staying in comfort at White's Hotel, near the Petit Palais.
From there he headed a letter to his dearest mother, using the new
style 'Tuesday, October 30th. 1st Year of the Republic, 1792', and
wrote with enthusiasm about his days with his new and dangerous
friend:

> we breakfast, dine and sup together. The more I see of his interior, the
> more I like and respect him. I cannot express how kind he is to me; there
> is a simplicity of manner, a goodness of heart, and a strength of mind in
> him, that I have never known a man before possess. I pass my time very
> pleasantly, read, walk, and go quietly to the play. I have not often been to
> see anyone, nor shall not . . . I can compare [Paris] to nothing but Rome
> in its days of conquest: – the energy of the people is beyond belief . . . I go
> a great deal to the Assembly; they improve much in speaking.[1]

Paine had been thrown out of England for his seditious writings in
the previous month, and was 'venerated' in France as greatly as he

was by the Society of United Irishmen in Dublin. He had already been elected as Calais' representative to the National Convention, and was about to help draw up a new revolutionary constitution.

There was nothing half-hearted about Fitzgerald's own embrace of the Revolution, nor in his delight at news of recent French victories, of the *invincible cavalry* of Prussia being 'eat up'. One must remember, of course, that this enthusiasm was very far from unusual at the time. Fox had called the French Revolution 'the noblest cause that was ever in the hand of man'. The King of France had not yet been executed, the worst of the Terror was still to come, and declaration of war with England was some four months away:

> I am delighted with the manner they feel their success; no foolish boasting or arrogance about it; – but imputing all to the greatness and goodness of their cause, and seeming to rejoice more on account of its effects in Europe in general than for their own individual glory . . . in the coffee-houses and play-houses, every man calls the other *camerade, frère*, and with a stranger immediately begins, '*Ah! nous sommes tous frères, tous hommes, nos victoires sont pour vous, pour tout la monde;*' etc.[2]

Other revolutions have been greeted with similar rapture.

Within a month a grand dinner was held at White's Hotel at which Fitzgerald declared his revolutionary beliefs, renounced his title, and in effect 'scratched himself out of' the Army. The occasion was widely reported. The *Dublin Evening Post* and the *London Chronicle* carried full reports. In the *Annual Register* of 1792 it is among the dozens of accounts of meetings of societies all over the world which celebrated the glorious achievements of the Revolution: the toasts and speeches are interspersed with '(Trumpets – "*Ça ira, Ça ira*")', '(Song – "*Oh Homme, mon frère*")', and so on. Moore quotes one report:

> Paris, Nov. 19th
> Yesterday the English arrived in Paris assembled at White's Hotel, to celebrate the triumph of victories gained over their late invaders by the armies of France. Though the festival was intended to be purely British, the meeting was attended by citizens of various countries, by deputies of the Convention, by generals, and other officers of the armies then stationed or visiting Paris, – J.H. Stone in the chair.
> Among the toasts were, 'The armies of France; may the examples of its citizen soldiers be followed by all enslaved countries, till tyrants and tyrannies be extinct.'
> An address proposed to the National Convention. – Among several

other toasts proposed by the citizens, Sir R. Smith and Lord E. Fitzgerald, was the following: 'May the patriotic airs of the German Legion (Ça Ira, the Carmagnole, Marseilles March, & etc.) soon become the favourite music of every army, and may the soldier and the citizen join in the chorus'.

General Dillon* proposed 'The people of Ireland; and may Government profit by the example of France, and Reform prevent Revolution'.

Sir Robert Smith and Lord E. Fitzgerald renounced their titles; and a toast proposed by the former was drank: – 'The speedy abolition of all hereditary titles and feudal distinctions'.[3]

Fitzgerald did not confine himself to toasts at this celebration of French victories and of the advent of 'The Great Republic of Man'. In his talks with Paine he discussed how the French might support an Irish revolution, and suggested that if 40,000 Irish volunteers could be financed and kept in the field for three months, Ireland could gain its freedom. The proposal was followed up, and an American Colonel Eleazer Oswald was commissioned to travel to Ireland to 'sound out the dispositions of the Irish people'. The route, via Norway, that Colonel Oswald chose took so long, however, that the initiative petered out. (But one result may have been that it gave new grounds for the Irish belief that French aid was there for the asking.[4])

Fitzgerald's understandable dismissal from the army met with a protest from Fox in the House of Commons which at least does justice to his family loyalty:

> that there might be good grounds [for his being cashiered] was possible, but they were unknown because they were undeclared . . . Lord Edward Fitzgerald was his near relation and of him he would say, from his personal knowledge, that the service did not possess a more zealous, meritorious or promising member; – he had served his country in actual service, and bled in its service.[5]

Fitzgerald soon took a step even more momentous than an embrace of revolution and a farewell to army life. Moore tells how at a theatre in Paris he saw through a *loge grillé* near him a 'face with which he was particularly struck, as well from its own peculiar beauty as from the strong likeness the features bore for those of a young

---

* Dublin-born, he was guillotined in Paris on 14 April 1794. (His toast does sound on the cautious side.)

lady for whom he was known to have a very affectionate regard' – a likeness, it became apparent, to Elizabeth Ann Sheridan, who had died giving birth to his child in June.

This young woman was called Pamela. She was popularly believed to be an illegitimate daughter of the famous and horrible Madame de Genlis,* by her lover the Duke of Orleans, that prudent but doomed advocate of the Revolution who called himself Philippe Egalité. Her real name, less romantically, was Anne – or perhaps Nancy – Syms. She had been taken by Egalité from an English foundling hospital in 1780, and been brought up with his own children from the age of six. Belief in her aristocratic parentage, however, appears to have done no harm to Fitzgerald's revolutionary credentials.[6]

Short, effervescent, addicted to ballooning dresses and extravagant hairstyles, Pamela had nothing in common with the Dublin ladies. She sounds as though she was, in equal measure, an embarrassment and an enchantment. In less than a month after their meeting in Paris, Fitzgerald and she were married in Tournay, safely beyond the borders of France in order to comply with the erratic wishes of Mme Genlis, her adoptive mother.

Fitzgerald, with understandable foreboding, wondered what his own ever-loving mother would make of her. The introduction came early next year.

Through the Dublin summer, Drennan had been following events in France with an enthusiasm equal to Fitzgerald's.

As the July commemorations of the Bastille grew near, Drennan threw off restraint. But he did think that enthusiasm alone was not enough. An element of religion should be added, some intimations of the spiritual. The panoply should have some mystic significance. Two of his letters to Sam McTier are full of advice for the Belfast festival:

> I think devotion should be mixed with [the celebrations], which is too much wanting even in French enthusiasm, and I should like to see . . . a sort of service for all the people to be read or spoken, and chorused with proper responses, in the open air, at a rustic altar, under the arch of

---

* 1746–1830. Mme Genlis was educated with extraordinary negligence and frivolity; she was famous for betraying her friends, for her greed, her pretentiousness and her lies. She accumulated several rich lovers and wrote many worthless books.

heaven, a liturgy of liberty. You should have something more *imposant* than a mere review. Your ladies should get some parts to perform, and the lower people should revive their garlands, etc . . .[7]

You ought certainly to have two days, one for the procession and another for the review. You should have four flags, for France, America, Poland and Ireland, borne by handsome boys in suitable dresses. Your dinner ought to have been where it was before [in the 1791 celebrations], not an expensive tavern, but so as to include all at a crown each. Tone, I believe, intends to propose a declaration of politics adherent to our Constitution and abhorrent of a republic . . . this declaration is by no means incompatible with a short address of good wishes to the assembly of France.[8]

There is an element of prevarication here. For its part, the Castle was uncertain how seriously to treat the Bastille celebrations. It was unseemly, even cowardly, to appear too disturbed. But it was a relief to see them pass without too much trouble. It was quite telling that the experienced and elderly Under-Secretary Sackville Hamilton, an official not prone to panic, wrote on July 16 to the Home Secretary in London:

On Saturday last the English mail was dispatched too early to admit of my giving you satisfactory Information of the Proceedings of the Day. I am happy to tell you it passed in perfect quietness without any attempt to a celebration of the French Revolution. Yesterday about twenty Volunteers headed by Hamilton Rowan Esquire paraded in Stephen's Green and fired three volleys, after which they dispersed and the day concluded without the least riot or disturbance.[9]

Drennan shared Paine's views on the absurdity of monarchy. He was, like many Presbyterians of the North, an instinctive republican. Even tyrannicide presented no great moral obstacles to him. Earlier in his life, in the title-page to his *Orellana*, there appears in Greek a testimony to the two Athenian cousins whose actions had (it was thought) eventually led to the institution in Athens of 'equality before the law'.* Much had to be sacrificed to the ideals of public good and public virtue.

Drennan was at this time so inspired by the French victories as to compose for his brother-in-law an address to be sent to the National Convention expressing the sentiments of the inhabitants of Belfast

---

* Harmodius and Aristogeiton actually succeeded in killing only the *brother* of the tyrant. But the legend nonetheless prospered, and their descendants received free meals for life from Athens.

'on the news of the Revolution's glorious completion'. McTier, he thought, should send a message saying:

> I feel myself emboldened in the sincerity of my heart to pray to that God whose ear is open alike to the first assembly on earth and to the humblest individual, that your arms may continue to prosper in the cause of France and of human nature . . . that, in fine, you may soon bring about a *civic union of the world* when all the sons of men and all religions shall join their worship in a temple of liberty which may have the earth for its area and the arch of heaven for its dome.[10]

It is difficult to disentangle, in such passages, the threads of Freemasonry, republicanism, and a sort of quasi-rationalist deism not much to do with orthodox or even dissenting Christianity. There is something reminiscent of William Blake in Drennan's attitude towards God: the Divine Reason being surrounded by a penumbra of mysticism, to be approached with aweful devotion and strange ceremony (though without pernicious priesthood). The God who loves Liberty is more important than the Christ who suffers Crucifixion.

By the end of the year, Drennan was reflecting on a more pressing question than celebrations of the Revolution. This was the petition that the Catholic Committee was preparing for Catholic emancipation, which they proposed boldly to submit not to the Lord-Lieutenant, but (if he was unwilling himself to transmit it to London) direct to the King. The growing predominance of the Committee in the political turmoil presented its own problems to Drennan. And he was confused.

The worm of mistrust between Catholics and Dissenters often emerges in his letters. Drennan was one of those who suspected that, once the former had gained their goal of emancipation, they might lose their appetite for the cause of parliamentary reform – and that was something he cherished most. (Indeed, had always done so, as he had declared in his *Letters of Orellana* eight years earlier.) Also, whereas the Catholics were in general well disposed to monarchy, by temperament and by religious upbringing, Presbyterians like himself wished to steer ever closer towards some species of republicanism.

One thinks again of Beresford's phrase about the artful perversion of minds – 'reform and republicanism for the Dissenters, emancipation and the ascendancy of popery for the papists'.[11] Drennan shows himself fairly well versed in cunning calculations: aware of the fragility of the alliance, and of the leading role suspicion has always played in Irish politics. 'Grandmother's footsteps' tactics are called for. One letter he wrote in December to his brother-in-law, is worth reading closely:

> Do not breathe any suspicions of the Catholics for the present. If they see we suspect them, they will suspect us. Let us not run a risk of losing them now when their business [of emancipation] is nearly decided and ours is but beginning . . . The cry of revolution and republicanism is raised against us. No King, etc. Take great care to obviate this. Our present pursuits ought to terminate in an equal and impartial representation of the people, and let posterity go on to republicanism if they choose.[12]

Drennan must have been aware that his new position as the President of the Dublin Society of United Irishmen (for three months from November) carried dangers. And so was his sister. The raising of a new regiment of Volunteers, to be decked out in a new national uniform,* understandably alarmed the Government, and soon led to a Proclamation suppressing any such new formations. From Belfast Martha advised:

> my dear brother be as guarded as you possibly can in your present situation . . . in any political matters you may publish, I hope the best *law* opinions may be your sanction. I would not like to visit you in Newgate, for glorious indeed ought the cause to be to gild such a residence. Patriotism seldom places anyone there. It is oftener the mistake of madmen.[13]

Drennan in fact well knew of one most inflammatory Address sent to 5,000 Presbyterians of the North. Collins had faithfully reported it as 'by one of our *gang*'. Signed by one of Paine's pseudonyms – 'Common Sense' – the author was rumoured to be Keogh:

> How long will the men of Ulster be duped by those who enslave them? How long will they bend their heads to the yoke . . . Are you free or are you slaves? – what is slavery? It is to be taxed, where men are not represented; are ye taxed? Yes; are ye then represented? – No! Are ye then free?[14]

Although Drennan later deplored the 'scurrility' of this pamphlet (for the distribution of which the printer was fined £1,000 and gaoled for two years), even more dangerous language was used the

---

* Drennan hoped that this would have inscribed on it a 'magnificent oriflamme, in glowing capitals UNIVERSAL EMANCIPATION AND REPRESENTATIVE LEGISLATURE'.

following month, during the period of his presidency of the Dublin Society, in an Address to the new Volunteers. This 'exceeded any other publications of the Society for violence not to say wickedness . . . with an express purpose of inflaming the nation particularly the north of Ireland and bringing about an immediate national Protestant convention' (the words used by Collins in his informer's report to the Castle of 14 December).[15]

This fateful Address, published in the *Hibernian Journal* on 17 December 1792, commenced:

> Citizen soldiers, you first took up arms to protect your country from foreign enemies, and from domestic disturbance; for the same purposes it now becomes necessary that you should resume them . . . from whatever quarter it arises, alarm has arisen; and you, Volunteers of Ireland, are therefore summoned to arms.

Although the Address contains many less insurrectionary sentiments about 'preserving the country in guarded quiet and preserving the blessings of peace', it does not seem unreasonable that the Government should have claimed, in their Bill of Indictment against its two signatories – the then President of the Society, Drennan, and its Secretary, Rowan – that the Address incited His Majesty's subjects to 'attempt with force and violence to make alterations to the government state and constitution of this kingdom'. 'Citizen Soldiers, to Arms', with its Parisian echoes, is a phrase that might reasonably alert any government. After the publication of the Address, steps were taken at different intervals to bring those responsible to trial for seditious libel. The wait both for Drennan and for Hamilton Rowan was very long and very suspenseful – the former's case did not come before the courts until the Easter term of 1794. Verdicts of guilty might well have led to their deaths.

All through the autumn, Drennan's movements and writings had been closely observed by John Pollock,* his former neighbour from

---

* He was *inter alia* Deputy Clerk of pleas in the Court of Exchequer, Clerk of Reports in the Court of Chancery, Transcripter and Foreign Apposer in the Court of Exchequer, Crown Solicitor for the Home Circuit and a JP. Many of these were sinecures and he held many simultaneously (see *The Trial of William Drennan*, p. 10). John Francis Larkin, Reid Professor of Law at the University of Dublin, is 'working on the career of this remarkable man', and I draw heavily on *The Trial* later on.

Newry, and a most ambitious and capable lawyer. More to the immediate point, of all the tribe of government agents he seems the most odiously ingratiating.

Pollock was the chief entrapper of all the informers of the age. He used the weapons of friendship and sympathetic advice to seduce countless men on the Castle's behalf. After the Rebellion, Edward Cooke, the Chief Secretary at the Castle, paid handsome tribute and recommended generous payment to Pollock for having done so well in recruiting and controlling informers (including, indeed, McNally). Now, in the critical month of November 1792, when the Castle had good reason to fear that rebellion might be about to break out, it was Drennan's turn to be approached.

Drennan's tale of this attempted seduction, told in two long letters, one to his sister and one to his brother-in-law, is a minuet of innuendo and pretence of bafflement. The first is dated 25 November:

> Our conversation, or rather his, turned upon the belief that we were all selling our wares to the best advantage, but in different manners, some exposing them at the window, others keeping them in the back shop to heighten their value, etc. He concluded with saying, 'Drennan, I am your friend, and whenever you wish to befriend yourself and get some good of your abilities, apply to me'. This was said more seriously than jokingly.
>
> I answered, 'I never will', and then went in [from the street]. On coming out again, and seeing him return on his step, I wished to coquet a little (for I really want an offer, but in a manner that could . . . give me the glory of refusing it, which, I suppose, he is too wary to make) and, therefore, wished he would walk in . . . the chief tenor of his succeeding conversation was the ruin of my practice, in case of persisting in any politics . . . My answer was that I was satisfied some would be so cruel as to wish to hurt me, and even ruin me, as a physician, merely because I differed from them in politics, but that I hoped that he and his friends would not lend them their assistance.[16]

A week later Drennan wrote again, this time hinting at Pollock's more peremptory tone. Menace began. Pollock was clearly in deadly earnest. He was taking up a great deal of highly valued time in order to win over the not-quite-so-innocent Drennan.

> at dinner time [Pollock] called upon me and said he wished to speak to me in private and that I would order myself to be denied to anyone that should call. I did so . . . he began to speak to me in pretty much the same

terms as he had before, concluding with declaring that what he had said was to be confidential and by no means to be revealed to anyone. I told him I thought this hard, that there were some persons such as my sister and my brother-in-law, Sam McTier, whose opinions I highly valued and might therefore wish to consult on anything interesting to my welfare. He protested against my sister, talked much against disclosing any important matter to any woman . . . I said I had early formed my principles in politics and that my father to his last hour had desired me never to forsake them, and here, on recollecting that best of men, and thinking that I saw that meek and venerable form bending over me with a placid and approving smile, I burst into tears and remained for some time much affected.[17]

We do not know how Pollock interpreted Drennan's plausible disingenuousness. He did, however, continue to question his victim closely on his views on granting the elective franchise to Catholics, on the preference of a republican form of government and particularly on the establishment of the 'new Volunteers called National Guards'.

There is a curious end to Drennan's letter, suggesting that it was just, just possible that Pollock's efforts had not fallen on completely stony ground. How else can one interpret:

I think I may be said to have had an offer indefinite indeed, because no one could expect anything written on the subject from anyone in, or under, government, but sufficient to give me the satisfaction of having refused it. *Whether advice or influence may change my mind, I cannot say, till I have heard or felt it. I am as I was, but I know not nor have the presumption to say what I shall be* [my italics].[18]

The fact was that Drennan's preoccupation with politics *had* led to a diminution of his earnings as a doctor; he felt the crib of genteel poverty, especially hard for someone who possessed his fair share of vanity, especially useful for an expert entrapper like Pollock. Not that Drennan was ever caught in the web; but his reflections upon the injustices of the world can only have been soured when, later, he learnt that his ingratiating 'former neighbour in Newry' had inherited a splendid estate in County Meath from one of his clients. In the end, however, we learn:

Mr —— S tells me he remembers having noticed, with some pain, the once swaggering and influential John Pollock reduced to comparative poverty and prostration. Mr Pollock did not long survive his humiliation.

In 1818 Leonard McNally saw his seducer [and the would-be seducer of Drennan, who died two years later] consigned to the grave.[19]

Intelligence derived from the business of tailors, in a time and country fond of uniforms, can be most useful; an accurate report of the numbers of cockades ordered may reveal more about deadly immediacies than the rhetoric of a dozen pamphlets. Collins's reports of the November meetings of the Dublin Society of United Irishmen go into great detail about the uniforms for the new First Battalion of Volunteers. These were provocatively modelled on those of the National Guards of the French Revolution. Rowan, as the then Secretary of the Society, took very great interest in their ordering and designing. He loved uniforms.

The idea of creating a new battalion was discussed at a number of meetings of the Society that autumn. Early in October one or two rudimentary measures of security were introduced; there should be fewer admissions of 'improper people'. A new seal was ordered, with the device of the harp (*without the crown*), and the motto: 'I am new strung and will be heard'. By the end of November Collins was reporting progress:

> I understand that there are already near 200 *Select Men* enrolled and the uniform fixed on is a dark green shirt cloth coat, white facing and cuffs, white waistcoat, green and white striped damascus trousers (*sans culottes*), a felt hat turned up at one side with a green emblematic cockade, the device a shamrock crowned with a [Phrygian] cap of liberty, the most perfect equality to subsist throughout the whole, they now talk of 8 or 10000 in the city of Dublin only . . .[20]

It seems extraordinary, given how it flaunted its parody of revolution, that the Society made so few attempts at concealment, or at discretion of any kind. How can they *not* have realized the deadly risks they were running with their inflammatory pamphlets, their mock-military preparations? ('Mock', since the scale of their preparations – probably exaggerated by Collins – was self-evidently too modest to pose a serious threat of grand upheaval, even if tiresome enough for the Government to nip in the bud.) There was as yet no sign that the wildfire of popular revolution could take hold in the country; on the other hand the Castle could scarcely ignore overt calls to arms, the flouting of proclamations that forbade illegal gatherings.

In those late autumn days of 1792 Rowan and his companions went their way visiting tailors, and the Government went on its way seeking more information. Collins gave a full report on 29 November. Before one or two rather general paragraphs stating that 'there are now a great number of arms in this city', and that 'there doesn't seem any plan for obtaining ammunition', five paragraphs are chiefly devoted to the ordering of the uniforms:

– Hamilton Rowan and Tandy have bespoke the buttons from Murphy but not any specific number . . .
– Bacon made a pattern suit for Tandy and another for Rowan one which is at the Irish Woollen Warehouse and another at Peebles and Spencer's in High Street exactly as I before described except that cuffs and collar and lapels are white, enclosed you have a pattern of cloth and a [*sic*] Buttons.
– The Volunteers are to pay individually for their clothes as the plan is to have them as select as possible in order to have credence with the mob, Bacon is making about 200 suits.
– Hamilton Rowan has ordered the cockades from [name missing] . . .
– One Grace in Cut Purse Row is making the hats.[21]

Within a week Collins was following up his alarums with a package enclosing a sample of the national cockades. He added more precise details:

Hamilton Rowan ordered one thousand hats at 5/5, the same number of cockades at 1/7½, and the same of white features at 2/2 . . . there are great numbers of common people calling every hour at Graces [in Cut Purse Row] to know if it's true they are to enlist – he delivered about 200 hats on Saturday, and exclusive of Mr Rowan's order there are already some hundreds ordered for different places in the north.
I think my Lord Lieutenant may find it prudent not to expose his person too much . . .[22]

On 8 December the Government made its Proclamation against the new armed force, pronouncing its assembly illegal and empowering magistrates to disperse all such seditious gatherings. The parade that had been planned for 9 December duly fell through. Only one enormous, unmistakable figure with two or three followers turned up. As Drennan wrote to his sister on 10 December:

[The Proclamation] did not prevent H. Rowan and one or two other *protestants* from walking in the streets with the green uniform and side arms. The mob surrounded them and huzzaed them much . . . The Catholics, who first originated the idea of this corps, are now afraid and would rather have prevented any meeting.

The Catholics, the Catholics, have damped the new Volunteers, which they originally moved, and Rowan, Tandy, etc. [are] left in the lurch . . . Rowan will be as mad as the rugged Russian Bear. Butler says that Tone has been bought off as *McKenna certainly is.* I don't know, but this I think, that the Catholics are *so for the present.*[23]

Suspicion was everywhere. The Catholic Committee had held their National Convention of Catholics in Dublin a week earlier. They had failed to reply to the message of good will which the Belfast Society of United Irishmen had sent them. Now, with the fiasco of the parade of the new Volunteers, they showed again how they feared that too close co-operation with the republican and potentially revolutionary United Irishmen might jeopardize their petition for Catholic emancipation. This struck Drennan as fearful timidity: fine rhetoric on the surface, wariness and resentment beneath. (How many beside Rowan ever wore their brilliant uniforms of the 'National Guard', their fine cockades at 1/7½ each, their expensive white feathers? By early 1793, Volunteering in Dublin had dragged to a close.)

Rowan's ardour had not, however, been cooled at all. Within a few days, in his capacity as Secretary to the Dublin Society of United Irishmen, he was overseeing the printing and distribution of Drennan's Address to the Volunteers which, as well as leading to his and Drennan's prosecution, eventually resulted, indeed, in wholesale changes in the composition and activities of the United Irishmen. Meanwhile the diligence of the informers, the rashness of the leaders of the Dublin Society and the deliberate waiting of the Government sometimes give the mesmerizing impression of watching a cat throwing doomed mice expertly into the air: no hurry to kill them.

Tone, as we have seen, had been appointed in July as the full-time Assistant Secretary to the new, radicalized Committee of Catholics. This gave him a most welcome source of income, but it meant that he saw little of his wife and family, to whom he vowed deep adoration on so many pages of his journals. For all the modesty of his title, he was now the Committee's principal organizer, and it was his job to do most of the groundwork for the grand National Convention of Catholics, due to take place in Dublin in early December.

He was disappointed to have to postpone an autumn weekend with Rowan and his wife in County Kildare, since he loved such country pursuits as hare-coursing. Instead he had to go on a long and uncomfortable journey to Ballinasloe in County Galway, to help in the selection of delegates to the Conference. No matter: 'Public business must take place of pleasure and vain delight.'

The plan had been that he should go with 'Gog' – John Keogh, the Committee's driving spirit. But Gog did not want to travel to out-lying parts, as he disliked wet sheets.

Tone's diary jottings of the perils of the expedition show his appreciation of the nature of courage (as well as of endurance):

> October 5, 1792. Left Dublin at eight in the evening in a post-chaise with Mr Braughall [in his sixties, and something of an intellectual]. Loaded with good advice by Gog in the morning, who has given me a broad hint to puff him in Connaught. An adventure! Stopped by three footpads near the park-gate, who threaten to exterminate the post-boy if he attempts to move . . . if they had persisted then we would have shot them, being well armed . . . Mr Hutton [Tone's nickname] in a fuss; his first emotion was to jump out and combat on foot; very odd! but his fear always comes on *after the danger*; much more embarrassed a quarter of an hour after, than during the dialogue . . . glad we did not kill any of the villains, who seemed to be soldiers. Drive on to Kinnegad – another adventure!! The chaise breaks down at three in the morning in the mud: obliged to get out in the mud, and hold up the chaise with my body, while the boy puts on the wheel; all grease and puddle! melancholy! arrive at Kinnegad at past four; bad hours![24]

Within a week Tone thought that he had 'secured' Galway and Mayo. News of the French successes of Dumouriez had given him the same cheer and prospects of glorious victory as they gave Fitzgerald in Paris and Martha McTier in Belfast: 'Huzza! Huzza! Brunswick and his army dying of the flux and running out of France, with Dumourier pursing him. Huzza! If the French had been beaten, it was all over with us. All safe now in this campaign. Huzza!'[25]

Despite the private words he committed to his diary, he conscientiously kept a certain distance in public from the United Irishmen, while the Convention was being planned. There were still conservative Catholics on the Committee who believed that emancipation – perhaps even including the right to sit in Parliament – was likelier to be gained if it was *not* mixed with the heady brew of parliamentary reform, the taint of radical if not revolutionary views. As the Assistant Secretary, he considered that it would have been improper to be seen to consort too closely with advocates of extremism, even if this politic caution ran the risk of disappointing such active United Irishmen as Drennan and Rowan.

Tone's hope, however, still remained that the United Irishmen and the Catholics should act in tandem. An excellent means might be the resuscitation of the glorious tradition of Volunteering. It would be 'once more the salvation of Ireland. A good thing to have 1500 men in Dublin. Green uniforms etc.'[26]

Sometimes he was carried away by his theme, afterwards confessing to his diary that he talked a great deal of tactics and treason (a word which now begins to edge into his jottings). He describes dinner at Warrens on 1 November:

> A long set of the chief United Irishmen. Mr Hutton endeavours, being *entre deux vins*, to delude the gentlemen present into forming a Volunteer company on good principles, civil and military. A.H. Rowan rises thereat ... Mr Hutton a little mad on the subject of volunteering; would be a great Martinet 'Army, d—n me!' Talks a great deal of tactic and treason. Mr Hutton grows warm with the subject; very much surprised, on looking down to the table, to see two glasses before him; finds, on looking at Hamilton Rowan, that he has got four eyes; various other phenomena in optics equally curious. Mr Hutton, like the sun in the centre of the system, fixed, everything about him in rapid rotation; perfectly sober, but perceives that everyone else is getting very drunk; essays to walk across the room, but finds it impossible to move rectilinearly, proceeding entirely from his having taken 'a sprig of watercress' with his dinner.[27]

The illusion sustained him, as it sustained Rowan and alarmed the Government, that the alliance between Catholic and Presbyterian was being erected on a solid foundation. Had he examined his own turns of phrase in his private jottings, he might have realized its fragility: for example, 'Dine with this Catholic, and that Catholic; very idle work'; and another entry, 'Dine with Magog (Mr McCormick); a good fellow; much better than Gog. Gog a papist'. Irony, yes; but one can detect a lurking streak of prejudice, and place a question-mark or two in the margins, beside his fervent championship of unity of the sects. This is not to doubt his sincerity:

> Dine at Macdonnel's with United Irishmen. Tandy tells me the Volunteers refused to parade round King William's statue, this being the birthday of

that monarch; they have also abolished orange cockades. Bravo! A few of them met today as at ordinary parade and wore national (green) cockades. This is a striking proof of the change of men's sentiments, when 'Our glorious deliverer' is so neglected. This is the first time the day has passed uncommemorated since the institution of Volunteers. Huzza! Union and the people for ever![28]

Tone did, however, admit unease about the adoption of the *garde nationale* as the model for the uniform of the new Volunteers. He seems to have been more aware than, for example, Rowan of the tremendous dangers in teetering on the edge of revolution. Behaviour should be moderated, more guarded, especially if one was confiding to one's diaries such beliefs and reports as:

the common people are up in high spirits, and anxious for the event. Bravo! Better have the peasantry of one country than twenty members of parliament. Gog seems disposed today for all manner of treason and mischief; separation of the countries, &c; a republic &c; is of opinion that this will not end without blows, and says he for one is ready.[29]

However, the Catholic Convention held in the Tailors' Hall, Back Lane, in early December was conducted with decorum: no whispers of disloyalty to the monarch, of revolutions and republics. Such ideas would certainly have alarmed many delegates: not the best way to gain the longed-for franchise, and entry into proper constitutional politics. The high drama of the Convention lay elsewhere, in its final moments: that is, in determining, after vacillations between the Castle and the Convention, whether the petition for complete Catholic emancipation should be sent, in the regular manner, to the Lord-Lieutenant, with the request that he should transmit it to the King; or failing his agreement, whether it should be carried to London, to be presented in person. 'A gross insult to the Administration', indeed.

In mid-December, a party of five, with Tone in attendance, gathered at the Donegal Arms in Belfast *en route* for London – no packet-boat having been ready in Dublin harbour. They had been met in the city, Tone wrote,

by a number of the most active and intelligent inhabitants, who had distinguished themselves in the abolition of prejudice, and the conciliation of the public mind in Ulster to the claims of the Catholics. On their departure, their horses were taken off [their coach], and they were drawn along with loud acclamations by the people, among whom were a number of an appearance and rank very different from what are usually seen on such occasions. To the honour of the populace of Belfast, it should be mentioned that they refused a liberal donation which was offered by the Catholic delegates; and having escorted them beyond the precincts of the town, and cordially wished them success in their embassy, they dismissed them with three cheers . . . it was an interesting spectacle, and pregnant with material consequences, to see the Dissenter of the North drawing with his own hands the Catholic of the South in triumph through what may be denominated the capital of Presbyterianism.[30]

6

Increasing boldness

The accounts of the County of Louth, with respect to the
proceedings of a banditti, calling themselves defenders,
grew daily more alarming – these daring insurgents met in
Dunbar, to the number of 1500 to 2000 men, some armed
with guns, some with pitchforks.

Annual Register, January 1793

The Catholic Committee's bold act of going over the head of the
Lord-Lieutenant, and carrying the petition for further relief
direct to the Palace, succeeded. Despite the snub to the Lord-
Lieutenant, the five petition-bearers, together with Tone, were
received in London with all the state they could have wished.

Lord Rawdon (soon to be Lord Moira) welcomed them ceremoniously. This had its effect. In his 'Account of the Proceedings of the
Delegation of the Catholic Committee which presented their petition to the King'[1] Tone shows no republican animus at all. He was
not at all averse to grandees, if they showed him courtesy and
consideration.

The petition-bearers themselves had determined to put on as
splendid a show as possible. Their instructions were engrossed on
vellum. They were resolute to give no impression of being suppli-
cants. Everything was to be done with the greatest dignity. They
stayed at the best hotel in Jermyn Street – Grenier's, in which the
Ambassador of Naples had recently committed suicide. They
dressed and paraded in style. All this was especially congenial to
Gog, in his silk stockings and curled and powdered wig.[2]

They had to wait long days before they were summoned to their audience with the King. But meetings with Henry Dundas, the Home Secretary (who in this capacity had the chief governmental responsibility for the affairs of Ireland, including the appointment – and dismissal – of Viceroys) helped them to assess the situation. So did frequent and magnificent dinners with Lord Rawdon, who offered to be their intermediary. Wolfe Tone wrote, in his account as Assistant Secretary to the Committee:

> when the Minister was dallying with the earnestness of the delegates to procure admission to their Sovereign . . . Lord Moira came forward and told them, that, if it became necessary, *he* would, as a peer, demand an audience of His Majesty, and be himself their introducer; adding, at the same time, with the frankness and candour of his profession and character, it was his wish that the Minister should rather have the honour, inasmuch as he thought it would better serve their cause. 'As an Irishman and a military man, it might . . . wear too peremptory an appearance were I to introduce you . . . if, however, he should persist in his refusal, you may then command me'.[3]

Whether or not they knew it, the door on which they were knocking was half-open. Pitt was already reconciled, for the sake of the quiet of the island, to the granting of Catholic relief (even if not *entire* Catholic relief). The difficult question that London had to face was not so much how to conciliate the Catholics, as how to press adequate measures on the Protestant Ascendancy. Ireland was naturally proud of its parliamentary independence, with some of its most powerful men, like Fitzgibbon, vehement in opposing concessions. Any encouragement of the Catholic deputation had to be cautious, and crafty.

Sharp-eyed though he always was, Tone's appreciation of the strength and weaknesses of the Committee's position might have been blurred by the flattery surrounding their reception. The words, but especially the manner, of their audience gratified him. Quick to take slights, adamant against forgiving them, he was also happy to smile if warmed by the sun of skilful compliments – although it would be unfair to say he was altogether *taken in*:

> the minister relaxed; and Wednesday, the 2nd of January, was fixed as the day of their introduction. On that day, the delegates were introduced at St James's in the usual forms by Mr Dundas, and, agreeably to their instructions, delivered into the King's own hands the petition of his Catholic subjects of Ireland. Their appearance was splendid, and they met with

what is called in the language of courts a most gracious reception; that is, His Majesty was pleased to say a few words to each of the delegates in his turn. In such colloquies, the matter is generally of little interest, the manner is all; and with the manner of the Sovereign the delegates had every reason to be content.

Thus had the Catholics, at length, through innumerable difficulties, fought their way to the foot of the throne . . .[4]

Tone wrote his formal account of the London deputation from the wings of the stage. He held conversations only in corners (he was after all only a paid servant of the Committee). He suspected, with some reason, that in secret negotiations behind the scenes Gog was hinting that the Catholics might settle for something less than the entire relief for which they were pledged to fight. His views on the emerging rift between himself and Gog give glimpses of petty distrust, familiar to all who have participated in cabals dedicated to single purposes. A sub-committee was formed to report to the Chief Secretary on their return to Dublin. One of the fragments of Tone's jottings written later in the month, after their return to Dublin, reads:

[The sub-committee was dispatched to the Chief Secretary to say] that nothing short of *unlimited* emancipation will satisfy the Catholics. They return, in about an hour, extremely dissatisfied with each other . . . it appears that so far from discharging their commission, they had done exactly the reverse . . . for the result of their conversation with the Secretary was that he had declared explicitly against the *whole* measure, and they had given him reason in consequence to think that the Catholics would acquiesce contently in a *half* one. And so Gog's puffing is come to this! I always thought, when the crisis arrived, that he would be shy.

. . . [The sub-committee's subsequent letter,] instead of putting the question on the true ground, only says that His Majesty's gracious intentions towards the Catholics cannot be fulfilled except by the repeal of the penal laws. I wanted to express it a great deal stronger and to hint at the danger of trifling, but was overpowered. Gog damped them by puffing his readiness, for one, to face any danger which might ensue from a strong representation . . . Gog asked [one member of the sub-committee], 'was he prepared to enter the tented field?' . . . but the fact is that [Gog himself] is not. He is a sad fellow, after all.[5]

Tone's Irish hostility to the 'sneaking spirit of compromise', his scorn of Gog's timidity 'to all intents as ruinous as downright treachery', propelled him towards ever more extreme opinions. 'Compromise' gave rise to a well-founded fear that the Catholics, once having accepted substantial measures of relief, might forsake the cause of the North, of parliamentary reform. So much for '*United* Irishmen!' He might be forgiven for fearing that the momentum towards republicanism, towards his covert hopes for eventual separation from England, would be slowed – even stopped altogether.

Meanwhile, on 21 January, the King of France was beheaded, and Tone wrote: 'I am sorry it was necessary'.

After the passing of the (partial) Catholic Relief Bill, the National Convention formally voted itself out of existence at the end of April. At its dissolution Tone was voted a payment of £1,500 and a gold medal. £2,500 was at the same time voted for a statue to the King: some estimate, one may presume, by the more cautious Committee members of the comparative value to their cause, of the support of Wolfe Tone and of King George III.

If, to outward appearances, Wolfe Tone might still be little more than a radical champion of Catholic emancipation – despite connections with the 'blasted Society' of United Irishmen – Lord Edward Fitzgerald could by now fairly be looked on as a fully-fledged republican, and a revolutionary in the making. He had renounced his title and forfeited his commission. He had sat at the feet of Paine. He had married the reputed daughter of Egalité. He lived in a high state of excitement.

Now, in January 1793, he recklessly provoked Parliament at the start of the new session. It was an act of bravado. People not surprisingly said he was 'cut' ('vehement tone' is the giveaway in the parliamentary report). James Stewart, MP for Killymoon in County Tyrone, had just finished a speech expressing strong disapproval of the behaviour of the new Volunteers:

> Lord Edward Fitzgerald rose, and in a very vehement tone, declared – 'I give my most hearty disapprobation to that address, for I do think that the Lord Lieutenant and the majority of his House are the worst subjects that the King has.'
>
> A loud cry of 'to the Bar,' and 'take down his words' immediately echoed from every part of the House. The House was cleared in an instant, and strangers were not admitted for nearly three hours.
>
> He was admitted to explain himself, and on his explaining, the House 'Resolved, *nem.con,* that the excuse offered by the Rt Hon. Lord Edward

Fitzgerald, commonly called Lord Edward Fitzgerald, for the said words so spoken, is unsatisfactory and insufficient.'[6]

He seemed to be carried along by the winds of insolence. This brought him a certain popularity outside the House. Great glamour attached to both himself and his young bride, newly arrived from France. An old lady remembers the vivid impression that the young couple made driving through the streets of Dublin:

> Lord Edward was seated in a very high phaeton, with the beautiful Pamela beside him. He held the reins, and was driving at a very dashing pace through College Green and Dame Street in the direction of the Castle; and having only just brought her home as his bride from France, Pamela shared with him the plaudits of the people . . . Lord Edward was vividly described as a smart, light, dapper-looking man, with boyish features, which beamed with delight at the cheers of the multitude, and the admiration excited by the beauty of Pamela . . . Lord Edward wore a green silk or tabinet round his neck, tied with very large bows, and very conspicuous-looking.[7]

Drennan, as ever impressed by social grandness, wrote to his sister that 'It is not unlikely that he and his elegant wife will lead the fashion of politics in a short time if he stays here'.[8] In rather a different tone of voice, Martha McTier wrote from Belfast to say, 'We have got Lord Edward Fitzgerald on our jugs here as the man of the people'.[9]

Rowan, long impatient with the mealy mouths of some of Dublin's United Irishmen, had nothing but admiration for Fitzgerald's outspokenness. He called at Leinster House, left his ticket for Lord Edward, and added 'A freeholder of the County of Kildare', telling the servant he had not the honour of being acquainted with Lord Edward, but he would understand his card.

This led to a meeting at Rowan's house in Dublin at which Drennan was introduced to Fitzgerald. He found much to approve of:

> He was as plain and familiar in his manners as in his dress. Entered into many topics, indeed. Not too talkative, seems honest, zealous and a republican. All his thoughts bend to France . . . He said Paine had nearly a design to come over here. We thought *at present* he would do more harm than good. He said there *would* be a war. Chauvelin had assured him there *would* and, if there was, there would be a landing. We hoped that

Parliament would intercept that by giving that reform which would satisfy the people. He said they would never please the people, and it was impossible they could . . . I believe he is a noble emissary from France, but an incautious one, and I fear he will be entrapped by some of our state inquisitors.[10]

Drennan found himself equally captivated by Pamela – not that it is unusual for men (even sons of Presbyterian ministers) to be swayed by exotic looks, youth, hints of aristocratic parentage, outrageous style. However, with her balloon dresses, her tininess, her French accent, her evident delight in shocking, Pamela became, understandably, the butt of Dublin ladies. Drennan reported to his sister, perhaps not bothering to think that she might easily hold the same views as the Dublin ladies, on this subject:

> She is a pleasing, interesting little girl, with enthusiasm of eye, manner and mind which is pleasing in her feminine size and form. She exclaims much, but her 'ahs' and 'ohs' seem all sincerity and, as she said of Mirabeau, when some one doubted of his patriotism, 'Oh, he was a patriot from the very bottom of his soul'. Her husband evidently dotes on her . . . *They say* she was received well by the Duke, but the ladies here will do everything to discredit her.[11]

Cautioning her brother against open republicanism and support of the French, Martha was unimpressed by his admiration of both the Fitzgeralds. When Drennan wrote to say that Lord Edward had called upon him and that he would return the visit 'as soon as respect required', adding, 'Were I not sure that they do not open letters, I think it would be best not to say anything about this great and, I am much inclined to say, good man . . .',[12] Martha showed a tart impatience at such fond and ill-judged adulation. On the jugs of Belfast he might be: 'He *may* be good, he *may* be great, for aught I know, but he is an irritated and degraded rash man of family, of one not famed for wisdom.'[13]

William, the cautious and temporizing Duke, was a dubious influence. But he did try, ineffectually, to hold Lord Edward back. When asked about his younger brother's intention to enter the Dublin Society of United Irishmen, the Duke 'negatived his desire with the utmost indignation'.[14]

The question remains: *was* all this imitation of French ways, his crop-cut hair, his wild talk, quite so much the consequence of innocent, wayward, generous youth as sometimes appears? There is no doubt he was spoilt by the crowd's adulation, and by his mother's doting. No doubt he was both credulous and rash. But there is one intervention in a debate in the House of Commons on 7 February which suggests that he was beginning to develop schemes for some form of insurrection.

The right to carry arms was under discussion in the Committee stage of the Gunpowder Act. No one with revolutionary credentials could be expected to favour restrictions on bearing arms. And indeed:

> Lord Edward Fitzgerald declared that the clause imposing penalties on the removal of arms from one place to another was an infringement on the liberty of the subject. He was informed by gentlemen of administration that the Defenders were now in arms. In case of an attack on his house, would he not be allowed arms, without licence, for its attack? Must Volunteers apply for a licence to the Lord Lieutenant, his secretary or the Commissioners of the Revenue as the Bill requires, as often as they wish to go through their evolutions? He therefore voted against this clause particularly, and considered the entire bill a penal one.[15]

The Catholic, peasant Defenders were indeed in arms, and growing fast. Their number, and their arson and looting and houghing of cattle became more terrifying every month. Not for them doctrinaire United Irish pieties about 'unity of the sects'. One may be allowed to wonder whether the reasons Lord Edward Fitzgerald gave for preserving his right to bear arms were entirely candid. Within a few years Defenders became the fiercest, most savage and effective, of United Irish allies in the field.

Drennan was still practising his medicine, quietly, cautiously and not unsuccessfully in Dublin at the beginning of 1793, but his letters begin to give the impression of a man in a very disturbed state of mind. There were many reasons for this. Partly there was the nagging fear of a knock at the door by a Sheriff, come to arrest him for his part in the distribution of that seditious Address for which Hamilton Rowan had already been charged and remanded. So would his turn come? (It did, later.) Meanwhile, his sister and he reassured each other – Martha wrote of the Government's 'fear of his pen', and Drennan wrote of his innocence, his certainty that he was in no danger. Whistling into the wind! His belief in his own rectitude, generally uppermost, was at this period not convincing, especially when Pollock reappeared, treading with delicate menace:

> He inveighed most outrageously against [our] publications, particularly *Common Sense*, in which I agreed with him . . . I again said I thanked him for his information but . . . Not being conscious of anything done, or at least with *malus animus*, I could not alter or correct my plan of conduct. I took my leave, and he said, 'God bless you, my dear doctor.' I think if on our former conference he meant to seduce, his aim at this was to terrify.[16]

Others, too, made uncomfortable and sarcastic remarks to him in the streets. Isaac Corry, the Revenue Commissioner said to be in close touch with the Government, had said to him, 'How many kings have you killed to-day?' He had been nicknamed 'the gentle Jacobin'. Others, again, asked him whether his medical practice was doing well, in obvious reference to the time he spent on political activities: 'Mrs Grierson asked me with a sort of sneer who all my patients were, to which I answered without the least acrimony, though it was pretty cutting.'[17] One cannot blame him for feeling surrounded, even persecuted. He was not in any case a born conspirator. He was too keen to write, to strike attitudes, to impress.

Then there was his distrust of his Catholic allies, so many of whom he regarded as 'cunning, uncandid, close, plotting and circumventing'.[18] There were his doubts about other allies' characters. Rowan was brave, certainly, but was he too rash, too lacking in circumspection, too *unafraid*? There had been rumours that he might be 'taken to Scotland to be tried and transported to Botany Bay. I mentioned this to Rowan but he seemed to think it a mere threat.'[19]

Certainly the attentions of Fitzgerald, 'this great, and I am much inclined to say, good man', were most gratifying. But it was worrying that he might he be an agent for the French, and that Rowan had 'evidently fallen in love with him'. By early March, amid more complaints about Catholic behaviour, he writes cautiously that 'Lord Edward wants to join our society, but we rather dissuade him'.

Most disquieting of all was the ease with which the Government seemed to be quashing the new Volunteers, their revolutionary uniforms hardly worn. The Gunpowder Act forbidding movement of arms had produced an immediate effect. Sam McTier had reported from Belfast that though the Volunteers' cannon had not yet been seized, they were expecting it to be every day; he had proposed to several corps that they should get wooden guns and exercise with them instead. A note of panic enters into one letter from Drennan to Sam:

> All you can do is to get as many arms as possible smuggled into the country. Let every man have a firelock in country and in town, that if ever anything requires their use, an army may start up at once. I do believe that if the Volunteers resisted . . . they would have the Catholics on their side; but I will not answer for this, after a few months have gone over and the impressions of gratitude [for the repeal of nearly all the penal laws] which they at present feel are worn away. It is hard enough, God knows, to be put down in this manner, and it even appears to me somewhat singular how easily it is done. I firmly believe Government is a bravo [a pity that this word has nowadays lost its meanings of 'ruffian' and 'assassin'] at the bottom, and putting all on the hazard to show Mr Pitt how easily the country can be kept down. Resistance at this critical time would, I allow, be dangerous . . . but the Chancellor may truly boast that this is the second time he has put down the people of Protestant Ireland.[20]

Even Drennan's sister comes in for criticism. She had failed to look at the execution of the King of France in the proper perspective. He had made his own opinion clear some months earlier: 'As for Louis, it is my opinion in two words that if he be not executed, there will be another massacre, and in mercy to the people, in mercy to the constitution, it ought to be cemented and consolidated with his blood'.[21] Martha had counselled moderation. Later, after the execution, he commented: 'the horror excited here by Louis' fate is amazing, particularly among the women'. It suggested to him that republicanism in Ireland was more 'seeming than substantial', and that aristocracy was ready to lift its head, even as Louis lost his.

If he was often fearful and bewildered during these months, he had not lost his puritanical compass. The Society, in its rotatory style, once again had elected Simon Butler as Chairman and Oliver Bond as Secretary – who had objected that the questioning of some of the witnesses by House of Lords' Secret Committee on recent agitations had been *ultra vires*. The reaction of the Lord Chancellor was predictable. They were themselves then summoned for contempt of the House, fined £500 each and sentenced to six months in prison, a sentence Drennan considered excessive. With his initial approval, the United Irishmen determined both to pay their fines and to make their stay in Newgate as tolerable as possible. Regular dinners for eight, with good wines, were arranged. Gaolers were paid to connive at unchaperoned visits by Butler's mistress. Drennan became ever more indignant at the size of their wine bill, writing 'Butler and Bond are living at too great a rate for our finances. I shall not subscribe one farthing more.'[22] (One must remember that the Hon. Simon Butler was described as 'the only man of fashion amongst us'.)

Rowan suffered from no such Drennanesque qualms and uncertainties. Throughout January he continued to walk the Dublin streets in his revolutionary green uniform, bearing a great club, occasionally barking at his dog. He even went to the theatre in his uniform; when the band played 'God Save the King' he stood up in the stalls and loudly demanded that the 'Volunteer March' should be played as well. The virtual certainty of a criminal trial for distributing the notorious Address did not seem to daunt him. Yet the information which the Government had could well 'touch his life', in the words of the Speaker.

But the proscription of the Volunteers daunted many others. However ferociously Rowan wished to challenge the Government's banning of the new corps, his own band never amounted to more than fifty men. The craven lack of spirit disgusted him so much that by the end of January he determined to resign his command, preferring to stay, if at all, as a private soldier. Drennan wrote:

> I prophesy Rowan will take off his uniform and burn it before their faces this evening at eight, if they do not meet somehow or other . . . Rowan is glad to get out of a set of men who have neither the spirit or manners of gentlemen . . . I wish Lord Charlemont were outed from the Volunteers and Rowan made their General. It is a place suited to him, and he to it.[23]

There was to Rowan something almost sacred about Volunteering. Six years earlier, having been unanimously chosen to command his father's Company in Killileagh, he had written letters about the strength of his feelings: on how 'among citizens armed for their constitutional as well as national safety, no superiority is known but that of daring most for the public good'.[24]

No wonder that Fitzgerald's enthusiastic recklessness, his dash, captivated him. (How different from Tandy's pusillanimous command of *his* corps, his 'shyness' in the face of the Government's ban!) Rowan played with the idea of raising a corps of 'gentleman Volunteers' to present to Fitzgerald.

Then in mid-February he set off with Fitzgerald to an Ulster

Convention which met, symbolically, in the Presbyterian church at that *mons sacer* of the Volunteer movement, Dungannon. They seem to have arrived, with an odd, cavalier incompetence, too late for the proceedings. Perhaps it was as well. The fourteen Resolutions of the Convention lacked fire. They included a vote of thanks to the Volunteers, of course, and a motion never to dissolve them. But they also included an expression of loyalty, an objection to republican principles applied to Ireland. Sam Neilson, the proprietor of the *Northern Star*, showed his disappointment in a letter to Drennan: 'Upon the whole, I think the proceedings prudent and useful, though not entirely up to my ideas.'[25]

Those who preface a comment with 'on the whole' generally mean the opposite of what they say. It is tempting to wonder how much fiercer the proceedings might have been had Rowan and Fitzgerald arrived on time. As it was, the only practical result of this Convention was to encourage the Government to proceed with the Convention Act, banning the way in which mass meetings could apply extra-parliamentary pressure.

Rowan's sudden and unsatisfactory excursions with Fitzgerald, his apparent sangfroid about the sword which hung over his head, could not have been to the liking of Mrs Rowan. There were tales of terrible rows. In April she complained that she was beginning to expect a gaol sentence for him, 'though certain that a few words of apology might save him from this and a fine, which she supposed, from the belief of his fortune, would be a heavy one'.[26] But though his letters to her at all times seem tender enough, disregard for wives' sensibilities is quite common to revolutionaries with great public causes on their minds. Certainly Tone shared it.

Ladies are often better, too, at detecting the falsities of charm. McNally could captivate a dinner table better than he could fool Rowan's wife, or Drennan's sister.

In early 1793 the sheer nerve, the *chancing* of Leonard McNally is seen at its finest. As always, he covered his tracks well, although, thanks to his addiction to sometimes unnecessary dares, he seems once to have come dangerously close to the edge of discovery.

One cannot be quite certain that at this time he was in the pay of Government. The informer Collins's single reference to McNally as 'one of *us*' is damaging but not, I think, conclusive. There is no mention at this stage of payments of secret service money in the Rebellion Papers. So we are looking at straws in the wind.

One such straw lies in his attendance at the twenty-odd meetings of the United Irishmen in Back Lane during the first six months of the year. His election to the important committees of parliamentary reform and the 'Committee of Constitution' (and all that might entail) ensured that he was prominent in the inner councils of the Society. What is, however, somewhat suspect (on the assumption that Collins recognized his fellow informer for what he was) is the former's letter to his paymaster on 20 February in which he suggested that some of the principal members of the Society should be examined by the Secret Committee of the House of Lords set up to look at the causes of recent disturbances. Collins's main list contains eleven names including Rowan's, 'from some of whom something may be extracted'. He adds:

> It will be losing time to examine Butler, Drennan, Keogh, Tone, Bond or Tandy, for I don't think anything will be got from them, though the present alarming situation of this country has been entirely caused by Keogh, Tandy, Drennan and Butler, yet you know them too well to suppose that they will ever confess.[27]

It is unsafe to place much reliance on the evidence of silence, but why was McNally not mentioned in the second list of names, beside Rowan and Tone? He was certainly important enough.

A more curious episode concerns a printer, McDonald, asked to print the Society's formal resolution to prosecute certain members of the administration for their sale of a peerage. Prudently, McDonald declined to print it; Drennan, as President, then signed an authorization for the printer to proceed. Somebody else added Rowan's authorization without asking him.

This has the ring of one of today's scandals. Reasonably enough, Rowan wanted the authorization back, and went with McNally to retrieve it. During the conversation, McNally asked for a private word with the printer and advised him not to surrender the authorization:

> as it was the only security he possessed. This you may be sure has forfeited McNally's confidence in our Society, and Emmet was inclined to denounce him to the Society, but all this is overblown, and the affair is quite over, nor do I believe there was any danger in it anyway.[28]

One can only guess what McNally was up to. He *might* really have had a friendly desire to protect the printer. Or else he might have hoped to ensure that a document, potentially incriminating to Drennan and Rowan (the latter already, it must be remembered, awaiting trial over distributing that fateful 'call to arms of the citizen soldiers'), was not destroyed, but remained available for later use against them.

McNally in any case never fooled Drennan's sister Martha, who wrote: 'Why does the printer keep that paper when he refused to print it, and what does he want security for? Are you or your Society safe with such a member as McNally?'[29]

Despite the French war, and the worsening of agrarian disturbances in the North, in other respects early 1793 seemed to go reasonably well for the Government. The Catholic Relief Bill, which all but abolished the great majority of the 'popery laws' or penal laws, eventually passed with surprising ease. Collins was able to report with self-satisfaction on two occasions that the 'serpents' teeth' were nearly drawn and that 'the nursery of rebellion is totally blasted'. He may even have been anxious about his future employment and source of funds as an informer, since at the end of February we find him writing:

> I think I may be of much more use elsewhere than what I can possibly be of here . . . I am confident from *particular circumstances* that I can get into a situation abroad that very few people may be able to attain; and are you not of an opinion that (provided the war continues) an invasion will be attempted in this country, perhaps by a diversion in Munster and a more serious attack northward?[30]

He need not have worried. For another year and a half he continued sending in his regular reports. (In his last list of members of the Dublin Society we see him writing beside the name of Leonard McNally, 'suspected of being a spy'.[31])

7

Fighting talk

He could not believe GOD ALMIGHTY meant that we
should bear to be insulted, or would be angry at a man's
taking revenge if he did it like a gentleman.
> Answer to Burke's observation that
> duelling was contrary to religion.[1]

Collins's reports sowed particular disquiet with his frequent, cryptic references to Rowan's correspondence with foreigners. Rowan often sent letters and addresses to such radical English and Scottish societies as 'Friends of the People', a convention of which had met early in the year in Edinburgh. These societies' rhetoric was quite as seditious as that of the United Irishmen. Disaffection in Dublin and Belfast was worry enough for the Government, but that – especially in times of war – the United Irishmen should play a part in spreading the disease abroad was intolerable (though increasing, it should be said, the value of the informer to his paymaster). Collins wrote:

> I find that Rowan keeps up a constant correspondence with Edinburgh and I believe, with Paris, and I have every reason to be confirmed in the opinion . . . that there is something in agitation amongst a few of those I mentioned last night which I have not yet been able to come to the bottom of, but you may depend on my not losing any time . . .[2]

The only foreigner to have been elected a member of the Dublin Society in its early days, apart from Paine, was Thomas Muir, Vice-President of one of the associations of 'Friends of the People'. In

August 1793, some time after visiting Dublin and attending a meeting of the Society of United Irishmen, he stood trial for sedition on his return to Edinburgh, and was sentenced to be transported to Botany Bay for fourteen years. The judge was said to have been a bully, the jury to have been packed, and the sentence to have been a salutary warning to other members of seditious associations.

In Dublin in September, at a meeting of the Society, Rowan read out a letter from Scotland. 'Muir glories in the punishment inflicted on him, and hopes that the Irishmen are ready individually to suffer the *same* or a *severer* punishment in so great a cause. He attended our society when last in Ireland.'[3]

But this was only the half of it. Several letters testifying to his character had been read out at Muir's trial, written by Drennan, his sister Martha McTier and Rowan. The court had expressed 'great satisfaction at one of Martha's letters and had enquired from Mr Muir the character of the lady who wrote it'.[4] However, Rowan did not emerge with such a favourable report. When the Lord Advocate read his letter to the jury, and referred to the Address which was enclosed, he described him as 'one of those wretches who had fled from the justice of their country'. He also judged that it had been written by a most ferocious person, since it had been sealed with the emblem of a human heart transfixed with a spear. This was plain misapprehension. Possibly the reproduction was poor. The United Irishman's seal was meant to represent the cap of liberty on a pole supported by two hands, one Protestant and one Catholic, united in friendship.* To Rowan's indignation, the Lord Advocate also mistook the shamrocks on the seal of the letter for *fleurs de lis*: a floral treason![5]

Had he been familiar with the ways of Dublin in general and of Hamilton Rowan in particular the Lord Advocate would have known what was bound to happen next. '*Fled*' indeed! Rowan's *Autobiography* continues:

A.H. Rowan, Esq., it is true, is indicted to stand a trial, but he had not *fled*. Mr Rowan wrote to the Lord Advocate, requesting to know if he had used these obnoxious expressions, and had applied them to him. A second letter was written to the same effect, and no answer having

---

* The editor of Rowan's *Autobiography* charitably observes: 'Among the emblems used [by] French revolutionists was a bull's heart transfixed with iron, bearing this epigraph "Coeur d'aristocrate". The Lord Advocate may have imagined the seal to be similarly emblematic.'

been received to either, on the evening of the 31st October 1793, Mr Rowan, accompanied by the Hon. Simon Butler, set out from Dublin, by way of Donaghadee and Portpatrick, to Edinburgh, and, after a most tempestuous passage in a small sloop, with three horses on board, arrived there at one o'clock on the afternoon of November 4th. Immediately after their arrival at the hotel, Mr Butler addressed a note to the Lord Advocate informing him that he had a letter to deliver from A.H. Rowan, Esq. and requesting to know when he might have the honour of waiting on him.[6]

Rowan's would-be duels often contained elements of fiasco, and this was a good example. When Butler called ceremoniously upon the Lord Advocate to convey to him the challenge, he was told that a reply to Rowan's letters had already been sent. The tempestuous, three-horse journey to Edinburgh had been unnecessary. Not indeed that the Lord Advocate in his reply acknowledged any fault in his expressions – he simply wrote: 'I do not hold myself accountable to any persons for any observation which in the course of my official duty I felt it proper to make.'[7]

That seems fair enough. Clearly, the challenge was not going to be taken up, nor would any apology be made. The Lord Advocate would not 'give Rowan a meeting'. A Scottish friend of Rowan's, Colonel Norman McLeod, MP, tried vainly to impress upon him the impolicy – the crime indeed – of duelling in Britain, begging him 'to weigh what I took the liberty of saying to you of the idea of appealing to the principles of private honour in public transactions'.

Meanwhile, worse was afoot. The Sheriff, having news of Rowan's arrival in Scotland, had him arrested at his hotel, on a charge of sedition relating to the original Address and the letter sent by Rowan to Muir. Rowan was now released only on Colonel McLeod's bail of £3,000 Scotch marks.[8]

What was gained by this insistence on satisfaction for words 'injurious to Rowan's honour' – for that phrase 'one of those wretches who had fled from the justice of their country'? Well, the fact of his return to Dublin at least demonstrated its falsity: he was *not* one of those wretches. And he had proved that he would put himself to great risk in defending the honour of the Society. He was also able to report (in the words of Collins) that 'the Scotch are full as ripe for the work of sedition as ourselves'.[9]

Scarcely very handsome rewards, then, for the expedition. Still, Butler and Rowan were both given a hero's welcome on their return to Belfast:

a select party waited on them, and entreated the favour of their company to dinner; with which request they obligingly complied. Accordingly they, together with Gawin Hamilton, Esq., of Killileagh [Rowan's father] were yesterday elegantly entertained to dinner, and the evening spent with that conviviality and heartfelt pleasure which the patriotic and the virtuous alone experience. Mr. Rowan's health was drunk in connexion with this sentiment: 'May the friends of liberty ever be found virtuous and BRAVE'.[10]

There are two footnotes to this episode. One is that Mrs Rowan believed that the Government had hoped to entrap her husband so that he, like Muir, would be transported to Botany Bay. It increased her determination to put an end, if she possibly could, to his rebellious escapades. The other concerns Thomas Muir himself. After escaping from Botany Bay, Muir did 'flee' via Mexico to Paris. There he created confusion in early 1798. Tone called on him at that later time, and wrote in his *Memoirs*:

> I begged him not to introduce the United Irishmen's business into any of his publications . . . of all the vain, obstinate blockheads that I ever met, I never saw his equal. I could scarcely conceive such a degree of self-sufficiency to exist. He told us roundly that he knew as much of our country as we did and he had as much the confidence of the United Irishmen as we had . . . after a discussion of nearly three hours, we were obliged to come away *re infecta*.[11]

On the return of the Catholic delegation from its audience with the King and the winding-up of the Catholic Convention, Tone was left at a loose end: so much so that he retreated to pamphleteering and spending time with his family. His third child, a son, was born in the spring. At least he could expect to get his £1,500 reward from the Catholic Committee (it was very late in coming). Perhaps a spell of country life, with her husband hunting hares in the fields and spinneys of County Kildare, was welcome to Matilda, too. Unfortunately we do not have many of Tone's own words at this period; the jottings are few; the *Memoirs* proper not yet begun.

In terrorem, however, over his head throughout most of the year were the fulminations of his kinsman the Lord Chancellor. Lord Fitzgibbon, now elevated to Lord Clare, was fiercer than ever in the House of Lords, in consequence of the report of their Secret Committee into the disturbances in the North. The question once again arose of Tone's authorship of that private covering letter back in 1791 – the one perhaps leaked by 'the scoundrel Digges' – in which he had expressed to Russell his belief that the English connection was the bane of Ireland, and that Ireland's salvation lay in separation from England. If indeed Fitzgibbon had originally covered up for Tone, as has been suggested, then his rage might well have been heightened by Tone's continuing betrayal of the Ascendancy: his lack of any sign of gratitude or remorse.

In any case, with the war against France now afoot, the Lord Chancellor could represent the sentiments in the letter, even more plausibly than when Tone had written it, as evidence of treasonable intent. In hot pursuit of his allegations of Catholic sedition, Fitzgibbon had even sent a copy of Tone's letter to the Prime Minister Pitt, saying of its author:

> The Catholics' cabinet minister and adviser, who first proposed an alliance between the Puritans and Catholics, is the son of a bankrupt tradesman, and has the merit of being the founder of the Society of United Irishmen. He was also the original projector of the Catholic Convention . . . And composes most of the seditious and treasonable libels which are put forth by the Society . . .[12]

During July Fitzgibbon maintained his attacks in the House of Lords. He held up Tone's letter. Responsibility for many seditious clubs and meetings in Dublin could be laid at the door of the 'worthy gentleman who wears a bar-gown, one of the leading members of the worthy Society of United Irishmen'. And so on. The treasonable desire to separate the two kingdoms, the contacts with lower orders to engage them 'in an insurrection which was to have taken place when France repulsed the allied armies' – all this and more could be traced back to the revolutionary tendency of that private covering letter.

Tone did not lie down feebly under this sustained attack. He did not have scruples about using personal, backdoor tactics. Why should he? He had already asked Lord Moira to be godfather to his third child. (This was the same Whig peer who, as Lord Rawdon, had entertained the Catholic deputation in London with some magnificence, and whose splendid town house in Dublin he often visited.) Now he wrote a memorandum to him on the state of Ireland, asking him to circulate it as widely as he could in London. Its principal burden was that, of all the pernicious influences under which Ireland was labouring, the man most responsible for the worst of them was

Fitzgibbon. Fitzgibbon was now the bane of Ireland. It was Fitzgibbon who had wrecked the dawning conciliation between Catholic and Protestant in prospect after the Catholic Relief Act. Unfortunately for Tone the move was fruitless: Fitzgibbon's connections with Pitt were far too good.

Whatever views Tone might express in his private letters, whatever talk of 'tactics and treason' he might indulge in over dinners, it was never convincing to paint him as a dangerous demagogue. He was not a populist. He never harangued a crowd. He would have scorned to put power in the hands of the rabble, even had such a temptation been offered. Indeed, he looked down on those who wore revolution on their sleeves. When in late autumn the Sheares brothers,* enamoured of their experiences in France, began to play an increasing part in the Dublin Society, Tone began to attend the Back Lane meetings less and less. He had little patience with their affectation of 'citizen' this and that. What did it really signify, any more than if everyone called themselves 'Lord' this or that?

Nor did the eruptions of agrarian lawlessness do anything to raise Tone's spirits. The Catholic Defenders had no strategy – even if 'Their Measures appear to have been concerted and conducted with the utmost Secrecy and a Degree of Regularity and System not usual in People in such mean Condition, and as if directed by Men of a Superior Rank'.[13] And their avowed sectarianism ran contrary to the fundamental principle of the Society whose name he had invented: that it was only by the union of the sects that Ireland could gain true independence. (There is no evidence for Tone's reflecting that, nonetheless, the combination of Defenders and United Irishmen might by sheer weight of insurrectionary numbers prove deadly.)

In his *Memoirs* Tone very seldom expressed disappointment. ''Tis but in vain for soldiers to complain' was his regular refrain. But he did show his distress from time to time. And, had he been able to skip a hundred years on, he would have been saddened by this summing-up by the great Victorian historian, W.E.H. Lecky:

---

* Henry, 1753–98; John, 1766–98. The father of the two Sheares brothers was a banker of Cork City, and an MP for Clonakilty. The brothers visited France in 1792. Though John was fascinated by the political principals of the Revolution, he once fell on his knees and vowed to plunge a dagger in the heart of every Frenchman he met, if a hair of the head of Marie Antoinette was touched. However, present at the execution of Louis XVI and returning in the same packet-boat as Daniel O'Connell, he disgusted him by exhibiting a handkerchief which he said was steeped in the King's blood (*DNB*).

[It was mainly through the Defender movement] that the great mass of the poorer Roman Catholics passed into the ranks of disaffection. It was ultimately connected with and absorbed in the United Irish movement, and formed one of the chief Catholic elements in the rebellion of 1798 ... There were two movements which were at first completely distinct. One was purely political, and was directed by educated men, influenced by political theories and aiming at political ends. The other was a popular movement which speedily became agrarian, and was to a great extent directed against owners of property. These two movements at last combined, and the result was the most bloody rebellion in Irish history.[14]

This is indeed the most succinct and convincing explanation of the mystery of the sheer scale of the Rebellion: the climax to these years of growling, smouldering insurrection. Without the radical but articulate pronouncements of Tone and some of his fellow United Irishmen insurrection might have remained for many more years a haphazard rash of country acts of arson and pillage and sporadic uprising. Without the great mass of Defenders, few of them literate, most of them oathbound, all of them prey to terrible resentment and dreams of millennial salvation, the fine words and dinner table conspiracies might have fizzled out into the sand. The fatal flaw was the incoherence of the links between the rebel head and the rebel body.

There was, in any case, a sense of uneasy drifting throughout that autumn. The news was contradictory. Tone wrote that 'the Government was apparently strong, the people subdued: probably both appearances fallacious'.[15] On the one hand the disturbances in the countryside, the burning and burglaries, the secret drilling by candlelight, the manufacture of pikes in every smithy, grew more fearsome. Large parts of Westmeath and Cavan were to all intents beyond the law. The Defenders were making the running. On the other hand, the Gunpowder Act, preventing the movement of arms, was being fairly firmly enforced, as also was the Convention Act (forbidding, as we have seen, the assemblies of large numbers of delegates set upon exerting extra-parliamentary pressure). And the Militia Act, for all its unpopularity, was helping to raise large numbers of men under the command of the local gentry.

Sometimes in this uncertain interlude Tone felt as if his future might, alas, have to lie in practising at the Bar once again. (Given his relations with the Lord Chancellor, that hardly sounds promising. Nor would he be helped by his reputation for 'having many talents, but unfortunately the law was not among them'.) And sometimes, in dispirited moments after conversations with Russell, who came to stay some summer days with his family, he felt like emigrating to America, land of freedom, opportunity and equality.

Lord Edward Fitzgerald's letters during the summer and autumn echo those of his Arcadian days spent, as a young officer, with the native Indians of North America. Now life was even more idyllic, with Pamela by his side. If we are to believe him, only the presence of his mother could have added to the bliss of his seaside days at Frescati. Banish memories of vehement interruption in the House of Commons, banish thoughts of war, prospects of revolution, forget the sporadic rashes of lawlessness!

> *Frescati, May 6.* Dearest Mother, Wife and I are come to settle here . . . the plants in the passage are just watered; and, with the passage door open, the room smells like a greenhouse. Pamela has dressed four beautiful flower-pots, and is now working at her frame while I write to my dearest mother, and upon the two little stands there are six pots of the finest auriculas, and I am sitting in the bay window, which all those pleasant feelings which the fine weather, the pretty place, and Frescati gives me, – with your last dear letter to my wife before me: – so you may judge how much I love you at this moment. Yes, dear mother, I am delighted to be at the Malvern party, and am determined to meet you there, or wherever you are. I dote on being with you anywhere, but particularly in the country, as I think we always enjoy one another's company there more than in town. I long for a little walk with you, leaning on me, – or to have a long talk with you, sitting out in some pretty spot, of a fine day, with your long cane in your hand, working at some little weed at your feet, looking down, talking all the time . . .[16]

In June the couple tore themselves away for a week to stay with his aunt Louisa and uncle Tom Conolly (the richest landowner in Ireland) at Castletown, but were delighted to return. More long letters about the magic of Frescati, more adoration of his dearest mother. What did Pamela make of it?

> All the shrubs are out, lilac, laburnum, syringa, spring roses, and lily of the valley in quantities, four pots full now in the book-room, – in short, the whole thing is heavenly. I believe there never was a person who understood planting and making a place as you do. The more one sees Carton and this place, the more one admires them; the mixture of plants and succession of them are so well arranged.[17]

All the time one wonders (since his letters and his biographer mention nothing else during these months), amid all these syringas and lilies of the valley, these flowers in every passage: where has all the revolution gone? Where is the spirit of Tom Paine? True, in part he may have been protecting his mother from the news of his dangerous inclinations. But there is another simple explanation: Lord Edward Fitzgerald, as usual, was throwing himself into a part. The extreme theatricality of life in upper-class eighteenth-century Dublin is almost impossible to exaggerate. Frescati was a beautiful stage.

By the autumn, when he descends to politics, some cares return and the style dulls. Rhapsodic midsummer dreams fade when he writes to his mother after a day up in Dublin:

> Our Parliament did business yesterday. What is to be done was partly told us, – a new arrangement of revenues, a pension bill, a place bill, – but the sums not mentioned. I am afraid we shall have only *form*, not *substance*; no saving of expense, no abolition of places, and a great increase of taxes. Ogilvie will explain it to you, if you wish to know it. What is to be done, though, will, I believe, take up a good deal of time. I don't think we shall be up these six weeks, which I am vexed at, as it will delay us seeing you, dear, dear mother; – but we shall enjoy Frescati. I wish Ogilvie was here now, and in parliament; he would be of use. I think we shall be bamboozled or deceived in this arrangement. I do not think our people understand what they are about . . .[18]

Some of this may be due to filial tact. He did not want to bore his mother with dry tales of parliament, to cloud the idyll of Frescati. But he did not want, I think, to bore himself either. What fired him most about radicalism and revolution was its drama. There was not enough of that in Parliament in Dublin – though he had done his best to provide it.

His mother, on the other hand, was by no means uninterested in politics by birth, family and connections. Emily shared many of the radical beliefs of her favourite son, even if she was careful about discussing them. She was a close friend of Lord Grey, supporter of the French Revolution even after the execution of the King and the beginning of the Terror; Grey, who had also founded the Society of the Friends of the People, one of whose officers was the Thomas Muir whose exile to Botany Bay had launched Rowan on his Edinburgh adventure; Grey, whose radical views on reform overlapped with those of the Society of United Irishmen; Grey, who will forever be associated with the Reform Bill of April 1832.

Emily also kept in her library the works of Joseph Priestley, thought by some people to be more subversive than those of Paine. Her views, however, seem to have been rather more sophisticated than those of Lord Edward (whose were not?). She did not share his dangerous belief in the beneficence of nature. She was not carried away by dreams of Utopia. But she could not bring herself to scold her favourite son for his fondness – anyway, not at all severely. After his return from Paris and his cashiering she had written:

> He is mad about French affairs – the levelling principle, and indeed seems entirely engrossed by these subjects, upon which he converses in a charming pleasant way. Though I fear he has made out a system to himself too perfect for this world, and which would be the cause of much disorder, and much blood would be spilt. This he denies . . . One must not say 'the mob' before him, but 'the people'. I think it charming to hear talked of, but I fear they will never realise it.[19]

In short, his adored mother spoilt him, as she always had and always would, and he loved it.

In the latter months of 1793, many of the rebels seem to have been engaging in pursuits generally regarded as more agreeable, if less heroic, than revolution. After the Catholic Relief Bill and the clampdown of the Gunpowder and Militia Acts, Ireland was becoming calmer: the Chief Secretary Hobart, who had in one month forecast the imminent outbreak of rebellion, reported the next month that order was so restored that Ireland could contribute troops for the war against France.

Tone was enjoying some family life in County Kildare, even while brooding on the possibilities of a new life in America; Fitzgerald was gardening at Frescati; even Rowan, in search of satisfaction, decided to take his combative spirit abroad to Scotland. And Drennan was seriously contemplating matrimony. (He was always serious.) At the end of September he wrote to his sister:

> The lady who is to form your brother's first, and, I trust, last attachment is Miss Swanwick (a name you will say made to be melted into another) of Wem, in Shropshire . . . I shall not speak of her beauty, of her wisdom, or her prudence, or any of her other qualities, real or imaginary, for the truth

is I have always thought there is something so secret and sacred in attachments of this nature that I feel an almost invincible repugnance in making a confidant even of you, my dearest sister.[20]

This was not good enough for Martha McTier, nowhere near good enough. After all, she had seen him through other entanglements. There had been those identical lines written to two different ladies. By return Martha wrote to him a nine-and-a-half-page letter, scolding him for the scanty notice he gave of his betrothed.

Over seven years were to pass, and letter after letter had been written worrying about such matters as his financial competence, before at last Sarah Swanwick and the doctor married. Reticence seems to have been in the Drennan blood. In his brief memoir which forms the introduction to *Glendalloch*, Drennan's son William confined himself to the solitary sentence in praise of his mother: 'Of her it is enough, and little enough to say, that [my father] could not have made himself a better choice of a help-mate for himself, or a mother for his children.'[21]

Yet Drennan did at least *versify* about the amorous side of his nature, poetry perhaps giving him some sort of licence, making him temporarily unafraid of either bathos or sentimentality:

When the friend becomes the lover
All the peace of life is gone,
Cares around us ever hover
When the friend becomes the lover
Newer stings we still discover:
Wake at night, by day look wan,
When the friend becomes the lover
All the peace of life is gone.

When the lover turns a friend
All the charm of life is past,
Oh! the scentless, vapid end
When a lover turns a friend.
Though Esteem's pale orb ascend,
Ah! the sun is setting fast;
When a lover turns a friend,
All our golden prime is past.[22]*

---

* It is fair to say that this claims to be a translation from the French. I have not been able to trace the original.

Surely, he must have been aware that his friends would attribute many sentiments in this verse to himself? Or was he? Drennan suffered from morbid self-importance, unalloyed by any sense of self-absurdity, which, looming gigantic from time to time, blocked out the possibility of any realistic vision of himself. He was disarmingly proud of his verse, although careful never to claim that it rose to the level of poetry: 'I am not a poet by profession, but only a gentleman amateur that writes verses for amusement.'[23]

But his attachment to Miss Swanwick did not occupy all his literary talents during this period. He may not have been quite so zealous in writing papers and attending meetings of the United Irishmen as he had been once; but Collins was able to report in late summer on the Address which Drennan had prepared celebrating the emergence from Newgate of Butler and Bond – where in six months they had run up bills of 'upwards of £2000 for their wine'. Drennan let this pass. His complaints about their extravagance (see p. 104) were made only in private. His public indignation was directed at the House of Lords' exercise of 'undefined privilege' – a repetition of the abuse which had first led to Tandy's escapades in 1792 and then to Butler's and Bond's spell in prison. Unless this abusive exercise was ended people would be well advised to emigrate from a land where they are *compelled to wear chains*.

The argument, and the metaphors of slavery, were familiar. Extravagant compliments were paid to Butler and Bond for their *fortitude and virtue* as being superior to Ralegh and other martyrs in the cause of liberty. As Collins said, it was 'like all his essays extremely prolix, but more violent and alarming to the feelings of the multitude than any of his writings that I have read'.[24] Irishmen must be willing to risk not only their liberty but their lives in the cause of freedom. So there was no question of Drennan's private life softening his public tone of voice. But the Society, and his participation in it, was undoubtedly drifting, and by the end of the year meetings were sometimes being attended by fewer than thirty people.

The informer Collins did not waste too much ink describing the lacklustre performance of the Society as the year drew to a close. And his reports grew more contradictory, as well as shorter. For example, after one meeting we hear that 'you may plainly see that the spirit of the Society is plainly lost, and that I apprehend that in future it will not as a body be capable of doing much mischief from its being fallen apparently into so much disrepute'.[25] But soon afterwards we are told that the members are more dangerous than ever. Collins alternately and sarcastically calls them the 'wild beasts' and the 'worthies'.

In these reports Collins makes cryptic references to some names being 'left out of the lists of attendance because you know them'. General nervousness was growing that the man in the seat next to you might be an informer. At least five and possibly seven of the 400-odd members of the Society, including McNally, *were* informers.[26] By 1793 voices began to be raised that security should be made tighter, and there was occasional reference to a 'select party' on the inside of things.

One must remember that the more thorough and better paid the sources of intelligence are, the more interest they have in exciting disquiet at all times, if only to justify their pay. This also increases the salary and importance of those who assess their reports. But Collins, who had once been declared bankrupt (see p. 75) and clearly felt the repeated stings of poverty, seems to have been particularly hard up; his letters grow ever fuller of pathetic requests. Sometimes these are for tiny sums of money; sometimes he uses the excuse (which McNally also stooped to in his time, and is a perennial feature of the spying trade) that he needed more pay in order to move in the appropriate circles and in fitting style:

> the present is a very critical time, and it's really impossible for me to be of as much service as I might if I was able to mix and enter into some of the expenses of a certain description of men, be assured when I make this observation that I put self totally out of the question . . . [we need to be] as active as possible, for I apprehend there is more mischief brewing than any of us are aware of.[27]

Paymasters having to assess the importance of informers' reports, and the urgency of their demands, have a hard task. It is probably wise to set time limits on their services, before their twists and turns and uncertainties unbalance them completely.

> The night can sweat with terror as before
> We pieced our thoughts into philosophy
> And planned to bring the world under a rule,
> Who are but weasels fighting in a hole.

We, who but seven years ago,
Talked of honour and of truth,
Shriek with pleasure if we show
The weasel's twist, the weasel's tooth.[28]

It is true that Collins never talked of honour. But he was probably nearing the end of his usefulness, as he recognized in his occasional, nervous request to be useful in some place other than Ireland. A turning point was coming, which Collins was too uncertain, too trapped perhaps, to recognize. The Societies of United Irishmen were about to be forced underground.

The Dublin Society, however radical and republican the views that its 'wild beasts' proposed, had in its early days operated more or less openly. Its meetings were advertised in the *Saunders' Newsletter*. Despite the 'Citizen Soldiers, to Arms' Address, its incitement to rebellion may be looked on as more rhetorical than practical. Leading members like Simon Butler had a lawyer's circumspection. Its Test was not blood-curdling: it was not even kept secret.

Given their disdain for concealment, the Society cannot have been greatly surprised when suspicion hardened that reports of their meetings were passed directly to the Castle. No wonder Collins became uncomfortable. The Dublin Society was soon to be reshaped into something much more conspiratorial and activist; no longer intellectual, middle-class and, in its fashion, politically principled. Quite how much, in policy and ideas, the latter-day Societies owed to their semi-respectable predecessors is debatable. More patently revolutionary – and developing ties to the Catholic Defenders which ran clean contrary to the Societies' original *raison d'être*, the unity of the sects – they certainly became more dangerous than the 'wild beasts' had been to the safety of the Kingdom.

The world is full of informers and the next double-crossing agent waiting in the wings to play his part in the break-up of the Society was a solicitor ready to betray his client, an Englishman for a change. W.J. Fitzpatrick, the nineteenth-century author of *The Secret Service under Pitt* and other works revealing the shady activities of agents of the time, wrote:

So many examples of treachery, perpetrated and prompted by Irishmen have been given . . . that it will prove to Irish readers at least, a refreshing relief to find Englishmen equally base, and that the legal profession had not been degraded exclusively in Ireland. It will also appear from the following that Mr Pitt, the prince of English statesmen, was not less unscrupulous an instigator than Castlereagh or Sirr.[29]

John Cockayne was the agent in the spring of 1794 responsible for attempting to destroy Rowan and Tone. At his door may also be laid the suicide in a Dublin dock of an Anglican clergyman, the Reverend William Jackson, on the verge of being sentenced for high treason.

Jackson in middle life had taken up residence in Paris (possibly for disreputable reasons), where he had espoused the cause of revolutionary France, become a disciple of Paine, and was a guest at the famous dinner at White's Hotel when Fitzgerald had renounced his title. Now his mission on behalf of the French authorities was to get in touch with revolutionary elements in England and Ireland and discover the lie of the land. Would a landing by the French meet with support from the native Irish?

Arriving in London, Jackson most unwisely confided in his old acquaintance Cockayne, to whom he still owed £300 for previous services. Cockayne went straight to Downing Street, saw Pitt and betrayed his client. (He may have taken the opportunity to double up the £300 owed to him by Jackson to £600, said to be owed by His Majesty's Government.) On the instructions of the Prime Minister he attached himself, with effusive protestations of help, to Jackson for the voyage to Ireland. Together, the spy and the spied-on arrived in Dublin on 1 April 1794.

8

Dispersal of the Dublin Society

I can have no other time to correspond as he (Jackson)
never permitted me to go to bed before two in the
morning or without having at least three bottles of Claret
– a mode so different from my living in London where a
pint of wine is my stint that I scarcely go through it; beside
the expense is so enormous.
                    Letter from Cockayne to Pitt, 18 April 1794

The Reverend William Jackson was a singularly hopeless spy. His
message to his French paymasters, sent through the public post,
were intercepted and never arrived. His carelessness, drinking and
misplaced trust sparked the train of powder that led to the seizure of
all the papers of the original Dublin Society and to its dispersal after
a raid on its offices in May; and, indirectly, to the scattering to the
four winds of many of its leading members, including Tone and
Rowan.

Ordained Anglican, Irish revolutionist, Jackson was a mass of
contradictions. Was he a pious man? His collection of sermons
suggest a religious orthodoxy; it is said he 'gained some notoriety as
a preacher' at Tavistock Chapel, Drury Lane. There are occasional
suggestions of odd sexual attitudes, or experiences. Consider this
brief passage from Sermon No. 9, 'An inordinate passion for riches
and sensual pleasures, shown to be incompatible with Christianity,
and the happiness of man':

As to the pleasures of the senses, when we have revelled to the full, when
we have tortured Reason for an ingenious device to act the brute with a

better grace, when we have ransacked sea and air, and ranged through the boundless regions of licentious appetite; each wild inhabitant of the woods, each beast and reptile, each despicable insect disputes with justice its superiority in this respect. Their desires are much keener, enjoyment much longer, and happiness uninterrupted by reflection.[1]

Whatever beliefs he expressed in the pulpit, charity would not appear to have been one of his virtues. When caricatured in a comedy by Foote as 'Dr Viper', his reply was to write a long poem called *Sodom and Onan*. 'Disgusting' and 'salacious' are some of the milder judgements passed on it.

Jackson's own apparent sexual ambivalence, and relish of spite, laid him open to innuendo. He served for some while as a chaplain and adviser to the mad, bad, and *lethal* to know Elizabeth Chudleigh, the bigamist Countess of Bath cum Duchess of Kingston.* At one point his enemy Foote wrote a letter to the Duchess saying 'pray, Madam, is not J—n the name of your female confidential Secretary . . . may you never want the *benefit of clergy* in every emergency'.

For all his poisonous attacks upon others, Jackson sometimes showed a delicate sense of honour. For example, when in Newgate awaiting trial he once escorted a visitor to the gate of the gaol. The turnkey was asleep, probably drunk. Jackson took his key and let his guest out. He could then easily have let himself out, too. But that would have compromised both his guest and the drunken turnkey. So he returned to his cell.

Was he a radical, revolutionary republican? Certainly he was a friend and admirer of Tom Paine, and was as impressed as Fitzgerald by the glorious dawn of the French Revolution. But he spent his long year in Newgate Prison awaiting trial writing a refutation of Paine's works.

Many spies may drink; surely few can have been quite so indiscreet. No doubt this was evident at the dinner which McNally, 'with an hospitality in which the Irish are never deficient', gave to Jackson and Cockayne on the evening of their arrival in Dublin, in April 1794. (He may have known both men from his days as a young lawyer in London; also Jackson and he had both in their time edited

---

* Elizabeth Chudleigh outdoes most of the brazen women of history. She never looked back from the time when as a young girl of fifteen, she caught the eye of Lord Bath when out riding. Among her very few respectable adventures, she had a yacht built at Le Havre, sailed to St Petersburg, met Catherine the Great, and opened a brandy distillery in Russia. (*DNB*)

the *Public Ledger*.) Here was a macabre *mésalliance*, with half the dinner companions playing a double game. Plans for gathering information were discussed. Butler, also present at dinner, seems to have insisted that 'Irishmen of property' would fail to support an invasion from France: a dusty answer, similar to the one already given to Jackson by his radical London contacts, about the prospects for a French invasion of England.

During a second dinner given for Jackson, as soon as the wine had 'sufficiently circulated' the butler beckoned the host to leave the room, and warned him to take care:

> for, sir, the strange gentleman [Cockayne] who has his hand over his face and pretends to be asleep is not so, but carefully listening to everything that is said, for when he was in the room just now, I could perceive the glistening of his eye through his fingers which he is covering his face.[2]

If Cockayne was secretly reporting to Pitt, McNally it seems was secretly reporting to the Castle. Neither of them would have known about the other. It is fair to add that though Cockayne may have been an assiduous listener and watcher behind fingers, he chose to remember very little in the eventual trial of Jackson. He came to repent of his part.

The climax of Jackson's drunken and indiscreet mission to Ireland came with his prison visits (together with Cockayne) to Rowan, after the latter had at last been tried and convicted for his part in distributing the infamous Address. Rowan was living with some show of gentlemanly comfort in the best prison apartment in Newgate. At a meeting on 12 April he openly expressed enthusiastic support of Jackson's mission – extraordinary as this may seem, in conditions of such doubtful privacy.

Also summoned to an early prison meeting along with Jackson was Tone, who took violently against Cockayne, remarking afterwards: 'This business is one thing for us Irishmen, but the Englishman who embarks on it must be a traitor one way or another.'[3]

It was agreed that the first job was to provide a clear picture of the state of affairs in Ireland, and that Tone was the man to draw it up. From the beginning Jackson was much taken with both Rowan and with Tone. He told Cockayne that 'he was very well satisfied with Mr Rowan; he was very much a gentleman': a familiar testimonial.[4] As for Tone, overnight he wrote an appraisal of the Irish scene (see p. 132). Jackson urged him to take it to France in person, but

Tone demurred. Nevertheless this was the first time that Jackson had received any encouragement for his mission since leaving Paris in January – that is, unless one counts Cockayne's treacherous incitements.

With a odd lack of judgement, Tone let Rowan take copies of his report for Jackson, although he at least refused to let him keep the original. That piece of evidence, in his own handwriting, might well have secured Tone's conviction on a capital charge.

On the interception of Jackson's cryptic reports, addressed to such names as 'Monsieur Chapeaurouge of Hamburgh' and signed by his *nom d'espion* of 'Thomas Popkin',[5] the way was now clear for the Castle to pounce. Jackson was arrested only four weeks after he had set foot in Ireland. His bedside table was piled with incriminating papers. Among them was a letter from his spymaster Hurford Stone in Paris addressed to the radical Horne Tooke in London, which referred to the French desire to invade Britain, saying that 'in the course of the summer Hurford Stone in Paris would have the pleasure of taking a cool bottle of burgundy (for Republicans love burgundy as well as other men) under the shade of Mr Tooke's tree'.[6]

A whole year passed before Jackson's trial for high treason was actually staged. It is convenient, however, to refer to it here, in the following brief and rather pathetic account.

Cockayne was the only witness at the trial. He was, in his own way, as unsatisfactory an informer as Jackson was a spy: reluctant to appear, extraordinarily vague in his recollections, and with a record of perjury in England. For example, he could not remember what was said at the prison meeting with Rowan and Tone:

> some pamphlets were read, some other matters were talked of, such as the dissatisfaction of parts of the Kingdom . . . I can't say more than this; that I understood from the general and constant conversation that [Tone was to go] with some papers to France, I can go no further than this, I can see it no other way.[7]

On the day before sentence was due to be pronounced, Jackson whispered to McNally, one of his junior counsel, as he passed by him in the court, 'We have deceived the Senate'. (These were the words spoken by Pierre in Otway's *Venice Preserv'd*, before he killed himself.) The next day Jackson was seen to vomit from the carriage window as he was brought back to court. In dock 'his body was in a state of profuse perspiration; when his hat was removed, a dense steam was

seen to ascend from his head . . . the hour of dissolution was at hand'.
Here is how the trial concluded:

> *Lord Clonmell*: 'If the prisoner is in a state of insensibility, it is impossible
> that I can pronounce the judgment of the court upon him.'
> Mr Thomas Kinsley, who was in the jury box, said he would go down to
> him: he accordingly went into the dock, and in a short time informed the
> court that the prisoner was certainly dying.
> *Lord Clonmell*: 'Are you in any profession?'
> *Mr Kinsley*: 'I am an apothecary and a druggist.'
> *Lord Clonmell*: 'Can you understand your profession sufficiently, so as to
> speak of the state of the prisoner?'
> *Mr Kinsley*: 'I can; I think him *verging to eternity*'.[8]

And so the drunken, revolutionary, betrayed parson spy crossed
over the river. He had taken a large dose of arsenic; it was thought in
order to safeguard, for his wife, his small patrimony.[9]

Back to spring 1794. By the time of the Reverend William Jackson's
arrival in Dublin in April, Rowan had already been in prison for
nearly two months. At his recent trial for distributing the Address he
had been ably defended by Curran; so much so that the lawyer had
been compared to Cicero, and carried home shoulder-high by the
crowd, by the light of carriage lamps torn from the Judge's wife's carriage. Nevertheless, the jury had taken just three minutes to agree to
their verdict;[10] and Rowan had been sentenced to two years in prison,
a fine of £500, and £4,000 surety for seven years' good conduct.

He had been lodged in the best-furnished apartments available.
(Money bought many legitimate amenities in gaols at that time.) He
paid for everything himself: unlike Bond and Butler, he made no call
on the funds of the Dublin Society. Mrs Rowan and his children
brought him dinner almost every day except Sundays, when he
'usually invited some of my fellow prisoners, who were of the better
order, to share it with me'. Although living in tolerable comfort, he
decided not to 'have any wine. I hear the water is bad. Let me have
Bristol water and good beer at my meals.'[11]

After those prison visits of Cockayne, Jackson and Tone, it had
been imprudent of Rowan, to say the least, to have taken two copies
in his own handwriting of Tone's memorandum on the state of
Ireland, especially since it discussed details of possible French help

for an invasion. His negligence of personal security may have a gentlemanly flavour to it, but what more damning evidence of treason could there be?

And this he realized at last, on Cockayne's final visit to his prison rooms, to bring him the news of Jackson's arrest. Cockayne, though having himself informed the authorities that the memorandum had been sent in the ordinary post, does appear to have shown some remorse about the turn of events. Rowan was now alarmed at the prospect of hanging, and set about his immediate escape from prison. He was scrupulous, however, in keeping Tone informed. No one should be compromised by his flight.

A man far better suited to adventures (especially waterborne ones) than to political intrigue, he makes a very good tale of his escape:

In the Fives Court [in Newgate Prison] I told Mr Dowell, the under gaoler, that I had sold a small estate, but my attorney had objected that, because I had signed the deeds when still in prison, my heirs might one day contest the sale. An extra expense of £50 or £100, he had said, might eliminate the risk.

Mr Dowell, I suggested, might easily assist by taking me out of prison just long enough to enable witnesses to attest that the deeds were signed out of the precincts of the gaol; if he could contrive that, I would gladly give the £100 to him instead of to the attorney. Dowell replied he would ask the head gaoler. I objected to this . . . shortly after he asked whether he might not tell his father, to which I immediately assented.

A little before dinner-hour he came and desired me to be ready by midnight. My friend Mat Dowling proposed to meet me at that hour on horseback at the end of Sackville Street. Our Swiss butler was directed to lay out a table above stairs, with wine &c. in a front two-pair-stair room, the door of which commanded a view of the staircase. He was told, when he came to the door, to show us up stairs, and to say the attorney and the witnesses would shortly arrive.

About midnight Dowell appeared in the prison with his sabre and pistols in his girdle, and accompanied me to my own house. There, I sat down with him to take some refreshment, and threw the purse I had prepared containing 100 guineas across the table to him, saying I was much better pleased with him having it than *Six-and-eightpenny* [as lawyers were nicknamed, because of their standard fee of one third of one old pound]. He put the purse back to me, saying he did not do it for gain; but I remonstrated, and he relented . . . At this moment I accused myself of my insincerity; but as Godwin describes in *Caleb Williams* under somewhat similar circumstances, I was not prepared to 'maintain my sincerity at the expense of a speedy close to my existence'.

I then said, if he had no objection, I would step into the back room opposite, where my wife and eldest boy slept. To this he immediately assented; and I desired I might be called when the attorney and the witnesses arrived. I entered, changed my clothes for those of my herd, who had opportunely come to town that day with a cow for the children. I then descended from the window by a knotted rope, which was made fast to the bedpost and reached down into the garden. I went to the stable, took my horse, and rode to where my friend Mat Dowling had appointed to meet me. Some of my friends had advised my taking my pistols with me; but I had made up my mind not to be taken alive, so I only put a razor in my pocket. After half an hour Dowling at last came up, and we set out for the house of Mr Sweetman, who was a friend of his, and lived on the seaside at Sutton, near Baldoyle, by whom, and his then wife, I was received with the utmost kindness. As soon as day broke Mr Sweetman set out for Rush, in hope of procuring a smuggling boat that would take me to France. On his arrival there, he found the place in great confusion, for Mr Dowell, with a military party, was searching several of the houses; in two of which he particularly expected to find me, as they belonged to some person who had been confined in Newgate, and had frequently dined with me; but they had been released, as it was only for some revenue affair they were in confinement . . . Mr Sweetman then said he thought I might be secreted somewhere in Ireland; but I persisted in my wish to get to France, both on my own and Mr Jackson's account. He then asked me whether I would risk myself in a little fishing wherry of his, which lay moored close to his house. This I accepted willingly; and ere long, he told me he had met with two brothers of the name of Sheridan, who agreed to land a person in France, and to find a third, if necessary, to man the boat.

In the course of this day, proclamations offering £1000 from government, and £500 from the City, with as much again made up of minor subscriptions from gaolers and others, for my apprehension, were dispersed through all the environs of Dublin.

It now became necessary to purchase several articles, such as a compass, charts, and provisions, for which he was obliged to go to Dublin. Shortly after his return, we were joined by the two Sheridans, one of whom, taking out of his pocket one of the proclamations, showed it to Mr Sweetman and said 'It is Mr Hamilton Rowan we are to take to France.' 'Yes', replied Mr Sweetman, and introduced me to them. Immediately the elder brother said, 'Never mind it: by J——s we will land him safe'.

The wind being fair, it was determined to sail that night, but not to mention anything to Murphy, who was the third person whom they had engaged, until we were all on board. Everything went well until we were near Wexford, when the wind changed, and blew so hard that we were driven back to take shelter under Howth. During the night, the elder

Sheridan told me that he had had some conversation with Murphy, which made it necessary that either he or I should always be on deck, to see the course of the vessel; 'for though his brother was as sound as steel, yet he loved a sup'. The weather had cleared before morning and we again spread our sail with a fair wind. In crossing the British channel, while we were nearer to England than to France, we found ourselves enveloped by a British fleet coming up the channel: but the ships which served as convoy kept between them and the French coast, so that we passed unobserved. As we neared France, we were saluted by the fire of one of the numerous small batteries which were erected along the shores. This was for want of colours; so I borrowed Sheridan's nightcap, which by chance was red, filled it with straw, stuck it on a boat-hook, and lashed it to the helm as a *bonnet de liberté*, and thus sailed unmolested to the mouth of a small bay under the fort of St Paul de Leon, called Roscoff. Here we saw a small fishing boat, which I boarded, and having divided what cash I had remaining in my purse equally among my crew, I ordered them to make for England, and the fishermen to take me to the town . . . I was taken up to the Hôtel de Ville, and very minutely searched for papers. The commandant of the fort, to whom I told my story coolly answered that as by my own account I had escaped from prison in my own country he would see I should not escape from him. I was confined in an upper room; and fatigued from the journey, I laid myself on a straw mattress and fell asleep.

At midnight the Mayor came to examine me. His eye turned to my hat, in which some person at the court-house had put a national cockade, which he tore out, as if in a violent rage against me, whom he *knew to be an English spy*, for thus having dared to profane the emblem of liberty.

I rose early the next morning, and on going to my garret window, was much mortified to see the little boat moored among the rest of the vessels in the harbour. I enquired for the sailors, but could get no account either of men or vessel, except that it had been pursued and taken.[12]

When after a while Rowan found that the Sheridans and Murphy had been imprisoned, he managed to buy their liberty at Brest, and saw that they were enabled to earn a little money, and were provided with board at public expense. In a letter to his wife, he wrote that they were 'as well, and as happy, as men kept from returning till spring, can be'.

His concern for his crew and conscience for the perils they had endured very properly continued to occupy his mind. Later, during his exile in the States, in another letter to his wife he talked of 'three men . . . whose honour, disinterestedness and integrity, do credit to humanity, and claim my utmost integrity. If I was this moment setting my foot on Irish soil, my first visit ought to be paid to these men.' And indeed, when he finally received his pardon and recovered most of his property more than ten years later, he paid Mr Sweetman £100 for the boat he had borrowed, and adjusted all the claims of the Sheridan brothers.[13]

For the present, he was embarked on a long exile in France and America.

Tone's part in the fateful Jackson imbroglio may be briefly rehearsed (although it has ambiguities). When he attended those early April meetings in Rowan's Newgate apartment Jackson had disclosed his mission at once. Although distrusting Cockayne, Tone agreed to write for French eyes a memorandum on the state of affairs in Ireland. This he appears to have written almost overnight on April 14/15. It discussed such *prima facie* treasonable matters as the desirability of simultaneous landings at several possible places. The Ulster Dissenters would then lead a general revolt. He had given it to Rowan to copy, although he had insisted on keeping the original.

Delighted with the memorandum, Jackson had tried hard to persuade Tone to present it in person to his masters in France. Tone, after some hesitation, rejected the idea, pleading domestic difficulties and the forfeiture which might result of some moneys still owing to him from the Catholic Committee. Vague references to French bounty were not good enough.

On Jackson's arrest, Tone, realizing the danger he was in, at once sought out his old friend Peter Burrowes, now a King's Counsel, an 'honest but eccentric genius' and an early campaigner for Catholic emancipation.[14] A letter, dated 1 May, from the young Marcus Beresford to his all-powerful father John, then in London, takes up the tale:*

---

* The Beresfords' eminence in the ranks of the Ascendancy is best illustrated by a later letter of John Beresford's. He had just had a conversation in 1795 with the new, brief-tenured Lord-Lieutenant. Lord Fitzwilliam had told him, 'No Lord-Lieutenant could exist with my [i.e. Beresford's] power; that I had made a Lord Chancellor, a Chief Justice of the King's Bench, an Attorney-General, nearly a Primate, and certainly a Commander-in-Chief; that I was at the head of the Revenue, and had the Law, the Army, the Revenue, and a great deal of the Church in my possession; and he said expressly, that I was considered the King of Ireland' (Beresford, *Correspondence*, ii, p. 51).

This was the first and only time John Beresford was threatened with dismissal. But it was the Lord-Lieutenant who was sacked, within a very few weeks.

Tone called on Peter Burrowes, and [requested him] to converse with me. Tone avowed to Burrowes that he had had two conversations with Jackson of a very criminal nature; that Jackson had pressed him upon the state of his circumstances, and had proposed to him to go to France, but that he had at once rejected that. He acknowledged that the object of several of his party had been to procure an invasion; but that he was positive there could be no evidence against him so as to affect his life, but he was well aware there was enough to blast his character. Under these circumstances, he made a proposal to Burrowes, which clearly shows the impression on his mind – that he wishes to quit Ireland, and migrate to America, under the imputation even of a traitor; that he hoped the Government would allow Hamilton Rowan to do so likewise. He wished to make reparation for his past conduct by giving such information to the Government as might be useful, provided he was not called on to accuse Rowan, which no inducement could make him do, and he did not wish to appear as a witness in a public court. I desired Burrowes to hint to him that I thought I should be able to procure not only his pardon, but also the means of transporting him to any part of the British settlements abroad, or to America, if he would consent to make a full disclosure of all he knew relative to these transactions . . . The truth is, he was brought up at the meeting at the Castle by a warrant issued for his apprehension; being examined, he told all he knew, but refused to swear any information, or appear as an accuser; at the same time, he said that if compelled to do so by compulsory process, he would declare what he knew. It is agreed that while the negotiation goes on between Burrowes, Tone, and me, he is not to be molested; nor will any circumstance which he discloses be made use of against his associates, unless he agrees to it.[15]

Tone undoubtedly did make a bargain, and recounted his version before he left Ireland the following year. He said that a defence was necessary because some said that he had *compromised* with the Government. Tone objected to the word: it was 'invidious'. But surely not unfair? In his own words, at the time of Jackson's arrest:

I felt the necessity of taking immediate and decided measures to extricate myself. I therefore went to a gentleman high in confidence with the then administration, and told him at once fairly, every step I had taken . . . it was certainly in the power of the Government, if they pleased, to ruin me as effectually as they could by my death; that on two points I had made up my mind; – the first was, that I would not fly; the other, that I would never open my lips, as a witness, either against Mr Rowan, to whom I felt myself bound by the strongest ties of esteem and regard, or against Mr Jackson, who, in whatever conversations he had held in my presence, must have supposed he was speaking to a man who would not betray him . . . What

I had done, I had done, and, if necessary, I must pay the penalty; but, as my ruin might not be an object to them, I was ready, if I was allowed and could at all accomplish it, to go to America . . . The gentleman to whom I addressed myself after a short time assured me that I should neither be attacked as a principal nor summoned as a witness . . . and this has been faithfully kept. I have betrayed no friend; I have revealed no secret; I have abused no confidence.[16]

There is a great deal more protesting. There seems nothing mean or dishonourable about Tone's accommodation with the Castle; but nor was there anything heroic. It was sensible, prudent. Where is the picture of himself, vividly seen on nearly every page of his *Memoirs*, as the light-hearted, daring, self-mocking – eventually tragic – protagonist of a great drama? This is not a part which he plays here.

It remains something of a mystery why the Government let Tone off so lightly. The Castle knew that he had played a leading part in preparing the memorandum given to Jackson, which (whatever Tone thought or pretended to think), might easily have led to his hanging. For certainly London wanted to see him brought to trial, whatever the Lord-Lieutenant's doubts that the evidence against him might not be quite strong enough.

It is true that Cockayne, the perjurer and informer, might not be a reliable witness in any trial – even although the Government in due course was forced into an unsatisfactory reliance on him in Jackson's trial for high treason. True, the bargain that the Government struck would at least remove Tone from the scene, perhaps for good: in the view of Chancellor Fitzgibbon, the document Tone had signed was 'a confession of his own treason, and would and was intended to hang him in case of his ever returning'.[17] True, leniency might be a pawn to play with the Catholics, given Tone's work on behalf of the Committee. But none of these points seems wholly convincing.

Two other possible explanations might have played a part, although they are seldom given much weight. One is that it is not unknown in any age for the Law to look after its own. The other and more agreeable one is that it might have been a matter of friendship. Peter Burrowes, the go-between for Tone and the all-mighty Beresford connection, had been a close friend of Tone in their days at Trinity College. In France in 1796 Tone wrote of him as a man 'whose talents I admire, whose virtues I reverence, and whose virtue I love'. Although disapproving of his actions, Burrowes tried to defend Tone until the very end – more so, indeed, than some of his associates.

In any event, by mid-May Marcus Beresford was able to write to his father again to say that, acting on the authorization of the Lord-Lieutenant, Tone 'by my directions, has withdrawn himself from town, to avoid the importunity of the Roman Catholics, who wish him to write for them . . . He is near Naas, and will come up whenever I send for him.'[18]

Tone sat down to write a history of Ireland at Château Boue, and to make the arrangements for the exile he had negotiated.

A note by Rowan, in his own handwriting in the margins of his copy of Macneven's *Pieces of Irish History*, comments that 'Lord Edward declined to have any conversation with Jackson'.[19] This seems very odd. Of all the rebels, Fitzgerald enjoyed the closest French connections. His mother's ancestry, memories of his visit to France in 1792, his belief in the Revolution, above all his marriage to Pamela might have been expected to make him eager to welcome an emissary from the Committee of Public Safety, and to hear the latest news from Paris.

Also, Jackson was carrying a letter from Nicholas Madgett, a Kerryman in the service of the Committee, addressed to Fitzgerald. Surely Jackson had more than enough credentials to have secured a meeting with him? At the time of that dinner at White's in Paris Fitzgerald had shown no reluctance to discuss French aid for invasion; quite the contrary. Helping to finance 40,000 Volunteers would do the job, he had then said. So now, in the spring of 1794, why did he decline to meet Jackson?

It cannot I think be put down to any sort of timidity. That would have been altogether out of character. Some said that there was a suspicion that the revolutionary clergyman might turn out to be an *agent provocateur*. Another suggestion is that he might have been disenchanted with the Committee of Public Safety for having guillotined his (then reputed) father-in-law Philippe Egalité five months previously. Who can tell? Concern, too, for Pamela in her pregnancy may well have played some part.

A little later in the year, after the birth of his 'little Eddy', who became the apple of his romantic eye, he described in terms of near ecstasy the 'pleasant, contented and happy' life he was leading. He wrote to his mother of how he was 'settling and arranging my little lodge' in Kildare, lent to him by his uncle Tom Conolly, owner of the magnificent nearby Palladian mansion of Castletown. Even if, aware of the possible interception of his mail by the authorities, he may have been careful to keep any seditious reflections out of his letters, the idyll sounds true to sentimental life. Not that dulcet eulogies of the joys of gardening by any means preclude the harbouring of revolutionary tendencies. Indeed it could easily be argued that within the boundaries of the romantic movement, they reinforced each other; or, even more, that sentimentalism in all ages opens the gate to ruthlessness.

For in his Rousseauesque love of the simple life, his obedience to the promptings of emotion and intuition, his rejection of social conformity, Fitzgerald was a conspicuous victim of late eighteenth-century romanticism. They were all so consistent and whole-hearted – his beliefs in the goodness of humanity, in the rights of man, in the breaking of shackles of tyranny. He was following, without a back-ward glance, one of the well-trodden paths to rebellion, and was held back only by his adoring mother, and by the temporary indulgences of generous, young family life. Throughout 1794 his letters to his mother continue to exalt the honeysuckle joys of well-provided-for country living.

Just occasionally we glimpse signs that his beliefs had not mellowed, even if his expression of them was kept in reserve. He hung a portrait of his friend and hero, Tom Paine, in the best posi-tion in his cottage, above the fireplace in the sitting-room. And he greatly resented the thought that improvements to his gardens might come to benefit the oppressor, the Lord-Lieutenant who was think-ing of renting Frescati as a country retreat. Before leaving that other idyllic spot for his Kildare lodge he had written: 'I have left off gar-dening, for I hated that all my troubles should go to that vile Lord W[estmorland], and my flowers to be for aides-de-camp, chaplains, and all such followers of a Lord-Lieutenant.'[20] But he still had a long way to go before rebellion. He still had to fall in with Arthur O'Connor.

Drennan stayed even more aloof than Fitzgerald from the Jackson imbroglio.

In part this may have been because he was, as always, on prickly terms with Tone, quick with author's jealousy. Early in the new year he had written to Martha:

I believe I will never hold any political communication with Tone, not only regarding myself, but from hearing him abuse and vilify the very man, as Keogh, whom the day or two after he joins with in the most intimate manner ... This in confidence, and I declare to God, without pique, at a man whose literary talents I know and admire.[21]

'Without pique' is unconvincing. Drennan never seems to have realized that self-congratulatory denial of one's faults is often tantamount to confessing them. He appears to have become disenchanted with Rowan at this time, too, being less than magnanimous about his escape from prison. He may have thought that such schoolboy adventure was demeaning, unserious, in some way unworthy of the high aims of reform and emancipation, of the goals of the Society on which one should always keep one's eyes fixed. Immediately after the escape he wrote a number of letters to Sam McTier in Belfast:

Most reproach Rowan. The hacks [do so] for want of honour ... Some say he has implicated himself with Jackson, the man who is closely imprisoned in Newgate on a charge of high treason. This man, though I called at Newgate daily, I never saw, and know nothing about. Others say Rowan has turned mad ... He will probably die in a storm of his own raising; nor would I be one bit surprised to hear of his quick return to Ireland, and for any *great* enterprise he has neither head nor conduct ... J. Magee, the madman, exclaimed today to a friend of mine 'That Rowan was born an idiot, and will die a fool. He is led always by the last advice ... I think Rowan's secession may lighten the party as much as Tandy's [who had fled and gone into hiding in London]; but for a short time we will suffer for the rashness and folly of this individual, as we did before for the other'.[22]

But in the early months of 1794 he had other important things to worry about. Not the least of these must have been himself. For months he had been reassuring his sister that he did not consider himself in danger, perhaps in tones too strong to ring altogether true. After all, he was the author and publisher of 'Citizen Soldiers, to Arms'. He knew that his 'friend' John Pollock was making enquiries likely to implicate him. It seems, however, that with his gift for self-deception, and his consciousness of rectitude, he may have managed to convince himself that the paper was not really seditious. Then again, a whole year had gone by; perhaps the Government had decided not to move against him. For all that, the confident note of various declarations in January does not really carry very much weight; the bell is cracked:

> Reading over it as impartially as I can, I think I never saw a paper that was fuller and stronger for peace and subordination . . . were I asked as exculpatory evidence whether I had any design of stirring up revolt or of exciting resistance to existing laws, I could answer No. Before God and my country, No. My single design was to endeavour to revive the Volunteer army of Ireland, and I wrote as if I had felt the departed spirit of 30,000 of my countrymen stirring in my breast . . . I do not think I could read a lecture more exhortatory to peace and tranquillity . . .[23]

Martha McTier did not pretend to be reassured. Her letters strike the familiar, protective note of the affectionate elder sister whose duty it is to care for a brother who is pretty hopeless in the ways of the world. She went so far as to write an agitated letter to the sinister Pollock (whom she had never met) begging him to desist from tracking her brother down:

> I find [that you pressed a printer] to declare Dr D. to be the author of that paper denounced by the Government . . . that you really aimed at the destruction of this *good-hearted friend*. Cease, 'tis a damning cause, nor can it come to good. Success in it could not . . . afford a lasting reward, for were you by it to place this Drennan in a gaol, you might lay up reflection, that at some future time might gall yourself, while *he* would remain materially unhurt, as you can never either make or prove him base. Leave then this friend to his humble fortune, tempt him not, neither betray him. You have chosen different paths, cross not each other, the world is wide enough for you both.[24]

This letter elicited an immediate reply from Pollock, then sitting at Trim Assizes, which is felicitously described by the author of *The Trial of William Drennan* as 'a masterpiece of vulpine elegance'. It is very long. He must have enjoyed writing it. But it could have done nothing to reassure Martha. Pollock would clearly not be dissuaded – not by one inch – from continuing his hunt to secure witnesses prepared to testify on behalf of the Government, that Drennan was the author of the insurrectionary Address: in short, to imperil his freedom, possibly his life. Here is an extract from Pollock's letter:

> Not having as I think the honour of being personally known to you, and never having had to my knowledge the honour of your acquaintance, I

confess I felt not a little surprise on reading a letter that the post brought me this day with your name signed to it. It is a composition, no doubt of great excellence and imagination, but as I have not yet submitted to the modern operation of being fraternised against my will, I should have declined answering it, were it not that it bears the name of a gentlewoman subscribed to it . . .

Dr Drennan's virtue or his honesty suffered no trial, save a strong remonstrance upon what I thought was a dangerous error in his judgement and in his conduct. I remember well he burst into tears. I say again his virtue was neither tempted or tried . . . as to what you mention of one Lewis, a printer, he has told you a gross and villainous falsehood.

As to the advice you have done me the honour to give me, I receive it with all due consideration. It is peculiarly kind in a lady to whom I have the misfortune of being wholly unknown, to take so much trouble on my account . . . allow me to assure you that whenever I shall venture to solicit your advice I shall most thankfully receive and attend to it.[25]

At about a quarter past eight in the evening of 13 May, two police messengers called on Drennan, who was reading in his rooms. He was shown a warrant demanding that he should appear before the Chief Justice, Lord Clonmell. Information had been laid on oath that he had caused 'a seditious libel to be published in the *National Evening Star* tending to disturb the public peace'. Drennan went with them immediately. The story of that trial straddles the midsummer of 1794, and takes us into the next chapter.

9

Trials and indignities

Integer vitae, scelerisque purus
Horace, *Odes*, 1: 22

The Chief Justice, Lord Clonmell,* was the same judge who had presided over Rowan's trial earlier in the year, and would next year try Jackson. He came into the hall of his house to meet Drennan, with the two police messengers, and instructed him to arrange bail immediately. But it proved too late to do so, and after some toing and froing, and another call even later at night at Lord Clonmell's, Drennan had to spend the night in prison, where 'he slept pretty well, considering the time, place etc, with a large bible by way of pillow, and the gaoler very civil in little accommodations'.[1]

Three people especially contributed to the defence, when Drennan's trial for publishing a seditious libel at last came to court in the Trinity term at the end of June 1794. One was the 'demure doctor' himself. One was Curran, his lawyer, 'the imp of pandemonium', as Drennan ungratefully called him. And one was the principal witness for the Crown, William Paulet Carey. Of these, ironically, the last turned out to be by far the most useful to his case.

---

* 'The Irish judges of the revolutionary era have not enjoyed a reputation for the virtues properly associated with their order . . . yet it is difficult to withhold admiration for their conduct in the trial of a man [Dr Drennan] committed, apparently, to the overthrow of that establishment of which they were servants. Presiding over the Court of King's Bench was the Chief Justice Lord Clonmell (1739–98), a man whose obsessive pursuit of success appears in his extraordinary diary. In this, along with his worries about flatulence and rivals for preferment, is revealed the demonic appetite for hard work . . .' (John Larkin, *The Trial of William Drennan*).

For his part, Drennan laid down in his 'Intended Defence' the principal plank on which he would have *liked* to build his case:

> It is certain that the very essence and pith of all criminality consists in the *intention*. It is the will, intention, or mind, with which the thing is done, that ought to be respected as constituting the guilt . . . my defence rests on the *purity of motive*, and that purity may be deduced from the character of my conduct and the consistency of my life. That little life has been rounded by a single benevolent principle, the object of which was to serve my country as far as I could serve her, in promoting a reform in parliament.[2]

Unfortunately it was simply not true that in law intention was the pith. Drennan took off so quickly into high moral altitudes. He declined to understand that 'purity' had nothing whatsoever to do with the case. As the author of *The Trial* drily observes, 'Drennan is probably confusing intention with motive . . . As the accused could not give evidence on oath, intention must be judged on the circumstances of the fact.'[3] (One need only reflect on the consequences, today, if the libeller could plead in his defence that he had not *intended* to defame so-and-so.)

In his 'Intended Defence' Drennan also inveighed against the activity of informers, whom he saw to have been responsible for his standing in the dock. His beloved Latin (and Italian) are often summoned up in times of stress:

> I am able, thank God, so far to overcome an instinctive moral antipathy as to [accept] that such odious creatures are in the order of nature; and that there is a use in all things most venomous, though we are not able to find it out . . . yet I cannot help lamenting that it should ever be necessary in any government to foster a set of informers, and to place them, as Locusta [employed to poison the Emperor Claudius] 'inter instrumenta regni'. I should have thought that an argument commonly adduced by modern as well as ancient Italian policy, would NEVER have found an advocate in this land. 'Egli è un huomo honesto, ma "La Ragione di Stato" racchiede che sia punito'.[4]*

Drennan's 'Intended Defence' runs to over 6,000 words in justification of his education, his modest virtues, his political philosophy, his debt to his mentors, Blackburne, Furneaux, and others, the

---

* 'He is an honest man, but reasons of state demand he should be punished.'

basis of his Protestant dissent and right to private judgement, his reading of Locke's 'Essay on Government'. This was all very well, but would the jury regard the following thoughts as at all relevant to the Doctor's innocence and guilt – even if, *per impossibile*, any judge had allowed them to do so – or as mitigation of his crime?

> From the earliest of my schoolboy days, from the delightful hours I voyaged with the patient, persevering Ulysses, and made his country the Ithaca of my wishes . . . the love of my country has been in my breast.
>
> I will ever think that a more equal representation of the people was absolutely necessary for their freedom, their virtue, their happiness and their *peace*. . . I thought the truest way for promoting peace was, as in the case of the Volunteers, to arm the people for their liberties [brave and disingenuous attempt to work in a direct reference to 'Citizen Soldiers, to Arms'].
>
> Though the paper may have been adjudged a libel, it may have been written without any libellous or seditious intention, and that may have been distributed with an intention of exciting commotion which the writer certainly meant as a preservative of the public peace. The best intentions are liable to be abused, the best purposes perverted, and things written with the most pure and sincere heart, have been conjoined with the worst actions. Men have taken the Gospel in one hand, and the sword in another; and the words of the Scottish rebels, under Montrose, were '*Jesus, and no quarter*'.[5]

As Sam McTier wrote, with evident relief, 'At last we agreed that it would be more dignified for him not to say one word, and his speaking might do him harm'.[6] The 'Intended Defence' was not used in Court.

Drennan was never well-disposed to the principal lawyer who conducted his defence. Yet Curran was most generous to him, even returning his fees. He wasted little time at the trial in 'troubling the jury as to the nature of the paper, whether it is a seditious libel or not'. This was wise of him, but it irked Drennan. The skill of Curran's handling of the case lay entirely in destroying the chain of evidence between Drennan's reading-out-loud of 'Citizen Soldiers' at the meeting of the Society, and its later publication in the *Hibernian Journal*. Did the published words precisely match the original? Would the principal Crown witness swear that they were word for word identical? Only one witness, William Paulet Carey, was in a position to answer this.

Or was he? There were two problems from the Crown's point of view. The first was Carey's unremitting candour. Under Curran's bludgeoning, he replied too often that he could not recollect, 'he was not positive', 'he could not swear to that set of words'. Then there was the fact that he was, after all, an informer, a turncoat. A jury in any age, asked to convict on the basis of evidence provided by one who has betrayed his colleagues for money (or his own personal advantage), is likely to have scruples. If the document as published was not the same as the document that Drennan had read out, it was reasonable for the jury to throw the case out. And so they did.

Drennan's acquittal, in the face of the Address's clearly seditious tendency, says much for the fair conduct of the trial and the impartiality of Lord Clonmell* and his fellow judges. Not that Drennan was optimistic as the trial proceeded. He believed that 'the jury will find as usual in such prosecutions', and at one time during its course wrote in a wobbly hand to his sister, 'I write this on my knee, but my heart does not tremble, though my hand does'. His anxiety was not surprising, given Rowan's recent conviction and imprisonment on the very similar charge of *distributing* the infamous Address.

Two hundred years after the trial, the character of the printer Carey has been reappraised. He was certainly an informer. But there are excuses for him, even grounds for some sympathy. And his story is illuminating, if only for revealing fissures typical of revolutionary movements in all ages.

William Paulet Carey belonged to a talented Catholic family of modest resources. His first triumph was to win two painting prizes in the Dublin Academy; and he ended life as a successful engraver, art dealer, versifier and critic, living in London until his death in 1834.† In between he was part of the turmoil of Dublin in the 1790s, becoming a United Irishman, an author of satirical verse under the enterprising pseudonym of Scribblerius Murtough O'Pindar, a

---

* Impartiality of which he was extremely proud. Apropos of Rowan's trial he had said, 'That gentleman would not have been better used by me, standing in the situation he did, if he was one of the princes of the blood' (Hamilton Rowan, *Autobiography*, p. 209).

† The British Library contains twenty-five of his works, with such varied titles as *Brief Remarks on the Anti-British Effects of Inconsiderate Criticism on Modern Art*, *Lines on the Lamented Death of Lord Nelson* and *The Dying Peasant and Other Poems*. See also Brian Inglis, *Freedom of the Press in Ireland* (1954).

printer and publisher who gave the Society much support – and, alas, one of the tribe of informers.[7]

Unlike the leaders of the Dublin Society, he was not well-born, not a professional, not a member of the so-called 'Law and the Physic', whom he accused of monopolizing the government of the Society. He resented this, and was angry at what he saw as its amateur direction, writing once to his brother: 'Our democracy here is unworthy of the name, it is nothing but a contemptible aristocracy in disguise.'[8]

Unfortunately, Drennan hated Carey, with a rare and poisonous personal hatred. And this was *before* Carey revealed himself as an informer, and gave evidence against him. Drennan expressed himself in a very undemure, unDrennanesque way, accusing Carey of having:

> a malicious mind, with vengeance on his tongue on all occasions, and virulence distilling from his pen . . . I can only exclaim with Brasidas, when a rat seized him by the hand, that even the most contemptible creatures acquire a portion of respect from their danger . . .[9]

True, that remark was made immediately before his trial; but in many of his earlier letters Drennan had descended into shameful abuse of Carey:

> [one of] the vulgar of our party which God knows . . . to be but a ragged set, as melancholy a motley as a beggarman's coat . . . Carey still threatens hard against me but I still think nothing can come of it and the fellow will damn his own soul to gratify pique . . . Carey has spoken the truth for once in his life . . . I said what was sufficient to prove that I had no personal pique against the man.[10]

For his part, Carey certainly felt resentment against Drennan, but not, I think, such personal animosity.

On the surface, the story is simple. As a printer, Carey had been of considerable use to the Dublin Society. His paper, the *National Evening Star*, had carried news of its meetings, and gave general support to republican and anti-English views. One article, for which he had been threatened with prosecution, had been devoted to a report of the Belfast celebrations of a French victory early in the war. Later, as a member of the Society, he had been asked by Drennan to copy his 'Citizen Soldiers, to Arms', from the *Hibernian Journal* into his paper, and had complied, although he must have guessed that

1. Lord Edward Fitzgerald, b.1763, military protagonist of the Rebellion, portrait by Horace Hone c.1795/6, from which the more flattering 'iconic' picture by Hugh Douglas Hamilton was probably taken: 'whatever faults he might have, he had a warm and affectionate heart . . . I cannot think it proper to judge the simplicity of his idealism too harshly, however terrible the consequences were to himself and others. Most will find it in their hearts to forgive, even if not to applaud, a man so gallant.' He was wounded during capture and died in 1798.

2. Theobald Wolfe Tone, b.1763, lifelong fighter for Irish independence, portrayed in Volunteer uniform: 'at the age of seventeen it will not be thought incredible that *woman* began to appear lovely in my eyes, and I very wisely imagined that a red coat and cockade, with a pair of gold epaulettes, would aid me considerably in my approaches to the objects of my adoration.' He died by his own hand in 1798, awaiting trial after the failure of the French '98 expedition.

3. Archibald Hamilton Rowan, b.1751, a giant and 'every inch a gentleman', in Volunteer uniform (designed by himself?), with a great green cockade. He escaped from prison to France and America, renounced revolution and was eventually pardoned. He died in 1834.

4. A montage of the United Irishmen (*left to right*): Samuel Neilson, Michael Dwyer, John Sheares, William Corbett, Arthur O'Connor, Archibald Hamilton Rowan, William Jackson, William Macnevin, Matthew Teeling, Robert Emmet, Henry Sheares, Wolfe Tone, Napper Tandy, Thomas Emmet, James Hope, Robert MacCracken, Thomas Russell and Lord Edward Fitzgerald.

5. William Drennan, b.1754, a son of the manse, coiner of the phrase 'emerald isle' and a principal founder of the Society of United Irishmen, whose resolute hope for the unity of the sects led him to demand that his coffin be borne to his grave, in 1820, by six Protestants and six Catholics.

6. Leonard McNally, b.1752, barrister, playwright and most skilled and deadly of the informers. He died with his treacheries undiscovered in 1820.

7. The Reverend William Jackson, b.1737?, betrayed spy and revolutionary, whose indiscretions in Dublin were followed by the collapse of the original Dublin Society of United Irishmen, and the exile of Tone and Rowan. He 'verged to eternity' at the end of his trial in 1795. Reproduced from *Walker's Hibernian Magazine*, 1795.

there was danger. Together with other printers, who were an easy target for the Government, he was immediately arrested – long before the law touched Drennan or Rowan.

Two friends stood bail for him, for £100 each. Others strongly advised him to jump bail and flee. Not wanting to let his friends down, Carey tried to persuade the Society to assume the responsibility for payment. The sum did not seem to him intolerably great, compared to the support they were giving to Bond and Butler in their well-fed incarceration. After all, it was for the sake of the Society, and at Drennan's particular request, that he had agreed to print the Address, and was facing prosecution.

But the Society prevaricated. At one meeting Drennan sat silent. Butler, principal beneficiary of the contributions made by members to his wine bills (a running grievance), refused to put the question of supporting Carey to the vote. Carey was disgusted: 'I could not have expected that these men would have abandoned the press and the printer, for the wine cask and the vintner'.[11]

At one stage Carey wrote a letter to the *Morning Post* (under the pseudonym of William Tell, that enemy of tyranny) criticizing the high-handed autocracy of the Society. At a subsequent meeting, reported by Collins, after a fracas involving McNally, a motion was passed:

> that there is good reason to believe that William P. Carey was the author of said letters signed W. Tell and that he be summoned to attend in his place next Friday to exculpate him from said charges if he has it in his power, otherwise that Carey be expelled.[12]

Carey's newspaper faltered. Advertisers withdrew advertisements. Creditors called in debts. Passing the hat round to members raised a paltry eight guineas. Collins, noting Carey's indignation with the Society's equivocations, reported to the Castle that he thought 'Carey might be easily *had*': he was right. Bought he was. Carey agreed to go into the witness box and give evidence under oath that, yes, Drennan was indeed the author of that fateful 'Citizen Soldiers' Address. Only the extraordinarily honest poverty of his memory, in the face of Curran's cross-examination, saved Drennan.

The Government rewarded Carey for his peaching with a pension and an annuity for his wife[13] – though it might well have given him more, had Drennan been found guilty. And, keeping to their side of the bargain, they subsidized a new newspaper for him. But the

Society, so it was reported, intimidated potential advertisers. Newsvendors selling his paper on street corners were beaten up. The informer Higgins claimed that by 1797 fewer than thirty copies of each edition was circulating. Even if the 'sham squire' was a notorious liar, the paper's life was short. In 1798 Carey wisely retreated to England, abandoned politics altogether and pursued his successful artistic career, all sedition spent.

The shadowy backdrop against which this part of Drennan's trial was played suggests tensions of *class* within the Dublin Society, not unlike those between the sansculottes and the 'bourgeois' Jacobins in the French Revolution. And the familiar division surfaced between revolutionaries concerned with organization and power, and others who clung with near-fanatical zeal to the purity of their idealism. The sheer impracticality of the latter advocates of 'direct democracy' (for example, the rotating of all offices by lot, in order to avoid the terrible corruption of power) seemed to them a small price to pay for preservation of their virtue.

It is risky to translate ideas of class into other countries, other centuries. But Tone, as the son of a coach-builder, complained of being patronized by the better-connected members of the Ascendancy, such as the Ponsonbys – even though he had the assurance of his Trinity College background. Drennan was certainly in awe of the high-born: one thinks of his visit to Lady Clanbrassill. Part of Carey's unhappy tale may be put down to a class resentment understandable among an emerging and talented Catholic middle class. Carey was only a little below the salt; but that is often the worst place to be.

Very much at the other end of the social scale, Lord Edward Fitzgerald continued to enjoy his long holiday from revolution throughout the summer and autumn of 1794, disturbed, so far as the evidence goes, by few thoughts other than those relating to married, aristocratic tranquillity, and the creation and tending of a cottage garden in his Kildare lodge.

Even his biographer Thomas Moore feels obliged to comment on this extended holiday from heroism:

> It is impossible not to feel how strange and touching is the contrast between those pictures of a happy home which they so unaffectedly exhibit, and that dark and troubled sea of conspiracy and revolt into

which the amiable writer of them, so soon after, plunged; nor can we easily believe that the joyous tenant of this little lodge . . . dividing the time between his child and his flowers . . . could be the same man who . . . placed himself at the head of rebel myriads etc., etc.,[14]

There are just one or two hints, however, of distant clouds. Some items of news entered his correspondence; there was talk of dissatisfaction over the raising of militia to aid England in the 'vile war' with France (by freeing more regular troops for service overseas); there were Dublin rumours of a change of ministry:

I intend paying a visit for a day to Castletown or Carton next week. We have been busy here about the militia; the people do not like it much, – that is, the common people and farmers – and even though Leinster has it [i.e. his elder brother is in command] they do not thoroughly welcome it, which I am glad of, as it shows they begin not to be entirely led by names. We are by no means so eager in this vile war as the people in England . . . I hear there is talk of a change here in the ministry.[15]

It seemed that a turning point was fast approaching in the latter half of 1794. The conspiracies of the 'blasted society' of United Irishman, in their original form, had been quelled; most of the leaders were in flight or exile, or at the very least cowed after successful prosecution. Even the peasant revolutionaries, the Catholic Defenders, appeared to be rampaging a little less, if by no means brought under control.

The responsibility for Irish affairs in London that autumn was rumoured in Dublin to be passing from the Prime Minister Pitt into the hands of the Whig partners of the new coalition. The Duke of Portland, as Home Secretary, would henceforth be the final arbiter of Ireland's destiny. On every side there was talk of a new Lord-Lieutenant. Lord Fitzwilliam (see p. 16), who had large Irish interests, was reluctant to accept the appointment at first. But if he did come, he would certainly be prepared to co-operate with Grattan: so everlastingly in opposition. He would be keen to encourage measures of parliamentary reform. He might even succeed in introducing complete emancipation, including the right of Catholics to sit in Parliament.

That at least was how the reformers (if not the revolutionaries) in Ireland imagined and peered into the future. But it was all seen in a haze. Not for the first or last time, everyone underestimated both the likelihood of confusion once plans had crossed the water, and the Ascendancy's connections and tenacity. In London, too, the extent of the powers, above all of dismissal, given to the new Lord-Lieutenant were less clearly laid down than they should have been. The Lord Chancellor Fitzgibbon and the Beresford family in particular were not to be toppled so easily. The worst of it was the uncertainty. Nothing was clearly written down. As Burke, now out of the main stream and grieving for the recent death of his son, wrote at the time:

'The Whig leaders undoubtedly thought that a very large discretion was committed to them', but they must have been strangely mistaken, for 'it seems Mr Pitt had no thought at all of a change in the Irish Government . . . these are some of the mischiefs which arise from a want of clear explanation on the first digestion of any political system.'[16]

Fitzgerald seems to have taken a revolutionary's view of the matter, even if a rather casual one. That is, part of him feared (at least when he walked about the streets of Dublin) that the coming of Fitzwilliam might put too easy an end to Catholic grievances and take the edge off the sharp executioner's blade; might retard the impetus towards a new, free Ireland in which everything was changed. He scorned the moderation of Whig clubs, he scorned all lukewarm politics. In a letter to his mother in early November he wrote:

There is no news here about our Lord Lieutenant with which people were occupied for so long a while. For one, I was very indifferent about it; and if anything, am glad Lord Fitzwilliam does not come, as perhaps it may make some of our opposition act with *more spirit and determination* [my italics].[17]

But Fitzwilliam was to arrive after all, early the following year. As will be seen, he came, saw and left – all in the space of a few weeks. Most of his attempts at dismissals were foiled. Moderate hopes were raised and dashed, reformers were cast into gloom, revolutionaries contrariwise given a new lease of life.

All through the summer and autumn of 1794 Tone contemplated eating 'the bitter bread of banishment', in the light of his agreement to leave Ireland following Rowan's prosecution. It was not until the following May, however, very soon after his fresh burst of notoriety (which arose from the revelations in Jackson's long-postponed trial, more clearly and publicly than ever implicating Tone in treason), that he set out at last for America with his family. What was he doing in this long meantime? He had, of course, to arrange to sell everything: his house and small property in County Kildare, and all his effects, apart from his books. These were a very good selection of about six hundred volumes which he determined to take with him. But there is no evidence of any progress on his project for a history of Ireland. Nor was there evidence of any new pamphleteering, of any great political activity apart from maintaining his connections with the Catholic Committee. He was keeping very scrupulously, perhaps fearfully, to his side of the bargain.

The Castle kept to its word, too. There were no threats, though there were discreet enquiries as to when Tone did propose to leave Ireland. That they asked him for no guarantee for his future conduct, once out of the country, is a puzzle. If the authorities had had any idea that he might stir up trouble in America, or even worse in France, they would surely have laid down some conditions. Tone himself was surprised that they had not even bothered to demand that he should desist from seditious activities outside Ireland:

> I told them that I considered my compromise with government to extend no further than the banks of the Delaware . . . that, undoubtedly, I was guilty of a great offence against the existing government; that, in consequence, I was going into exile, and that I considered that exile as a full expiation of the offence.[18]

The claim of 'expiation' strikes a disingenuous note in one who was probably contemplating a further 'great offence'.

Several reasons for his lack of harassment suggest themselves. One is that Tone, the heroic martyr of the future, had not yet become important or dangerous enough for the authorities to bother to hound. There had, admittedly, been that letter at the time of the foundation of the United Irishmen in 1792. And exile would answer for his assessment of the Irish situation handed to Jackson. He was, in the eyes of many at the Castle, little more than a spirited hack. And in the eyes of the Catholic Committee, too. When the Committee finally paid their debts to him, and even consulted him over future activities, they referred to their sadness at losing his 'literary talents'. A very good hack, a rather poor lawyer, a rather amateur traitor: that was how it may have looked to many at the time.

Another, complementary likelihood is simply that he was regarded with affection by a great number of friends (not only Peter Burrowes), many of them from his Trinity College days or the Middle Temple in London. Some of them were friends of the Government. Others, such as George Knox, were at least of the respectable Opposition who sought emancipation and reform by acceptable constitutional means. Thus his friend William Plunkett was to write to him before his departure about:

> the great pain at being deprived of the social, happy and unrestrained intercourse which had for so many years subsisted between us ... it is not without a degree of melancholy that I reflect that your present destination makes it probable that we may never meet again, and talk and laugh together as we used to do, though it is difficult to determine whether these *jumbling* times may not again bring us together.[19]

Circumspect as Tone was in this wilderness of brooding (a sad time, too – their fourth child died soon after birth this year), there is some suggestion that he was beginning to contemplate a more active revolutionary and republican future. Conversations with his dearest friend Thomas Russell would certainly have helped to lead him down this path. Russell had attitudes more like those of Carey; he was a man who believed that revolution, if it was to be serious and successful, needed to be based not just on an urban, intellectual élite but on a mass, popular movement. Later, after the closing-down of the original Dublin Society, with its well-conducted meetings run by the 'Law and the Physic', this was indeed to be the future of the resurrected Societies of United Irishmen: oath-bound, conspiratorial, secret, unafraid of violence. It was a future, however, that Tone would be able to observe only from other lands.[20]

There are some even more speculative explanations, all of which may contain grains of truth. Senator Frank MacDermot in his attractively written biography of the 1940s thinks that the Castle may have been happy to watch the Catholic Committee run the risk of compromising itself by continuing to deal with a proven revolutionary. But this seems to attribute to the Ascendancy a Machiavellianism out of character with its arrogance.

Then, finally, it may be that the Lord Chancellor Fitzgibbon wished to spare his kinsman from the worst consequences of his delinquency. Judicial thunder does quite often cohabit with personal kindliness (we shall see this in Fitzgibbon's last dealings with the dying Lord Edward Fitzgerald). So while certainly not intending to spare Tone from his compact over exile, or to moderate his language in condemning him in public, Fitzgibbon may have been content to see Tone's punishment stand exactly as agreed: no less, no more.

The suspicion that Rowan was a spy, entertained as soon as he had landed at Roscoff in late May 1774, was hard to dispel. He was sent under the escort of 'three cavaliers and a rascally nag, with an equally sorry equipage' to Brest. The cavaliers passed the journey by recounting the most recent atrocities they had been proud to commit. But at Brest, Jeanbon St André, a member of the French 'Committee of Public Safety' whom Rowan had hoped to see, had gone aboard the French fleet that hoped to break the English blockade. In his absence, the unfortunate suspect spy was taken to the Military Hospital, and left in the care of some galley slaves:

> This part of the building was furnished with beds on each side, about four feet from each other, most of them occupied by invalids, and some British and other prisoners whose health did not allow of their being sent into the interior. The galley slaves were designated as such by a slight wire round the left leg, just above the ankle. They registered my name, and gave me a pewter porringer and cup ... after about an hour the galley slaves drew into the room two tumbrells, in one of which were cauldrons of soup, as they called it, and on the other boiled kidney beans and potatoes, and flagons of the *vin de pays*; the prisoners ranging themselves, each at the foot of his bed, with the cups and porringers in their hands; I did the same ...
>
> During the night I detected one of the slaves rifling my pockets, when he thought I was asleep, whilst he pretended to be settling my bedclothes. I told the person in the next bed that I would complain to the *concierge* next day; but he advised me to hold my tongue, for these people had the perquisite of all the clothes etc. of those who died in the hospital, and it was strongly suspected they had been the death of some invalids, by giving them the wrong medicine during the night.[21]

It is surprising how long it took Rowan to realize that he himself was now one of the prisoners, and not, as he had hoped, a revolutionary ally, bringing valuable information. The slaves refused to listen to him. Nor was it any better when, after several days, six poor priests were brought in from the hold of a prison ship, 'in a miserable condition, covered with sores, from lying in the cable tier without any bedding'. His gentlemanly instinct to be helpful to those in distress asserted itself. But:

one of the priests was placed in the bed next to mine, and I constantly assisted him when [he was] obliged to leave his bed on different occasions. This, in the opinion of my companions, was a decided proof of my being an English spy; for who but such a person would pay any attention to a *refractory priest*?[22]

Days of imprisonment turned into weeks. It was only when a gaoler pleaded with a visiting Inspector of Prisoners of War, an Irishman named Sullivan in the service of France (*'débarrassez-moi de cet homme là, qu'on le renvoie ou que le guillotine, car il m'ennuie'*) that Rowan was at last set free. Then a letter arrived from Paris, full of apologies for the detention of the distinguished Irish patriot, who might well be bringing them useful news. His credentials at last established, he set out with Sullivan

> in a *Berline à quatre chevaux*, with the tricolour flying from the roof as usual, as a representative of the nation, and at its expense . . . as we passed along, in various demesnes we saw hanging on the trees and on most of the substantial looking houses notices of *Propriété Nationale à Vendre* [I wonder how the owner of one such grand estate in Ireland looked on these sinister notices of expropriation?]
>
> On our arrival at Orleans, the decree acknowledging God, and the immortality of the soul, which had just passed the Convention, was about to be promulgated by a great fête . . . about half way up the very handsome steeple of the church, on which the words *'Le peuple Français reconnoit L'Etre suprême et L'Immortalité de l'Ame'* were blazoned in large gold letters . . . at a signal the screen fell, amidst the firing of cannon and musketry, and bands of music playing, while the multitude responded, *'Vive Robespierre!'*, who was supposed to be the framer of the decree.[23]

Alas, a fever which he had caught in prison, hardly improved by the tearaway rattling of the coach to Paris (seventy miles in ten hours, on a day of tremendous heat), made his appearance before the dictator fruitless and unmemorable. Robespierre, finding him practically speechless, waved a dismissal at him. But at least he was lodged in a suite in the Palais Royal, and was courteously laughed at for his anxiety over the expenses, which were all paid.

Otherwise the Terror, now at its height, struck him unfavourably. Very soon after, toward the end of July, Robespierre was himself executed; the crowd attending his wagon, so Rowan learnt, went 'so far as to thrust their umbrellas into the wagon against his body':

two days [afterwards] the whole commune of Paris, consisting of about sixty persons, were guillotined in less than one hour and a half, in the Place de Revolution, and though I was standing above a hundred paces from the place of execution, the blood of the victims streamed under my feet. What surprised me was, as each head fell into the basket, the cry of the people was no other than a repetition of '*A bas le maximum*'.[24]

This seems an extreme example of popular revenge for an economic doctrine: price controls on grain had led rural areas to refuse to supply food to the capital.

Rowan had by now begun to receive fair sums of money from his resourceful wife, and found lodgings in the rue Mousseau, in the house where his eldest son had been born. Here he 'witnessed several of the inconveniences of a revolutionary government' – something of an understatement. The house he was living in

had been bought by a locksmith. He had been ordered to prepare carriages for four heavy guns. He had no plan or model given to him, nor was it in his line of business; yet he was made responsible for the wood as well as the iron work. I saw one of these carriages rejected four times by an inspector who could not even point out its faults.[25]

To judge from his indignant tone Rowan, his boyhood passion for watches and all things mechanical still alive and ticking, may well have found this incompetence not *much* less distressing than the blood of the Terror. But in any case all enthusiasm for popular revolution had faded. His wife must have been relieved to read a letter that ran:

I own to you candidly, when it is of no avail, that my ideas of reform, and of another word which begin with the same letter, are very much altered by living for twelve months in France; and that I never wish to see the one or the other procured by force. I have seen one faction rising over another and overturning it; each of them in their turn making a stalking horse of the supreme power of the people, to cover public and private massacre and plunder; while every man of virtue shuddered and skulked in a disgraceful silence.[26]

By the early part of the next year, he had determined to change his place of exile, and leave for the less tarnished prospects of the New World.

10

To the New World

> The next Augustan age will dawn on the other side of the
> Atlantic. There will, perhaps, be a Thucydides at Boston, a
> Xenophon at New York, and, in time, a Virgil at Mexico,
> and a Newton at Peru. At last, some curious traveller from
> Lima will visit England and give a description of the ruins
> of St Paul's, like the editions of Balbec and Palmyra.
> Horace Walpole, letter to Horace Mann,
> November 1774

Hamilton Rowan, disillusioned but still in Paris in early 1795, secured a passport from Nicholas Madgett, a sly and circumspect Kerryman serving off and on in the French Foreign Ministry (whom Tone later came to know, disdainfully). It was made out in the false name of James Thomson, an American businessman, a precaution against a possible arrest by a British ship on the high seas.

Very much in character, 'Thomson' decided to buy 'a little Thames wherry . . . at the sale of the Duke of Orleans' effects'. (From this time he began often to call himself by his assumed name, even signing 'Thomson' in some letters to his wife.) He hoped to 'fall down' the Seine at least as far as Rouen, taking only his dog Charles – he never, ever, forgot his dog – and the least possible luggage. It was a crazy enterprise. He set out on 17 April 1795. He was threatened with musket fire, had his boat forced into the bank, was shouted at by a posse of washerwomen, hauled (twice) before the mayor of Passy, and accused of being a spy and of escaping from France with the country's gold.

Once he had reached Argenteuil, where he spread his things to

dry, and paid a visit to an old friend, prospects brightened, reminding him of what days on the river ought really to be like:

> On the 18th I resumed my course, which was extremely pleasant. My
> mode of travelling was certainly novel, and created more suspicion along
> the whole route than I was aware of. In about four days I reached Rouen
> without any remarkable occurrence.[1]

Four days in a Thames wherry to cover nearly a hundred miles is
good going. By then he had had enough, and completed the rest of
the journey to Le Havre in a diligence. There, an obliging Captain
Dillon of Baltimore (of Irish origin, to judge from his name) drew up
some new bills of lading under his false name; his ship, the *Columbus*,
was due to sail for Philadelphia in a few days' time.

These few days he stayed at a house which Mary Wollstonecraft
had put at his disposal. The mother of Mary Shelley and author of *A
Vindication of the Rights of Women*, she was the first English feminist.
Rowan had recently enjoyed several evenings with her in Paris – or at
least I hope he enjoyed them, given her tone of voice, which is rather
familiar today. One remark in particular of hers, 'Minute attention to
propriety stops the growth of virtue',[2] might have run counter to
Rowan's gentlemanliness, implying as it does that manners are inim-
ical to higher ideals, and may with advantage take second place.

Touchingly and teasingly, Rowan had in the previous month
written a letter to his wife (whose own letters so often scolded),
dwelling a little on his acquaintance with Wollstonecraft:

> she has unknowingly given me many a heart-ache, since I had the pleasure
> of being acquainted with her. There is an avowal for you! Was anything so
> impertinent? Yes, she has made my heart ache, when she has persisted
> that no motive on earth ought to make a man and wife live together after
> mutual love and regard were gone . . . she said in the end that I had no
> reason to be alarmed, for when a person whom we have loved was absent,
> all the faults he might have were diminished . . . her prophecy has been
> fulfilled by the kind and affectionate letters you have sent me . . . and I am
> now as happy as a man can be, whose dearest, and almost his only
> comfort is withheld from him.[3]

On the slow-sailing, wallowing *Columbus*, occasionally beset by
equinoctial gales, he found plenty of time to keep his journal, writing
in the corner of the steerage where he had rigged up a few private
square feet, guarded by an English flag hung across some hand-

spikes, with his cot slung in the middle: 'my *dejuné*, writing-box and trunk, on the one side; on the other, my two camp-chairs and a little writing table; I enjoy my corner to myself and my dog Charles'. Two days out of Le Havre however, before the long tedium of the voyage had set in, he had a narrow escape:

> we were brought to by a British frigate, the *Melampus*. The officer who boarded us examined the ship's papers, and went into the hold with the Captain. On returning to the quarterdeck, he accosted me, saying, 'Your name is Thomson, Sir, I understand this cargo belongs to you' . . . He asked me from what part of America I came from. I replied, 'From Charleston: but going to settle in Philadelphia'. I mentioned South Carolina, as from the visit I had formerly paid that province with Lord Charles Montague, I was the better able to answer any further questions he might put to me . . . We were now under the stern of the frigate, and I retired to the cabin, which I thought it most prudent to do, as I found that the ship he belonged to was commanded by my old Cantab friend, Sir John Borlase Warren.[4]

The journey took so long that the ship almost ran out of provisions other than bread. Rowan filled his time (after writing his letters and his journal whenever the weather allowed him), by becoming 'a seamstress, I have made myself near a dozen pair of socks, besides mending shirts, stockings, trowsers, &c'. This is in good seafaring tradition – though I wonder where he learnt such skills. Not in his comfortable mansion in County Kildare, surely?

Towards the end of June, after they had been at sea over five weeks, Captain Dillon saw a vessel floundering, her sails all ahoo, and wondered 'what the devil was doing'. At first he thought she was a whaler that had a whale alongside, which was being cut up. That would explain her heavy list. Suddenly, she entirely disappeared. Then the men in the tops

> cried out that they saw a boat, in which three masts were rigged, and besides which there appeared to be a raft. This in a great measure allayed our fears for the safety of the crew; and the captain said he hoped they had taken the precaution to bring some beef and water with them, for we had bread enough. I could not help thinking the wish was somehow ill-timed, while we were as yet so uncertain of the fate of the crew; his anxiety, however, proved sufficiently that it was not for want of feeling for their distress, but a proper foresight, which seafaring persons naturally acquire.[5]

In fact, confusion taking its toll, the ship turned out not to have sunk at all, but was lying on its side. At one point Captain Dillon declared he could see but one man upon her quarter, 'which man was found soon after to be a wooden gun'. But no one was rescued, and Rowan was left with his solitary reflections, writing immediately afterwards to his wife:

> You may recollect my saying, that two circumstances had in my life made an effect upon me, which I had never felt at any other time . . . these were, the first person whom I saw executed, and the first balloon which I ever saw go up with [a] man. The emotion I felt on seeing the ship go down, as I thought, was exactly similar. I ran down between decks, and Tony Lumpkin [nickname for a lecherous fellow passenger, lifted from Goldsmith's *She Stoops to Conquer*], almost pushed me off the ladder in running by me, to announce to the females that a ship had perished in sight . . . when I was left alone, I put up an ardent prayer to the Omnipotent for the safety of my dearest love.[6]

Another three weeks passed before, on 15 July, they came up with a pilot-boat at break of day; by the evening they had entered the river with land on both sides and a fair wind. It was a crossing which extinguished Rowan's love of watery adventures, at least for a time.

In Philadelphia he stayed in a house where Mr Adams, who succeeded George Washington, and Mr Jackson – another future President – were fellow boarders. Unfortunately for us Rowan was not a man to push himself forward. He did not utter a single word to them. Worse still:

> [I had meant] to have waited on the President; but being informed that Washington had declined receiving Talleyrand, I gave up that idea; and having determined on retiring into some country situation, I fixed on Wilmington, in the state of Delaware, about thirty miles from Philadelphia.[7]

During the weeks when the *Columbus* was wallowing in the mid-Atlantic, Wolfe Tone was being given a generous and consoling farewell from Ireland. He had secured the agreement of the United Irishman that he would, on their behalf, act as an emissary first to the American Government and then, if things could be so managed, take ship from there to France and engage her to help in the liberation of Ireland. It is not clear how he reconciled this plan with his undertakings made the previous year – apart, that is, from his unilateral assertion that his agreement with the Castle could not be construed to reach beyond the banks of the Delaware.

He took several members of his family with him: Matilda, his three children, his sister and his brother Arthur. He had determined to sail from Belfast, where he arrived on 20 May 1795 and passed almost a month, much of it in the company of Thomas Russell:

> [while we were there] we were every day engaged by one or other; even those who scarcely knew me were eager to entertain us; parties and excursions were planned for our amusement; and certainly the whole of our deportment and reception at Belfast very little resembled those of a man who escaped with his life only by a miracle, and was driven into exile to avoid a more disgraceful fate . . . the most agreeable day we passed during our stay, and one of the most agreeable of our lives was in an excursion we made with the Simms's, Neilson and Russell, to Ram's Island, a beautiful and romantic spot in Loch Neagh. Nothing can be imagined more delightful, and we agreed, in whatever quarter we might find ourselves, respectively, to commemorate that day, the 11th of June.[8]

Not all in Belfast was innocent pleasure and the poignancy of fond farewells. Gone were his former reservations over alliances with the 'rabble'. He had some contact with the Defenders, and took the new oath of the re-formed United Irishmen. It can be argued – just – that the oath itself was not overtly republican, and so, in itself, not treasonable. But it nevertheless aimed at full independence. And, by his own account, solemn hilltop undertakings were made:

> I remember, particularly, two days that we passed on the Cave Hill. On the first, Russell, Neilson, Simms, McCracken and one or two more of us, on the summit of M'Art's fort [from where you overlook a magnificent panorama of Belfast, its Lough and, on fair days, a vast expanse of the lands of Ulster] – took a solemn obligation, which I think I may say I have on my part endeavoured to fulfil, never to desist in our efforts until we had subverted the authority of England over our country, and asserted her independence.[9]

It was Thomas Russell more than anyone who helped to instil into him such uncompromising resolution, Russell who persuaded Tone that the future for Irish independence lay less with the professional United Irish leadership than with the poor, the peasants in their cabins. If a revolution was to be feasible they needed to listen to men and women in these classes. Before he left Belfast, Tone pronounced himself as competent to speak 'fully and with confidence for the Catholics, for the Dissenters, and *for the Defenders* of Ireland [my italics].'[10]

Tone at one time had called the Northerners cowards and braggadocios: 'nothing was to be expected from this country except from the *sans culottes*, who are too ignorant for any thinking man to wish to see in power'. Whether or not this was ever his real opinion, it was certainly quite different from that of his dear friend Russell, who in one entry in his *Journals* writes of a journey he once made to a mill near Belfast:

> Talking politics with one of the mill men . . . go to his cabin to drink whisky with him. A wife and two children. Says, 'I think liberty worth risquing life for. In a cause of that sort I think I should have courage enough from reflection to brave death'. One of his children was climbing on his knee. 'As for my part', says he, 'it does not much signify now as to myself but it grieves me to breed up these children to be slaves. I would gladly risque all to prevent that.' When will a man of fortune in Ireland reason thus? Our senators and great men think of nothing but their own sordid interest. Here was a peasant interested for the freedom of mankind.[11]

Russell walked everywhere through the streets and countryside. He could seldom afford to travel on horseback. And he walked alone. But he found it easy to talk with strangers. He was interested not only in politics and economics and Ireland, but in geology, archaeology, chemistry, agriculture, new factories. The character of this gaunt and solitary man, this ex-officer who had served in India, this pauper gentleman – was equally many-sided. Intensity – intensity above all – melancholy, passion of all sorts, reticence, self-critical lacerations for his many backslidings, lust and hopeless yearnings, occasional very heavy drinking; these are a few elements. Generosity, too; if the only pennies he had were his last ones, he never hesitated to give them. He was sensitive and proud. He was profoundly religious. He was unsuccessful in love, indeed in most walks of life. Perhaps surpris-

---

* The text of the *Journals* have only recently been rescued by the heroic diligence of C.J. Woods: their handwriting not much easier to decipher than Linear B or the Oxyrhyncus papyri. Russell evidently suffered from some form of dyslexia: egregious misspelling, transposed letters etc.

ingly in the light of this agonizing catalogue of virtues and vices, he was excellent company. He had a gift for friendship. His heart was sometimes light. He was utterly loyal.

In turn, he was much loved by his friends, who often had to support him. (I am glad that these included distant ancestors of my own, the Knoxes of Dungannon, who appointed him Seneschal of the manor court, and a Justice of the Peace for County Tyrone.[12])

Tone, as well as embracing many of Russell's extreme republican and revolutionary views in the mid-1790s onwards, looked on him with undying affection. One of the first letters which he wrote on arriving in America read:

> Believe me, dear Tom, the greatest of the numberless heavy losses I sustained in leaving Ireland . . . was the loss of your society . . . You know how exactly how our humours concurred, and that particular style of conversation which we had framed for ourselves and which to us was so exquisitely pleasant; those strained quotations, absurd phrases and extravagant sallies which people in the unreserve of affectionate intercourse indulge themselves.[13]

The two men never met again.

On June 12 Tone boarded the *Cincinnatus*. He at once began making the cramped quarters as comfortable as he could for his family. How he managed for money is a mystery. He had certainly had a final payment of £1,500 from the Catholic Committee, but it is not known whether the Government had provided the funds they had at one time proposed (as is stated in some of Tone's obituary notices). There are unexplained discrepancies between the capital which he states he had, and his expenditures in America. In any case he was not unduly short of funds for his uncertain future:

> I had hired a state room, which was about eight feet by six, in which we had fitted up three berths; my wife and our youngest little boy occupied one, my sister and my little girl the second, and our oldest boy and myself the third. It was at first grievously inconvenient, but necessity and custom by degrees reconciled us to our situation; our greatest suffering was want of good water . . . which we found impossible to replace by wine, porter, or spirits of which we had abundance.[14]

The seafaring lot of Tone was, however, at least happier than that of Rowan: 'The 1st of August [we] landed safe at Wilmington, not one of my party, providentially, having been for an hour indisposed on the passage, nor even sea-sick.'[15]

While Tone was being given his memorable farewell on his way to contractual exile, and Rowan was making his own, lonelier passage from Paris to the banks of the Delaware, Drennan, still shaken after a capital trial that had led to so fortunate an acquittal, prudently lay low. His letters to his sister and brother-in-law could be read without incrimination if opened by others. He might have taken to heart the words of the Attorney-General at his trial: 'I say again, gentlemen, that every man has a right, and I hope we will long exercise it, of discussing political questions – but not in such language as is calculated to excite tumult and sedition.'

So no undergrowth of treason is visible, only the fruits of his listening and observation. And at the beginning of 1795 there was plenty to observe in Dublin. It is often looked upon as one of the turning points of Irish history. It was expected that Catholics would find themselves admitted at last, under the new Lord-Lieutenant, to seats in parliament. The final coping-stones of emancipation would be put in place. The 'blasted society' of United Irishman might be taking new shape underground, its more or less public meetings in Back Lane a thing of the past. But one of the Society's founding ambitions, of securing reform through a firm alliance between the Catholics and Dissenters of the North, did seem, tantalizingly, to be within view. The dawn, of course, was false.

The Lord-Lieutenancy of Fitzwilliam enjoyed a very brief day indeed. He was outgunned by the powerful connections of those of the Ascendancy, like Beresford and Fitzgibbon, whom he had so abruptly sought to dismiss. By the end of February the appointment that had aroused such high hopes among both Catholic emancipationists and parliamentary reformers, was over and done with.

As to who had given what precise (or imprecise) undertakings, dissertations are still being written today. Perhaps the Duke of Portland, who as Home Secretary in the new coalition bore the principal responsibility for the appointment of the Viceroy, had been more opposed to total emancipation than Fitzwilliam believed? Perhaps Fitzwilliam had wilfully exceeded the terms of his agreement with Pitt? Perhaps Pitt had contemplated, with cool equanimity, a débâcle of this kind as a prelude to the union which, three years later, was to be carried through, after the bloodiest rebellion in Irish history? Or was he simply too engrossed in larger questions to do with the war with France? All one can say for certain is that, leaving aside imputations of bad faith and Machiavellian scheming, everywhere there were eddies of misunderstanding, confusion, recrimination, bitter grievance.

Drennan's own observations display his customary ambivalence about the Catholics. Thus, just before Fitzwilliam's departure (less than two months after his arrival) he described the pressure they were exerting:

> Grattan and the Catholics are [now] all in all. They use all instruments that are malleable, and perhaps they will submit to some compromise, to something less than all. In the meantime they use every means of getting addresses to Fitzwilliam. Their own address will go up in grand procession from the Rotunda on Thursday . . .[16]

Here was his familiar suspicion of a plot whereby the Catholics, once granted total enfranchisement, might be weaned away from the causes of the Dissenters (from radical reform, from revolution, from the assistance of the French, from independence). Nor were United Irishmen's fears unreasonable. Edmund Burke was not alone in favouring such Catholic policies.

Burke was, at the time, thought to be dying. Drennan reports a comment, made in February 1795, which shows how revolutionaries can often be guilty of wishful thinking:

> Orr writes to me: 'Burke is certainly mad . . . the progress of the complaint was gradual, but distress for the death of his son completely subdued his understanding. Unhappy as this event is to his family, fortunate is it for his character with posterity. He will appear the bold patron of American liberty, the eloquent advocate of Indian suffering, and the successful pleader for Catholic emancipation. His political principles will be inferred from his exertions on these occasion, and his work on the French Revolution will be considered as the ruin of a mighty mind.'[17]

Obviously Drennan enjoyed listening to the rumours that swirled round Dublin early in the year. His letters to his sister are full of high politics and hint at all manner of conspiracies. Some of his guesses are wild:

I think it probable that a strong representation of the dangerous consequences of total emancipation, not only to the established church, but to
the *Union* of the two kingdoms, was sent over from the Law and the
Episcopal benches . . .[18]

Drennan was interested in the constitutional propriety of total
emancipation, given that the King's Oath of Accession promised, as
it still does, to uphold the established religion. Drennan's doubts are
laid bare; on the one hand lay his distaste for Catholic politicians
('they use all instruments that are malleable'), on the other hand
his United Irishman's credo that the Catholic alliance might be
necessary to secure parliamentary reform:

it is said that the Marquis of Buckingham groped his way a second time
up the backstairs and told the King he would violate his Coronation Oath
by granting a total emancipation to the Catholics, and subvert the
Protestant religion as by law established, upon which the King, who is
very religious, altered his opinion on the subject entirely; and, besides,
condemned much the dismissal of Mr Beresford etc., etc . . . so it is that
the compact entered into by Mr Pitt and Lord Fitzwilliam on the other
side [of the water] is on this side to be broken . . . the Catholics are to miss
their bill, and all is again topsy turvy. They talk of calling a meeting, in
order, I suppose, to expatiate on the auspicious prospects this Lord
Lieutenant held and their discontent at being blasted. All the aristocrat
Catholics with Byrne, Keogh etc., were to have dined at the Castle on
Saturday.[19]

It sounds as if Drennan was not altogether displeased by the
Catholics' discomfiture.

In the spring the new Lord-Lieutenant, Lord Camden, had been
greeted by riots in protest against the dismissal of his predecessor.
Other Dubliners as well as Drennan realized that the hoped-for
progress towards Catholic emancipation would be halted. So would
steps towards parliamentary reform. Camden was in any case a man
prone to alarm. Stories of the disturbances confirmed, in his eyes,
the wisdom of the peremptory instructions he had brought with him
from London.

Equally disturbing to the Castle was the news that the United
Irishmen were busy reconstructing themselves on a more frankly
revolutionary basis, after Tone's departure for the United States. And
more links were being established by the Society with rapidly spread-

ing Defenderism. All the more reason to resist reform, to put down disaffection.

Drennan had come to treat Fitzgerald with reserve, probably agreeing with his sister (as who could not?) that he was a rash man. His meeting with him, in the aftermath of his trial, sounds more cautious than ever. He recounts Fitzgerald's calling on him in early 1795, when Fitzwilliam was still Lord-Lieutenant, to sound him out on how the North might look on a call to take up arms:

> Lord Edward came with an *air* of great friendship. He said he was resolved at this critical time to continue in opposition even to his brother, and although a place [of profit] was offered to him, which might be deemed convenient, the usual remittance from France to his lady being stopped, yet he would still persevere.[20]

Fitzgerald was one of the few who were happy to see the speedy departure of Fitzwilliam. The Lord-Lieutenant's readiness to make concessions and envisage *total* Catholic emancipation, slowed the desirable revolutionary momentum.

It was about this time that Fitzgerald's intimacy with Arthur O'Connor took shape.* They were both thirty-two, born within four months of each other. Soon Fitzgerald was calling him 'the twin of my soul'; Pamela, called his 'dangerous little wife' by O'Connor's friends, was devoted to him too. O'Connor seemed finally to have shaken him out of his protracted rustic interlude. Even so, Fitzgerald wrote that he did not greatly enjoy life in Dublin:

> I confess Leinster House does not inspire the brightest ideas. By the by, what a melancholy house it is . . . a poor country housemaid I bought with me cried for two days, and said she thought she was in prison. Pam and I amuse ourselves a good deal with walking about the streets, which, I believe, shocks **** a little.[21]

On these walks, Fitzgerald may also have reflected on the revolutionary possibilities of the city. These were certainly very much in the mind of the Castle and of the military. A letter in March from the Commander-in-Chief Lord Carhampton to the Home Secretary in

---

* See Introduction, p. 18.

London shows the alarm that was felt about the defenceless state of Dublin:

> a body of 3000 men and a few field pieces might be equipped unknown to us . . . and be landed in the vicinity of Dublin and possess it, before the inhabitants were well aware of the attempt. In the space of 24 hours, a million of money at least might be raised in contribution, the city handed over to a municipality formed of the dregs of the people who armed with pikes and whiskey would probably plunder and burn the town, and the whole United Kingdom then be undone for a century to come.[22]

Although Fitzgerald and O'Connor were already thinking of insurrection, neither had yet come out completely into the open. The latter's very long speech in May on the laws that still 'disabled papists to sit and vote in either House of Parliament', attacking the idea of the so-called '*immaculate* nature of the constitution in church and state' was acclaimed as a great oratorical triumph. Today it is hard to see why. O'Connor compared the representatives of the people of Ireland to traders:

> I will suppose those wholesale dealers in our rights and liberties, coming from their rotten boroughs, and from the counties they had debauched with their attendant supporters on 'Constitution in church and state' to discharge their cargo at the seat of government, at the counting house of an English factor. What shall I suppose the price of this infernal cargo, like Pandora's box, a collection of every ill that can affect mankind? . . . The men who oppose the abolition of religious distinctions are the men who usurp the whole political power of the country. Catholic emancipation would be incompatible with their accursed monopoly.[23]

Burke did not think quite so ill of this rodomontade as one might expect. He was more lenient to *Irish* Jacobins, because of their circumstances:

> It would seem as if young O'Connor gave himself his full swing. I am sorry for it: he has good parts: and on his Uncle Longfield's death he will have a large fortune. I saw him at Bath three years ago. He was then an enthusiast, an admirer of Rousseau . . . I saw he had a mind of great energy, and was capable of much Good or of much Evil . . . That speech, though full of fire and animation, was not warmed with the fire of heaven. I am sorry for it. I have seen that gentleman but once. He is certainly a man of parts, but one who has dealt too much in the Philosophy of France.[24]

How often Fitzgerald, like 'the twin of his soul', had invoked Rousseau's name in those long-ago letters to his mother, written during his expeditions to the wilderness of North America, his dalliance among the 'noble savages'!

Sometimes O'Connor and Fitzgerald escaped together from the cares and covert excitements of Dublin. Here is a record of their more or less innocent flaunting of rebellious colours, as told by Thomas Moore:

> At about this time there took place on the Curragh of Kildare a well-known *rencontre* between his lordship and some dragoon officers . . . Mr Arthur O'Connor being, at that time, on a visit to his noble friend, they rode together, on one of the days of the races, to the Curragh, – Lord Edward having a green silk handkerchief round his neck. It was indeed his practice, at all times (contrary to the usual custom of that day) to wear a coloured silk neckcloth, – generally of the name of Belscher; he chose to wear the national, and, at that time, obnoxious colour, green.
>
> At the end of the race, having left the stand-house, in a canter, to return home, the two friends had not proceeded far before they found themselves overtaken by a party of from ten to a dozen officers, who, riding past them in a full gallop, wheeled round, so as to obstruct their passage, and demanded that Lord Edward should take off his green cravat. Thus accosted, his Lordship answered coolly, – 'Your cloth would speak you to be gentlemen; but this conduct conveys a very different impression. As to this neckcloth that so offends you, all I can say is, – here I stand; let any man among you, who dares, come forward and take it off.' This speech, pronounced coolly and deliberately, took his pursuers by surprise; and for a moment they looked puzzled at each other, doubtful how to proceed; when Mr O'Connor, interposing, said, that if the officers chose to appoint two out of their number, Lord Edward and himself would be found, ready to attend their summons, at Kildare. The parties then separated, and during the two following days, Lord Edward and his friend waited the expected message. But no further steps were taken by these military gentlemen, on whose conduct rather a significant verdict was passed at a Curragh ball, shortly after, when it was agreed, as I have heard, by all the ladies in the room not to accept any of them as partners.[25]

In the early months of 1795 the informer McNally played an ignoble part in the epilogue to the affair of the Reverend William Jackson. McNally, as one of the defending counsel, had agreed with a grateful Jackson, just before his suicide, to look after his widow's interests as best as he could. She had three children, and was expecting another. Jackson had hoped that the French nation would care for them, and had begged McNally to see that this was done. He had written at the bottom of his will: 'signed and sealed in the presence of my dearest friend, whose heart and principles ought to recommend him as a worthy citizen – Leonard McNally'. About three weeks after his dearest friend's death, McNally placed all the documents in the hands of the Irish Government.

The new Lord-Lieutenant Camden then wrote a secret letter to the Home Secretary, the Duke of Portland. He believed that having this most trusted of the United Irishmen's lawyers so completely in the Government's power might be very valuable, and, curiously, that he could even be used for double-agent overseas missions:

> It has occurred to me that an excuse might be made for Mr McNally's being allowed to enter France for the purpose of attending to this woman's fortunes, that he should go through London, and in case your Grace should wish to employ him, I will inform him when and where he will be found.[26]

But the Duke of Portland was wiser than to place such confidence in an informer, all the more so because McNally was so very skilled a deceiver. If, he wrote, Camden thought that McNally really could be trusted, then indeed the Government might be ready to make use of his services in France. But surely this was most unlikely. Nor could their close control extend to a foreign country. Meanwhile McNally would continue to be most useful in Dublin, where he could be overseen.[27]

And useful he was. His work as lawyer took him to all parts of Ireland. The stories of those whom he defended were of increasing interest to the Castle as the tide of violence rose: as revolutionary movements extended outwards beyond the professional and middle-class ranks of the United Irishmen. His reports on the organization of the Defenders were particularly useful. And he showed understanding about their grievances:

> The sufferings of the common people from high rents and low wages, from oppressions of their landlords, their subtenants, the agents of absentees, and tithes, are not now the only causes of disaffection to Government and hatred to England; for though these have long kept the Irish peasant in the most abject state of slavery and indigence, yet another

cause, more dangerous, pervades them all, and is also indeed almost universal among the middle ranks, by which I mean the upper classes of artisans and mechanics in the cities, and farmers in the country. This cause is an attachment to French principles in politics and religion lately imbibed, and an ardent desire for a republican government . . .

So sudden a revolution in the Catholic mind is easily accounted for. *I impute it to the Press* [my italics]. The publication of political disquisitions, and resolutions by the Societies of United Irishmen of Belfast and Dublin, written to the passions and feelings of the multitude, affected them with electrical celerity. These papers affected them with Paine's politics and theology . . . I believe it to be true that in the County of Cork, Paine's works are read by the boys of almost every school, and that in most houses they now supply the place of the Psalter and the Prayer Book.[28]

Lecky, strangely, manages to find good words to say about McNally, despite his diligent betrayal of clients' secrets:

As a lawyer in considerable practice, constantly going on circuit, McNally had excellent opportunities of knowing the state of the country, and was able to give very valuable warnings about the prevailing dispositions . . . few men would have been thought less capable of long-continued deception than this good-humoured, brilliant and mercurial lawyer . . . he was the most constant and apparently the most devoted defender of the United Irishmen . . . from no other quarter did the government obtain so many useful warnings, and if the advice of McNally had been more frequently listened to, some of the worst consequences of the rebellion might have been avoided.[29]

True, Lecky also writes of his 'strangely composite character, in which the virtues of impulse seemed all to live, though the virtues of principle had wholly gone'.[30]

I ask myself whether one can, just possibly, defend a lawyer who provides the Government with information he has happened to accrue during his work, about the methods and operation of a secret, oath-bound organization intent on overthrowing the Government of his country: a Government fearful of the threat of imminent and bloody revolution? After all, the spy is one thing, the informer another. To some degree in his earlier dealings with the Castle, McNally may have managed to justify himself on these grounds. As he appeared at the Assizes in every part of the country, he saw at first hand the mounting barbarity of the Defenders' murders, arson, plunderings, their avowals of subversion, their declarations of loyalty to an enemy with whom the kingdom was at war. Just possibly he excused himself, as he informed to the Castle, by reciting to himself the convenient doctrine that 'there is no confidence in iniquity'.

I believe however, that there is a likelier explanation of McNally's character. As he pondered on his promises of friendship, his gift for arousing and for giving sympathy, his duties of confidentiality – and on the other hand the importance of the secrets to which he was privy, the sheer power of information, properly handled – he may well have found himself *enjoying* the tug between the contrarieties of his nature. He revelled in temptation, relished his skill at deceit. It was a theatrical gift. He was in charge of the beginning and of the end. He was his own *deus ex machina*.

His next victim was to be the poor Lawrence O'Connor.

I I

Tumultuous risings

'Money is good and a girl might be better,
No matter what happens and who takes the fall,
But a good strong cause' – the rope gave a jerk there,
No more sang he, for his throat was too small;
But he kicked before he died,
He did it out of pride.

　　　　　　　Yeats, *Last poems*: 'Three Marching Songs'

A dozen or so miles south of Dublin lies the garrison town of Naas, not far from the Curragh canters and challenges of Lord Edward Fitzgerald and Arthur O'Connor. More banefully, Naas was also the seat of the Assizes where the schoolmaster and Defender Lawrence O'Connor (no relation of Arthur) was tried for high treason in the late summer of 1795.

The trial proved an opportunity for McNally to pass on a great deal of information to the Government about the Defenders, who were again rampaging, after a relative lull. (He was, however, unable to save his client.) His warnings to the Castle about the growing threat of Defenderism became more and more insistent through the summer and winter of 1795; and Camden did not hide his alarm.

Defenderism had become a spreading patchwork of millennial dreams: a brotherhood 'almost as sacredly kept as freemasonry'. Lawrence O'Connor himself had been initiated into the Grand Lodge. He was described as 'Sir Lawrence O'Connor' in another Lodge. And he was a member of a 'Knot of Friendly Brothers'.

The movement had many oaths. Most were a bizarre mishmash:[1]

What have you in your hand?
The rod of Aaron at command
What do you intend to do with that glorious rod?
To clear our passage through the Red Sea.

Are you concerned [i.e. sworn]?
I am.
To what?
To the national convention.

What do you design by that cause?
To quell all nations, dethrone all Kings and plant the true religion that
    we lost since reformation.
Where did the cock crow that all the world heard?
In France.*

One evening in July 1795 O'Connor had fallen in, on the streets
of Naas, with Bartholomew Horan, a private soldier in the North
Mayo militia. They talked of the likelihood that the French would
shortly invade – the reason for their recruitment. O'Connor then
took Private Horan to a house where there were between twenty
and twenty-five Defenders present, most of them 'in liquor'. They
drank one or two pots of porter. They also shook hands, rubbed
their fingers down the sides of their faces. O'Connor pulled out the
oath, on a paper with the illustration of the tree of liberty. The oath
began:

> I AB do swear, in the presence of Almighty God, that I will be true to the
> present United States of France and Ireland, and every other kingdom in
> Christianity, or will become hereafter, without it being hurtful to soul or
> body, as long as they prove so to me.

The illustration showed the trunk of a tree of liberty marked out
in three divisions, on which were written the three words LOVE
LIBERTY LOYALTY: over the word 'loyalty', near the branches, was the

---

* Bartlett compares some of these oaths to the *aisling* or 'vision poem' which transmitted millennial notions . . . 'the Gaelic mind, essentially the outlook of the lower orders, found no
difficulty in assimilating French developments into the by now time-honoured themes of
deliverance from abroad, besting the Saxon and destroying the Protestants' ('Defenders and
Defenderism', *IHS*, xxiv, p. 378).

cap of liberty; at one side of the trunk was written JACOB'S LADDER; there was a large seal of red wax at each side, and at the foot the words 'OF LIBERTY'.

O'Connor offered to write Horan's name in English, Irish or Latin, and asked him to swear that he would be 'loyal to all brother defenders and to the French, and they would soon have the Kingdom to themselves'. But Horan drunkenly protested that he had sworn to be true to King and Country. He escaped and ran back to barracks. There he reported to his Commanding Officer, Captain Burke. He 'looked as if he had been boxing'.

A posse was dispatched. O'Connor was discovered. He was stripped, and a paper fell on the floor beside him. In his trial McNally, who pleaded as expertly as he betrayed, made much of the incomprehensibility of the oath, the gibberish of 'the present United States of France and Ireland', the nature of the book on which Horan had been asked to swear. What was it? Just a tattered pocket book, of no consequence. And what was this on this paper, which the prosecution refused to allow anyone to inspect? But it was hopeless, and O'Connor was found guilty. The speech O'Connor made to the court before he was sentenced was eloquent on the concern for the miseries of the poor that had driven him to become a Defender. He did not attempt to justify himself. He talked instead of the great and understandable resentment of tithes collected from Catholics for the support of comfortable Protestant clergy (a subject on which his namesake Arthur O'Connor had dwelt at length in his speech in the House of Commons earlier in the year). He dwelt on rack rents, landlords who refused land for cottages, the exorbitant rent asked for small potato plots, the utter wretchedness of peasant life.

O'Connor's trial, however, is worth remembering not only for the selflessness of his pleading, nor for the professional skills of McNally in court, but for one rather 'Irish' exchange between Judge Finucane and himself:

Judge Finucane interrupted the prisoner by saying that *he* at least 'had always let his lands to cottagers, and not to men who relet them to rack renters, by which his tenants prospered'. 'God bless your Lordship for that!' exclaimed O'Connor; 'you will yet feel the benefit of it; but you must allow there are few rich men like yourself in the country'. McNally told the story that O'Connor had been offered a provision for his family if he would make discoveries [i.e. give names of other Defenders). He answered, 'He who feeds the young ravens in the valley, will provide for them'.*

O'Connor was convicted, and the ancient, complete sentence for high treason was carried out to the letter by direct order of the Lord-Lieutenant:[2]

prisoner to be drawn to the place of execution, the gallows, and there be hung up by the neck, but being yet alive, should be cut down, his bowels be taken out and burned before his face, his head be severed from his body, his body to be divided into four quarters, and his head and body to be disposed of at the King's pleasure.[3]

Although O'Connor had been decapitated 'with no great dexterity', his head was then fixed on top of an iron spike seven feet long, and exhibited on top of the prison wall for a few days.

Thoughts of a similarly bloody end after a trial for his treason did enter Tone's head occasionally, though the shame of it, as we shall see at the end, made him queasier than the agony.

Within a week of his landing at Wilmington in early August, he was in touch with Rowan at Philadelphia (then the capital of America). Rowan had helped to arrange a meeting with the French Minister to the United States, Pierre Adet. Tone took with him 'the two votes of the Catholics, engraved on vellum, and my certificate of admission into the Belfast Volunteers', by way of credentials. Adet asked him to write a memorial on the state of Ireland, a familiar task, which nevertheless took him two or three uncomfortable days. It was his first experience of 'the burning heat of the climate, so different from what I had been used to, the thermometer varying between ninety and ninety-seven'.

But Adet did not, at this time, take him up on his proposals.[4] Tone waited for weeks and began to believe that he could do no more for Ireland. A little later, however, he began to write *The Memoirs of the*

---

* This is as quoted both in Lecky's *History* (iii, p. 392) and in Fitzpatrick's *The Secret Service under Pitt* (p. 181). But surely it should read 'He *whom the young ravens feed* in the valley . . .': a suitably messianic reference to Elijah? 'He went and dwelt by the brook Cherith, that is before Jordan. And the ravens brought him bread and flesh in the morning, and bread and flesh in the evening; and he drank of the brook.' (I Kings, 17:5.) O'Connor was referring to the tradition that Elijah would return to earth to proclaim the coming of the Messiah.

Catholic Committee, and worked out the money that a 'large octavo volume with a copious appendix' might earn him. This refuge in literary work never to see the light of day was reported to Dublin. Informers were everywhere. McNally reported to the Government, with apparent satisfaction: 'Study is his object and he is preparing a work for the press.'[5]

Meanwhile, Tone was restless. He did not like Americans. He found the unadulterated pursuit of money, the mercantile spirit which pervaded all their conversation, uncongenial. The aristocracy, or rather plutocracy, and the corruption reminded him of those aspects of the Protestant Ascendancy that most disgusted him at home. There may have been many hundred coffee-shops, but where was there any theatre, any gaiety? It was a far cry from the more civilized entertainments of Dublin.

He cast round for a small plantation, somewhere which would be cheaper and more agreeable, a better place for his wife and children. At one time he was tempted to become a frontiersman. Land would be cheap. But unlike Fitzgerald, he was not attracted by the Indians. Hardly surprising – their raids were fierce and merciless, savage nobility not much in evidence. He wrote to Russell, 'As I have no great talent for the tomahawk, I have given up going into the woods'. Still, farming might serve as a *métier*.[6]

> I made divers excursions, on foot and in the stage-wagons, in quest of a farm ... at length I agreed with a Captain Leonard for a plantation of 180 acres, beautifully situated within two miles of Princeton, and half of it under timber. I was to pay £1180 for it ... Then I moved my family to Princeton, where I hired a small house for the winter, which I furnished frugally and decently. I fitted up my study, and began to think my lot was cast to be an American farmer.[7]

Princeton was then a handsome small town of some eighty dwellings and a Presbyterian church. And the College meant that there was some civilized company. Tone was susceptible to the beauty of the countryside and the town was set 'in picturesque wooded surroundings, with large black walnut trees and plantations of Italian mulberries for the culture of silk-worms. The area was also noted for its abundance of partridge and wood pigeon, and for its cider presses.'[8]

His preparations for farming sound rather lost and desperate; he wrote letters to Russell requesting quantities of furze seed, Lucerne seed, sainfoin, haw stones and a gardening dictionary. He had hoped by the spring to have moved to his small estate and begun farming at last. He was not however whole-hearted about his new career. He talks of being roused from his lethargy by letters from many of his friends, including Keogh and Russell, stimulating him with news that the mood of republicanism in Ireland was growing. They pressed him to 'fill the engagement he had made with them at his departure and to move heaven and earth to force my way to the French Government, in order to supplicate assistance'. Thus, Keogh's letter recalled him to the solemn promise he had made that day they had climbed to the top of M'Arts Fort and sworn an oath 'never to desist in our efforts until we had subverted the authority of England over our country, and asserted her independence'. His compact with the Government was of lesser concern, as has been remarked:

> A man of high and delicate honour, who had left his country under such circumstances, would have considered himself under a tacit obligation. Such feelings, however are very rarely found among men who have once drunk the intoxicating cup of political conspiracy.[9]

Whatever Tone's reservations about life in the States, America's successful war of independence, only twenty years previously, was always before his eyes, an ever-present example of what might be won for Ireland.

In October, a second visit to Adet (who was now impatient to wean his Government away from making accommodations with Britain) gained him letters to the Minister's masters in Paris, together with money and plans for an early sailing to France. This was a surprising triumph. By late autumn, Tone was spending a day back in Philadelphia with Rowan and 'my old friend and fellow-sufferer' Napper Tandy, who, after a long concealment and many adventures, was recently arrived from Hamburg.

> On the 13th December at night I arrived at Princeton, whither Rowan accompanied me, bringing with me a few presents for my wife, sister, and our dear little babies. That night we supped together in high spirits, and Rowan retiring immediately after, my wife, sister, and I, sat together till very late, engaged in that kind of animated and enthusiastic conversation to which our characters, and the nature of the enterprise I was engaged in, may be supposed to give rise. The courage and firmness of the women supported me; we had neither tears nor lamentations . . . at length, at four

the next morning I embraced them both for the last time, and we parted with a steadiness which astonished me.[10]

While waiting ship in New York a few days later, at the very end of the year, he wrote 'continually' to his family. Their hardihood does seem extraordinary:

> a day or two before my departure I received a letter from my wife, inform-ing me she was with child, a circumstance which she had concealed so far, I am sure, lest it might have had some influence on my determination.[11]

He sailed on New Year's Day 1796, with nine fellow passengers, all French, bound for Le Havre.

As soon as Rowan had arrived in America he wrote letters to his wife which were, at first, faintly reassuring. But only faintly; reservations can be read between every line:

> Were it not for the terrors of the sea, I would to God you were out here. The changes from heat to cold are certainly to us, Europeans, very terrible; but, upon the whole, it is a fine country, and there are great opportunities for settling a young brood; and, although expensive, we could get some place in the country, and be very happy.[12]

He talked of his irksome situation in a house crowded by captains of ships, 'each more impertinently inquisitive than the other'. Little of this could have made Mrs Rowan easy in her mind, especially as many of his letters seem less than tactful. For example, he talked of his seeing Tone, and of messing with Tandy (who lodged in the same house), although he knew that his wife disapproved of him. Nor would his very next, well-meaning, sentence have raised her spirits: 'I need not tell you that his society does not make up for what I have lost . . . I have seen but one handsome woman since I came here; and she is from Shropshire, and something like the wife of A.H. Rowan.'[13]

Mrs Rowan's letters were, however, much more chilling than her husband's. He had found a bundle of them, one containing her picture, waiting for him on his arrival. Soon other, long letters fol-lowed, urging him to abstain from all politics, for which she thought him dangerously unfitted. She congratulated her 'best beloved' on his overdue conversion to saner counsels:

It is with the highest satisfaction that I learn your residence in France has so altered your opinions on political subjects. It would have been well, most certainly, had this happy change been brought about at a less price than it cost you . . . No person, indeed, who knew you well, could doubt that when you were removed from those whose interest it was to deceive you, both your head and heart would lead you to see things, as you now do, in their true colours . . . if you stay quietly where you are, and do not meddle with politics, which I am sure you will not, all will be well . . . Reynolds and Tone are not exactly the people you ought to make your constant companions; though there is no reason for absolutely shunning even Tone; however, you ought to beware of him, and I hope he will not again fall in your way . . .[14]

Leading-strings stretched all the way across the Atlantic. But evidently Rowan did talk often with Tone. He had introduced him to the Governor, given him that letter of recommendation to the French Minister Adet. Rowan shared Tone's dislike of the all-pervasive culture of money-making, and wrote:

I do not promise to remain here; indeed I cannot, disgusted as I am with the rough manners of the people; the great expense of procuring those mental gratifications which are so superior to eating and drinking; the universal rage of money-getting . . . [and, later,] What would you propose to yourself in this country, where, if I had a child unchristened, whom I would wish to be caressed, I would call him DOLLAR![15]

But the other side of the coin was his grateful acknowledgement of that wonderful, perennial New World virtue of hospitality:

I have met with more than civilities; I have met with a degree of friendship which I could not have conceived. The Governor, General Mifflin, has been particularly attentive; he says I am melancholy, and will drive me out of it; that I am formal, and he will not be treated with formality.

Governor Mifflin took him down to the river to shoot reed-birds 'supposed by some of our epicures to equal the ortolans of Europe'.[16] As the autumn went by, Rowan asked everyone for advice on what he should do. There was no question of his returning to Ireland; he was a refugee, an outlaw. He hated dependency. He had forsworn continued rebellion, after his recent experiences in France. By the end of the year, with more resignation than Tone, he decided, if he had to remain in America, to 'go to the woods', whatever the dangers. Decency, as usual, as well as the desire for independence, prompted him:

> Now let me assure you, that I am acting quite by myself, and contrary to advice; for one wants me to remain in Philadelphia, and another, to buy a small farm in a settled country. But I will do neither; I will go to the woods; but I will not kill Indians, nor keep slaves. Good God! if you heard some of the Georgians, or the Kentucky people, talk of killing the natives! Cortés, and all that followed him, were not more sanguinary in the South, than they would be in North America.[17]

And who will blame him if, occasionally, he allowed himself a small sting in the tail of his letters? Mrs Rowan, so many of whose lectures he had to endure, might not have been amused when she read in a letter early in the following year, after her husband had spent six lonely months in America, that

> last night at a little ball I was under the necessity of twice refusing the hands of two young ladies, who, by their uncle and father, had asked me to dance. After that, have I a right to complain of my situation in this country? or, rather, ought you not to be a little jealous of your husband?[18]

'Reform' was the natural banner under which to beat an honourable retreat from the tented field of revolution, whether for Rowan, pursued in his days of exile by the thin-lipped strictures of Mrs Rowan, or for Drennan, still bruised by the experience of a trial that might so easily have earned him a long imprisonment (or even worse).

We have seen how Rowan stood:

> As to my sentiments they have been nearly always the same, as far as I can remember. The fact is, that from education and principle, I was led to assert, and attempt to support a reform of parliament, and equal liberty to all religious sects. *Association* [clearly referring to Tone and/or Tandy] may have, and certainly did lead me into more active life than I wished for, or will ever, in any case on this side of eternity, fall into again.[19]

Drennan felt very much the same. One thinks of the 'demure doctor', imagining the ghost of his father over his shoulder, urging him on with study of Tacitus' *Annals*, and of Cicero's speeches inveighing against extortion and tyranny.[20] Drennan certainly read; but there is no evidence of any revolutionary sentiment, let alone activity, during this latter half of 1795. The letters do not lack reference to high aims, but they are most respectable ones: a new institute for educating poor girls, a suitable inscription for his brother-in-law's tomb (Sam McTier had died near Inverary in summer). It is all a far cry from those of two and a half years earlier, when he had felt able to write to McTier: 'All you can do is to get as many arms as possible smuggled into the country. Let every man have a firelock in country and in town, that if ever anything requires their use, an army may start up at once'.

Reform, at least, could continue to be argued, however many spies were about. It may still be hard fully to comprehend the intensity of indignation which the spectacle of jobbery (that is, every kind of casual, unashamed buying and rigging of votes, inside and out of Parliament) aroused in the breast of Irishmen of principle at the end of the eighteenth century. It was a running, everyday sore, before which recent scandals pale.

Maria Edgeworth's novels, set in these years, catch something of the contemporary scorn for the corruption of political life. A character in her *Ormond* recites at dinner a lampoon in which the slippery Sir Ulick O'Shane, caricature of an Ascendancy place-seeker and jobber, is contrasted with the unreconstructed man of honour, the Catholic 'King' of islands off the West Coast, 'King Corny'.

> To serve in Parliament the nation,
> Sir Ulick read his recantation;
> At first he joined the *patriot* throng,
> But soon perceived he was wrong,
> He ratted to the courtier tribe,
> Bought by a title and a bribe;
> But how that new-found friend to bribe
> With any oath, of any kind
> Disturbed the Premier's wary mind.
> *'Upon his faith – upon his word'?*
> Oh! that, my friend, is too absurd . . .[21]

Drennan never lost his distrust of Catholics who hoped to advance their political careers by recanting from their beliefs. Martha McTier wrote a letter to him one day in autumn:

old Lord Kenmare said 'it was much for the interest of both govt. and country that the Catholic Lords should remain unconverted, as a link in the chain and a useful interest with the lower orders, over whom they would lose all influence if they change their religion, the bad effects of which appeared so transparent that he wished, unless it was for conscience sake, they might not change'. I agreed with him, that they should take care of the remaining links, for I feared there were but few left.[22]

He seemed to share his sister's sentiments. Not only did he despise the easy, self-seeking changecoat; he also preferred dealing with Catholics of rank than with the lower orders.

Another disease was eating at the doctor's soul during these months: the besetting canker of suspicion. Not that one can blame Drennan for the feeling that he was constantly watched. It was all too probable. His letters were innocuous, yet betrayed more and more unease:

Do you know that there is a society of 'staunch friends' in this place who have one of their members stationed in every coffee house, in every literary newsroom, in every club to report conversations and to denounce names to the Castle? Many of these are directed to talk as they choose and have received a plenary indulgence . . .[23]

In writing about an outbreak of rioting among some of the regiments he talked of 'Government spies endeavouring to trap as many as they can who speak to the soldiers . . . Regiments, reduced to 100 in number, have shown symptoms of mutiny . . . [soldiers] were to be either flogged or sent in to the transports, handcuffed, tomorrow.'[24]

In a mood of sorrowful reflection rather than revolution, Drennan published in 1795 his best-known poem, 'Erin', in which he was proud of having coined the phrase 'the Emerald Isle'. Disarmingly, he wrote: 'It may appear puerile to lay claim to a priority in the use of an epithet, but poets, like bees, have a very strong sense of property.' He might not, however, have been pleased to see how future generations failed to endorse his poem's two most-quoted lines:

> Nor one feeling of vengeance presume to defile
> The cause, or the men, of the Emerald Isle.[25]

In September 1795, a terrible act of sectarian savagery between agrarian Defenders and Protestant Peep O'Day Boys took place at the Diamond in County Armagh. This was immediately followed by the formation of the Orange Society, from which Orange Lodges are descended. There is no telling whether Drennan wrote 'Erin' before or after this pitched battle. Twenty or thirty men were left dead on the field.*

While Drennan was seeking refuge in mournful verse, in quiet advocacy of reform, Fitzgerald was advancing on the opposite course, towards revolution and rebellion. Would reform, or a republic, ever be achieved without *real* revolution? It did not seem likely.

Contemporary descriptions of the state of mounting insurrection in Ulster sound very fearful: tumults, riots, plunders, murders. The Attorney-General stated in the House early in 1796 that he was sorry to say that 'conspiracies to murder were frequent now, and the idea of assassination as familiar as fowling'.[26]

Mr Serjeant Stanley described life in the province of Connaught, where so many of those chased from their homes in Armagh, Tyrone and County Down had fled:

> the spirit of Insurgency was not that of a private or a mere constructive nature, but shewed itself in open Rebellion, bodies of insurgents marched in array through the country, and offered battle to the King's troops; others of them attacked and plundered of arms . . . another body stormed the iron works at Arigna, put the workmen into a state of requisition, and obliged them to make Pikes, Spears and other Weapons.[27]

In the same debate, John Rochfort, the Member for Coleraine, thoughtfully 'did not wish to violate the feelings of the House by a detail of the horrors committed in the County where he resided':

> In many cases the miscreants styling themselves Defenders attacked people's houses in the dead hour of night, tied ropes round their necks to force out their tongues, which they cut off to prevent their informing – and in some instances where persons had been induced to prosecute these miscreants they were dragged out of their beds at night, found tied together on a dung hill, and fired at like marks, till shot to death.[28]

Fitzgerald attended the session when the introduction of the Insurrection Act was debated. He was the only Member of Parliament to vote against it. His speech was brief:

---

* In fact, it is now accepted that the Catholics were the undoubted aggressors at the Battle of the Diamond. But outrages in Ulster at the time were boundless on both sides. For a brief account of the savage battle see Lecky, *History of Ireland*, iii, pp. 425ff.

The Bill appeared to him a violent, unnecessary and useless violation of the liberty of the subject – and was also one of the most vague Bills he had ever heard read in Parliament – there was no man, not even a lawyer, who could attach a meaning to the phrase 'tumultuous risings' and yet on 'tumultuous risings' penalties the most severe were attached.[29]

Later, on the second reading, we are told that 'Lord Edward Fitzgerald declared his opposition to it in the same open and manly manner as he had done on a former occasion'.[30] (In passing, the editor of the *Register* allows himself occasional mild ironies, such as 'observed, in a speech of some length', 'drew an elegant and affecting picture, and would beg leave as one of the humblest of the college', and so forth; I read 'manly manner' as one such euphemism.)

Some at least of the rampages would have been known to Fitzgerald from accounts of neighbours in County Kildare. Indeed his uncle Thomas Conolly confirmed 'the alarming Spirit of Insurgency', and added that if a member wished for proof of the necessity of the Bill, he himself would call for the attendance of the widows and orphans who had been left to survive the crimes and outrages of those miscreants who had disgraced the country'.[31]

Every night, indeed, brought fresh atrocities. Why, then, did Fitzgerald see fit to cast his solitary vote against the Bill? It may be some slight extenuation that the Attorney-General himself, in introducing it, had admitted that parts of it were repugnant to his feeling. It was a 'bloody, penal code'. But 'the Act now in force against administering of illegal oaths was not sufficiently strong and was the source of all the treasonable acts which had taken place in this country; this should now be 'a felony of death'. All arms were to be registered. No one could emerge from their houses or cabins when it was dark. And a clause to empower magistrates to take up all idle vagrants and persons who had no visible means of earning livelihood, and send them to serve aboard the fleet, gave them freedom with impunity to bundle suspicious persons into transportation for life.[32]

Fitzgerald's single, dissenting vote may perhaps be regarded as a badge of revolution rather than any objection in principle to the harshness of the Act. He was brutal in general judgements, sentimental in particular ones: a common and unsatisfactory combination. It may be one reason why many of his fellows (as well as the editor of the *Register*) failed to take him altogether seriously.

His eyes were on France. That may be another explanation of his vote. He was one of those Irishmen referred to in the debate as 'anxious to pluck the Diadem from the Temples of Royalty, in order to invest themselves with something like the Sway of Robespierre'.[33] The more terrible the tumult in his own country, the easier it might be successfully to solicit an invasion from France. Then would come the longed-for separation from England, an independent Republic – and Liberty at last.

This was the mission on which Fitzgerald was soon to embark, in the late spring of 1796.

12

French connections

I am, I flatter myself, completely a citizen of the world. In my travels through Holland, Germany, Switzerland, Italy, Corsica, France, I never felt myself from home.

Boswell, *Tour to the Hebrides*

Lord Edward Fitzgerald's expedition to Switzerland and France in the spring and summer of 1796 had two faces. One brings to mind Thomas Cooke, the other Baroness Orczy. They are not incompatible. Each may contain many elements of truth, and is founded on record.

Both Fitzgerald and Arthur O'Connor had, at last, been enrolled as members of the reconstituted version of the Society of United Irishmen early in the New Year, and were sanctioned to seek help from the French Directory for an early invasion of Ireland. Thus they were now indisputably plotting high treason, rather than merely making fiery speeches in Parliament. They did not find justification too hard. Any crime perpetrated in the name of liberty was excusable in the aftermath of the French Revolution. (It is worth remarking that the fifth-century Athenian tyrannicides, Harmodius and Aristogeiton, invoked by William Drennan in the frontispiece to his *Orellana*, were also invoked by Dr Priestley in a letter he wrote to Fitzgerald's mother.)

By May, Fitzgerald and his wife had crossed to London. They explained their proposal for their planned expedition to the Continent on the grounds that Pamela was expecting their second child and they wished to visit her foster-mother in Hamburg. While in London the couple naturally moved in the most aristocratic of Whig circles. The daughter whom Pamela was expecting* recounts a family tale of one dinner in particular:

> My Mother told me that when they were going to Hamburg in 1796 she supped at Devonshire House, and the Duke of York took her in to supper, and speaking kindly about my father and regretting the course of politics, he at last said: 'Allow me to advise you as a friend most seriously, use your influence, your whole influence, to deter Lord Edward from going abroad. More is known of the plans of those he thinks his friends than you can imagine, in short,' he added, 'all is known.'
> She tried on returning home to persuade him to give up Hamburg, but she did not succeed, and early in May they sailed, ostensibly so that my Mother might visit Madame de Genlis and her niece . . . who had married a Hamburg merchant; but in reality, I fear to meet Hoche or Pichegru, the French Republican Generals.[1]

It is fair to assume that, although Fitzgerald was careful *not* to travel to Hamburg in company with the 'twin of his soul', both his and O'Connor's efforts at concealing their movements and purposes were at best casual. Fitzgerald enjoyed disguises, but rather more in the manner of amateur theatricals than of serious espionage.

Ensconced in Hamburg by June, Fitzgerald visited Reinhard, the French Minister to the Hanseatic League, whose acquaintance he had made earlier in the 1790s when he was serving in the French legation in London. Reinhard was an intelligent and civilized man, who at one time corresponded with Goethe, and who, on his death, was eulogized by Talleyrand. He was said to be master of five languages.

Fitzgerald reminded him of his 1792 visit to Paris; his speech which had led to his cashiering from the army; his discussions with Eleazer Oswald on the ways and means for the French to discover the lie of the land in Ireland. Then, the French republic was still young, barely out of its swaddling-clothes. Now it was strong and growing in power; and Ireland was ripe for insurrection. Discontent there was universal. Recall of the Lord-Lieutenant who was to bring salvation to Ireland, Lord Fitzwilliam, had been a crowning disappointment for the majority. A French expedition could not fail to carry all before it. He, Fitzgerald himself, would gladly risk a journey

---

* The Fitzgeralds christened their children after themselves: one son, Edward, always called 'Little Eddy', and a daughter, 'Pammy' or 'Pamy'.

to Paris, if necessary, to conduct detailed negotiations. He talked of 150,000 men eventually rising, of 10,000 Defenders already armed and waiting. Cannon, guns and gunpowder were needed, it was true. Until the French arrived a scantily armed people could do little. Irish priests would be no trouble, might even assist the invaders. Thomas Paine could be relied on to help plan the internal organization.

Reinhard had the measure of Fitzgerald. He reported to his master in Paris that

> he was a young man incapable of falsehood or perfidy, frank, energetic and likely to be a useful and devoted instrument, but with no experience or extraordinary talent and entirely unfit to be chief of a great party, or leader in a difficult enterprise.[2]

On the other hand, Reinhard was very much more impressed when, a few weeks later, he held a conversation with O'Connor, whom he represented to his Foreign Minister as one of the first orators in Ireland, a politician of great position and weight, altogether a far abler man. O'Connor was very good at making himself seem a man of formidable authority, and now he added further powerful arguments in support of invasion. He said he had recently travelled widely in the North, and found the Dissenters there even more determined to rebel than the Catholics of the South. The militia would side with the people. Cork, Waterford, and even Dublin might be seized. Yes – guns, munitions, artillery officers and a few troops were certainly needed. But that was all. 'We only need your help in the first moment; it is in your clear interest to give it.' An insurrection in Ireland would make it impossible for England to continue the war. The fleet, so many of whose sailors were Irishmen, would mutiny. There were, furthermore, fewer than 12,000 English troops of decent fighting quality stationed in Ireland.[3]

Finally, O'Connor announced that he hoped to travel secretly with Fitzgerald to Paris. He had told his friends in London that he was going on a tour in Switzerland (the word 'tour' occurs often in accounts of this episode). He hoped that Barthélemy, the French Minister in Basle, would be able to issue the appropriate permission; they intended, for the sake of cover, to travel through Switzerland, taking a holiday *en route*.

Reinhard appears to have had all doubts dispelled. Even although O'Connor's representations had the greater weight, he was convinced of the truthfulness of Fitzgerald, even to saying that he would answer for the sincerity of Fitzgerald with his head. His honour was clearly unimpeachable, even if his talent and authority needed some reinforcement.

One is reminded, as so often in following Fitzgerald's adventures, of his aunt Louisa's judgement after his death: 'his natural, charming and excellent character that has gained him so many friends that those who differ most in sentiment from him, lament more than blame – oh, what dreadful times we do live in'.[4]

News of the mission of Fitzgerald and O'Connor, sent to the Directory via Reinhard, never reached the ears of Tone, even when he was deep in discussions with the French Government. Hints, cryptic or garbled, were sometimes made, though. Once, Tone was stupefied to find it suggested that *Fitzgibbon* might be a useful contact for a French army of invasion: surely a slip for Fitzgerald!

At first, however, Tone's own mission to France went better than he could have dared to hope. Within days of his arrival in Paris on 12 January, the American Ambassador James Monroe received him courteously and openly, made friendly enquiries about Rowan, and gave him introductions to men in power. At one visit Monroe suggested that he must not be fobbed off by dealing only with underlings like Nicholas Madgett; that was a *subaltern* way of doing business.

Madgett was the Kerryman in the French Affairs Ministry who dealt with such things as passports, *noms de guerre*. He had given Rowan the name of Thomson; now he dubbed Tone Smith. But confined to looking after Irish affairs, Madgett was of little real importance. Tone soon confided his growing disillusion to his diary: 'Madgett has the slowness of age, and at present the gout, about him.' On another occasion, confronted with his fussiness: 'Madgett's scheme is just like my countryman's, who got on a horse-back in the packet [-boat], in order to make more haste.'[5]

Tone was gratified soon to find himself given audiences with the great Carnot, the so-called 'Organiser of Victory' and one of the three members of the Directory. Plans for invasion seemed on the verge of taking off in February. Discussions were mostly about the size of any French contribution. Would they need 5,000 men or 20,000? Ten sail of the line or twenty? Should they attempt landings near Belfast, if the force was only modest? Head straight for Dublin with an army of 20,000?

Early hopes faded as Tone was shunted from pillar to post. His first impressions of General Clarke,* to whom Carnot had sent him on, changed to annoyance, distrust. He was asked to write memorandum after memorandum. Some were lost by Madgett, others left untranslated or unread for days. One project, urged upon him, came up time and again. This was to disgorge bands of Irish prisoners, held by the French after being captured in English ships, into the countryside of Ireland to foment disturbances: in imitation of the royalist risings, or *chouannerie*, of an estimated 100,000 rebels in the west of France that had created so much trouble for the Republic. (The 'chouans' were so called after the nickname of their leader, who imitated the screech-owl or *chat-houant* as a signal to his followers.) Tone urged, with irony, the futility of such a diversion: Clarke should abandon

> the old scheme of debauching the Irish prisoners. His idea is, that they should be put aboard privateers, and landed in various part of Ireland . . . this is the six-and-fiftieth time I have given my opinion on this head, yet he [Madgett] still returns to the charge. I know the Irish a little. The way to manage them is this: If they intend to use the Irish prisoners, let them be marched down under other pretences to the port from whence the embarkation is to be made. When everything else is ready, let them send in a large quantity of wine and brandy, a fiddle and some French *filles*, and then, when Pat's heart is a little soft with love and wine, send in two or three proper persons in regimentals, and with green cockades in their hats, to speak to them, of whom I will gladly be one. I think, in that case, it would not be very hard to persuade him to take a trip once more to Ireland, just to see his people a little.[6]

Like 'Pat', Tone solaced his cares with drink. And he was lonely. He longed for the company of Russell:

> St Patrick's Day. Dined *alone* in the Champs Elysées. Sad! Sad! . . . If I had had the pleasure of PP's company, we should, indeed, [have taken] a sprig of water-cresses with our bread [an unusual euphemism].[7]

Like 'Pat', too, he was easily transported by ladies, especially theatrical ladies. One thinks of his first love in Galway, Eliza, the 'neglected' wife of Richard Martin. Now, in Paris:

---

* Clarke was half-Irish, thirty years old and officially head of the War Ministry's *Bureau Topographique et Historique Militaire*. Later he was created Duke of Feltre by Napoleon in acknowledgement of his campaign in the Veneto in 1799. Tone understood him to be in charge of all military operations.

It is inconceivable (I lie, I lie, it is not at all inconceivable) the effect which the admiration or contempt of a woman has on the spirit of a man. Hector, when he is balancing in his mind whether he shall stand or fight before Achilles, is determined by the consideration of what the Trojan ladies shall say of him: – 'Troy's proud dames, whose garments sweep the ground'.[8]

Tone's martial ardour was thoroughly aroused in the theatre: he would dream of a glory he was set on fulfilling in real life after the curtain was rung down:

the performers [in the opera] were completely Grecian statues animated, and I never saw so manifestly the superiority of the taste of the ancients in dress, especially as regards the women. Iphigénie was dressed entirely in white without the least ornament, and nothing can be imagined more truly elegant and picturesque. The acting admirable, but the singing very inferior to that of the Kings' Theatre in the Haymarket. The French cannot sing like the Italian . . . Achilles sang in the old French style which is destestable, shaking and warbling on every note: vile! vile! vile! . . . one incident crowned the whole. At the repetition of the words *aux armes, citoyens* the music changed again to a martial style, the performers sprung on their feet, and in an instant the stage was filled with national guards, who rushed in with bayonets fixed, sabres drawn, and the tri-colour flag flying . . . *I never knew what enthusiasm was before.*[9]

Love of the theatre sat naturally with his love of uniforms and dressing-up, and Paris in 1796 gave Tone plenty of scope. He was delighted by the Guards in the Tuileries – 'their uniform blue, faced white, red cape, cuffs and shoulder knots, plumes in their hats, with white belts, vests and breeches, black stocks and gaiters'. He was amused by the style of the Foreign Minister Charles De La Croix – 'a respectable-looking man with very much the air of a bishop . . . he was dressed today in a grey silk robe-de-chambre, under which he wore a kind of scarlet cassock of satin, with rose-coloured silk stockings, and scarlet ribands in his shoes.' And Carnot 'appeared in the petit-costume of white satin with crimson robe, richly embroidered. It is very elegant, and resembles almost exactly the draperies of Vandyke.'[10]

Such vanities extended to an ingenuous delight in converting his own role into theatre. He sometimes seems to pinch himself to check that his part was real, however serious he knew his ambition to be:

I am a pretty fellow to negotiate with the Directory of France; to pull down a monarchy and to establish a republic, to break a connection of 300 years standing, and contract a fresh alliance with another country! . . . I have not got my commission yet, and it will be quite time enough when I am Colonel to dream of being an Ambassador. A Colonel of horse in the service of the Republic! Is it not most curious . . . eighteen months ago it was a million to one that I should be hanged as a traitor, and now I am like to enter the country in which I was not worthy to live, at the head of a regiment of horse. It is singular.[11]

When he switched to such play-acting he gave pleasure to others as well as to himself; and some of the dark clouds that hung over his impatience to get into battle momentarily lifted. He was even able, on these occasions, to treat the detested schemes for *chouannerie*, on which the Government seemed so 'plaguy fond', with a light heart. He describes an interview in June with General Clarke, who obviously knew his man. First of all he told Tone the good news that within a month the Irishman might expect an appointment in the French army. Action at last seemed near:

I then asked him, if he had many prisoners remaining, as I thought they might be usefully employed in case of the landing being effected. He laughed at this, and said, 'I see you want to form your regiment.' I said I should like very well to command two or three hundred of them, who might be formed into a corps of Hussars, to serve in the advanced guard of the army, not only as soldiers, but as éclaireurs to *insense* the country people. He seemed to relish this a good deal, and I went on to say that, in such case, they should be as an Irish corps in green jackets, with green feathers, and a green standard with the harp, surmounted by the cap of liberty. He bit at this, and made me draw a sketch of the device, and also a description, which he took down himself in French, from which I infer the standard will be made directly.

After five months of delay, he was still hoping, making plans and changes of plan. There was plenty more of this to come. When *would* the invasion begin? And meanwhile he was down 'to his last louis'.

The iridescent gaiety of Tone's writing in the face of endless delay seems to come from whistling to keep his spirits up, and trying in his imagnation to comfort his dear, far-away, wife Matilda. But the gaiety conceals the canker of suspicion. This may be fair enough in the circumstances, even if it is a vice shared neither by Fitzgerald, with his aristocratic preference for outright expression of his opinions (and be done with it), nor by Rowan, with his gentlemanly reluctance to think ill of others.

Such suspicion can be sudden, irrational and as irreversible as malice. We see it at Tone's meeting with De La Croix at the end of February. When he arrived at the Foreign Office in the rue du Bacq, he found the Minister engaged with Neri Corsini, envoy of the Grand Duke of Tuscany. Tone writes:

> I waited accordingly in the antechamber. A person came in, and after reconnoitring me for some time, pulled out an English newspaper and began to read it. Looked at him with the most interesting indifference, as if he was reading a chapter in the Koran. Did the fellow think I would rise at such a bait as that? Neri Corsini being departed, I was introduced, leaving my friend in the antechamber to study his newspaper.[12]
>
> . . . I [told De La Croix I] kept the most rigid guard on myself; that I formed no connections, nor desired to know any one . . . he said I was very right, and asked me, did I know the person in the antechamber? I answered, I did not. He said he was an Irish patriot, named Duchet (as he pronounced it,) who was persecuted into exile for some writing under the signature of *Junius Redivivus* . . . I mentioned the circumstance of his pulling out an English newspaper, and setting me a trap therewith, and how I avoided falling into his snare. The Minister said again, I was quite right, but that person had delivered in several memorials on the state of Ireland. This is very odd! I never saw the man in my life, and yet I rather imagine he knew my person. Who the devil is Junius Redidivus? or who is Duchet, if his name is Duchet? I must talk a little to Madgett on this resurrection of Junius, of which, to speak the truth, I have no good opinion.[13]

The suspicious (and suspected) man was William Duckett, whom ever afterwards Tone regarded as a rascally adventurer, probably an informer, certainly to be avoided. In fact, the newspaper reader was a Kerryman intermittently in the pay of the Minister of the Marine, a more or less ordinary ex-student of the Irish Theological College turned fervent revolutionist, and as dedicated as Tone himself. He had been among the guests at the famous dinner at White's.

An eye had been kept on him by the Foreign Office in London as one of the 'parcel of young fellows just escaped from the seminary'. Together with his companions he had been arrested in London but had been let go as too green to be dangerous. Nor would his few subsequent articles in the *Morning Chronicle*, for all their high-flown invective, greatly have alarmed Ministers – even if they did lead to his exile:

> the millions slain in the fields of Belgium . . . the industrious Youth of the Provinces dragged from the Plough and shipped off by *hundreds*, to oppose in a strange and hostile country, the enthusiastic movements of an ARMED NATION . . . argue forcibly the ignorance and wickedness of the Minister; for wicked and corrupt must that man be, who sacrifices to his pride and obstinacy the lives of one class of his fellow Citizens, while he wantonly sports with the fortunes of the other etc., etc.[14]

Duckett was, however, nurturing dangerous schemes that were bound to attract distrust. No one in his life seems to have given him any credit for loyalty. Generally his plans involved double-dealing, pretence, false information, subterfuge of all sorts. His main ambition was to wean Irish sailors away from their allegiance to the Crown. Still, had Duckett enjoyed greater success then – bearing in mind that Irish sailors probably accounted for about a quarter of the lower deck – he might indeed have dented the legendary English sea-supremacy. On the face of it, was the French Directory so misguided in using Duckett as Tone thought it to be? (One cannot say for certain how much credit Duckett should be given for the mutinies at Spithead and the Nore in May 1797.) In another conversation with the Foreign Minister Tone talks of

> the old scheme of debauching the British navy, which seems a favourite scheme of De La Croix, and is, in my mind, flat nonsense . . . he then mentioned that it would be necessary to send proper persons to Ireland to give notice to the people there of what was intended. I answered, one person was sufficient. He asked me 'Oh, you know Duckett?' (the fellow who pulled out the English newspaper to decoy me). I answered I knew nothing at all about him.[15]

If Duckett earned Tone's dislike for the crudity of this decoy, Duckett for his part resented Tone's airs. We see something reminiscent of William Paulet Carey's touchiness against the 'Law and Physic'. Is this an aspect of *class* – the instant taking of offence at slights, real or imagined, when delivered by 'superiors'? After the end of the 1798 Rebellion, Duckett wrote in disgust that the French should never again place their faith in upper-class United leaders, who had deceived France and the Irish people alike. To others, too, the high politics of the United Irish movement became irrelevant to the crisis developing in Ireland.[16]

Trusting immediate acquaintances, despising duplicity, Rowan was a most implausible suborner of others. He would have made an utter innocent in espionage, too (witness the imbroglio over the Reverend William Jackson). So it is an irony that he came near to being charged, in Philadelphia, with the craft of William Duckett: the seduction of British sailors from their allegiance.

This suspicion was groundless. He seems to have observed his promise to his wife to steer well away from political activity in America. He tells the tale in a letter later in the year:

> A severe charge might have been made against me, upon the most plausible grounds, viz. the encouragement of desertion in the British navy, by giving a certificate and recommendation to thirty or forty persons who said they had deserted from the fleet on this station. Luckily a gentleman in Maryland stopped the bearers and took the paper from them, knowing it not to be my handwriting. Having obliged them to confess that a schoolmaster in this town had forged it for them, he sent it to me. This would have been a charming story for my friends in your island . . .[17]

It was a doubly lucky escape since, had the false charge stuck, it might have blighted the splendid naval career of his son, Gavin William, who became a Captain and a Commander of the Bath.*

Rowan never overcame his dislike of American social life, grateful though he was for the general hospitality, and the particular kindness of one or two 'families with Quaker manners, but elegant withal': He writes to his wife:

> [America] is a heaven for the poor and industrious but a hell, compared to any part of Europe, for any other rank of society. The climate, the manners, the state of society, the pride and ignorance . . . are against all idlers coming here. Yet I wish you out of Ireland; I dread the moment when ignorance and despair there, without any one to appease or keep down the storm, may burst from their shackles:[18]

---

* Captain William Rowan Hamilton, RN (who reverted to the original – and present – ordering of the family name), spent large sums of his own money in emancipating numbers of Greeks who had fallen into Turkish hands; evidently he had inherited his father's generosity (and quixotry).

He found pitifully little company to his taste. Once he dined with the 'famous traveller Volney whom I much liked', but he formed very few friendships. Even after a year he was writing:

> I do not say, however, that there are no agreeable persons to be found; but they are so rare, and it is so nearly impossible to keep off the others, that I still think the woods the most eligible situation [that is, if his wife came to join him in exile]. But the woods with a young family will not be fair towards them.[19]

It is, as before, hard to judge whether he struck the right note in his continued attempts to reassure his wife about his conduct in the face of such loneliness. Did he indeed want her to be *wholly* reassured?

> the influx of French has been of no service to American female morals; and you know the French from the islands are always the most dissipated. I came down this country [from his farm] hoping to get a lodging in a house where I was disappointed, for there has been a death, a birth, and then a marriage, besides a runaway match in the same house. I can tell you nothing of the American ladies, as I have seen but few.[20]

In late April 1796 a letter quoted in his *Autobiography* reads a little more reassuringly. Perhaps his wife was pleased, this time, by the news of her husband's healthy outdoor exercise:

> I have bought a boat, which I hope will not be so much money thrown away; yet I must allow I begin to sicken at having four miles to walk to it in the morning, and the same distance in the evening. It is not like my excursions on the Seine, where I could row the whole day, and be within a short walk of my bed at night.[21]

One wonders sometimes if Mrs Rowan grew tired of her husband's obsession with boats. So much of his youth had been spent in or on rivers and seas. There are one or two echoes of 'improved' political beliefs, but his watery adventures always seem to come first:

> I continue faithful to my boat; but in this land of liberty nothing is understood of *yours* or *mine* in that way; so that my boat is nearly knocked to pieces by those who want to bring hay from their marsh, or onions from the Jerseys to market, or take sheep from the pasture; nay, while I was washing her out, and preparing for a fishing party, a man carried off my

oars and sail! There may be liberty here, and certainly the lowest class, when industrious (for there are poor here as well as with you, but not miserably so) have a fine field to work on for their advancement in life ... I return to my boat. I was extremely astonished at being broken in upon a person who still further excited my admiration by asking my leave to take the boat. The answer was, 'Yes, with pleasure'. 'But', replied he, 'she is full of dirt; how shall I get her cleaned?' By G——, he wanted me to go down and wash her out for him!!![22]

Rowan almost always behaved well to his fellows, and obeyed the dictates of fraternity, but his sense of *égalité* was more narrowly focused. The presumption of boors was too severe a test.

Rowan was prudent in his anxiety not to dip, or be seen to dip, his toes into political waters in America. But there was nothing he could do to prevent his becoming a folk hero in Ireland; he was rumoured to be the future Irish King about to come from over the water, heading an army of the French. Myths were woven round him. The Castle were keen for news – even gossip – about his intentions. Edward Cooke, the powerful Under-Secretary at the Castle, wrote a worried letter to Pelham about the United Irishmen's 'keenness in enlisting and embracing the Catholics':

They have intercourse with Rowan and other rebels in America and there is a report to which I give some credit that Rowan is coming from America to head them; this intelligence comes from a maid serving Dowling the attorney who says she has seen a letter to the purpose in her master's possession.[23]

And the Lord Chief Justice, Lord Clonmell, according to Drennan:

spoke for two hours yesterday [in delivering his sentence of hanging on College Green, on a boy of seventeen], and I hear the whole scope of his speech to the jury was in endeavouring to connect and weave together all the plots, privy conspiracies and seditions of this country into one mystic web, on which he inscribed the name of H. Rowan.[24]

For his part Drennan, still scalded after his trial for seditious libel, was also steering clear of anything to do with active politics. Irish nationalism may have been in his thoughts, but his letters and verse now contain few traces of revolutionary zeal. Gone are references to slavery, to tyrannicide in the name of liberty, to citizens taking arms. Now he turned more of his thoughts, like the good Presbyterian he (like his father) was, to the Christian religion. His instinctive mistrust of Catholicism, which always sat so awkwardly with his fervent United Irish belief in the necessity for the unity of the sects, shows itself in one letter to his sister in February. (This letter probably refers to a proposal for collaborating in a criticism of Paine and his *Age of Reason*.) Drennan writes with some magisterial irony, about those who held that Christianity was founded on *miracle*:

> the Romish church are consistently politic in, as it were, denouncing knowledge and debate and disquisition; for the restless power of reason, once introduced, brings in doubt, and is apt to beget incredulity in the place of that serene and all-confiding faith which makes everyone a Christian in exactly the same degree, and thus preserves the unity and the peace of the Church universal. Trust like a papist, for if you doubt as a dissenter, the same restless faculty that rejects the Athanasian Creed (which, by its so perfect exclusion of reason, is the fitter subject for measuring the capacity and sounding the depths of human credulity) will begin to nibble at the Incarnation, the Miraculous Conception, etc., and thus Priestley lifts the latch for Paine to enter.[25]

'Romish' is a giveaway. Drennan himself was comforted by his own '[liking of] the *morality* of the Gospel so well that I have not the least occasion for the supplementary proof of miracle'.

He had, however, by no means lost all his capacity for indignation, or his sorrow and foreboding at the way the country was going. In particular he was dismayed by the Government's creeping purchase of loyalty among the professional classes: in short, by their bribery and corruption. Presciently, he writes in April:

> [we are] verging to what may be called civil anarchy, and from that to civil war, where the contending parties will be too equally balanced to hope for a speedy termination or a happy one. The parties appear to me to be busy recruiting without beat of drum, and mustering their forces without calling them into the field . . . in law there is a gradation and scale of promotion for all ranks and abilities, from £2500 for a judge, to a sergeant and a silk gown . . . in the established church they are as faithful as Caesar's tenth legion . . . in *our* [Presbyterian] churches I have always considered the increase of the Regium Donum [the government grant given to Ministers of the Dissenting churches] as hush money . . . the Catholic College, which is patronised pretty much for the same purpose, got a large grant from Parliament this session, for I believe their clergy in

general have been too proud to receive an annual stipend from the state, though much poorer than the Dissenters . . . in short, a man cannot live well enough at present like a gentleman without acting as a rascal, and for his daily bread he must not pray to God, but to the Devil . . . in a little time every man that can read or write will be forced to assume the character of a Government man, and every man that has his senses, but not a letter, will be deemed a Defender . . .[26]

Although Drennan could no longer be called an active rebel, nostalgia for the ideals of the French Revolution lingered. He had not, like Rowan, drawn back in utter horror from all its excesses. He still looked on Burke, for example, as having a disordered mind:

In his invective he is as coarse and vulgar as one of Robespierre's hirelings. He is very much the Marat of Pitt, equally vulgar, equally vainglorious, and much more venal . . . with the mixture of venality he joins the wiliness of a crafty politician.[27]

In a verse of upright indignation, and with an absence of modesty or self-mockery, Drennan delivered what he may have thought a *coup de grâce* against his great, dying adversary:

In an imitation of one of Juvenal's satires, which I once made, but left unfinished in the middle, I took notice of Burke in a line or two which I shall copy:

> . . . Jack is cleans'd by CLARE
> But how could wash of heraldry efface
> The name of BURKE, and dignify disgrace!
> Could peerage blazon o'er the pensioned page
> Or give a gloss to ignominious age?[28]

'Jack' Fitzgibbon, now elevated to Lord Clare, gets off lightly. What most offended Drennan's high-mindedness, was Burke's venality – or rather, the charges of venality which were so widely circulated. To Drennan, corruption was always a principal enemy. One wonders what comment he would have made on Gibbon's famous definition: 'Corruption, the most infallible symptom of constitutional liberty'?

13

Failure of an invasion

The Irish are not yet sufficiently enlightened to bear the
sun of Freedom. Freedom would soon dwindle into
licentiousness; they would rob, they would murder. The
liberty which I look for is that which would increase the
happiness of mankind.

Daniel O'Connell on the French in Bantry Bay,
Irish Monthly Magazine, x.

The closeted, thoughtful existence of William Drennan – this
exemplar of the early 'Law and Physic' of the United Irishmen –
now gives way to the headier, active conspiracy of Lord Edward
Fitzgerald and Arthur O'Connor.

The pair conducted negotiations in midsummer with Barthélemy,
the French Minister in Basle, after their meetings with Reinhard in
Hamburg. By transferring the talks to Switzerland, they hoped to
shake off the underworld of agents of all colours (*émigré*, British,
Royalist etc.) who were concocting Irish connections to discover
what the two flamboyant visitors were up to.

At some time during their month's stay in Switzerland, it seems
to have been settled that the French Directory would prefer to deal
only with O'Connor. Fitzgerald was left behind. As the supposed
son-in-law of the Duke of Orleans (the guillotined Philippe Egalité)
he was thought to have too many French connections, be altogether
too conspicuous. There was a near certainty of his movements
becoming known to British intelligence. (As indeed they were:
secrecy and Fitzgerald were strangers to one another.) At a meeting

in Angers, O'Connor duly gave General Lazare Hoche* a résumé of the position in Ireland; like Tone, he had a clear idea both about the desirable size of any French invasion force (preferably 20,000 men) and the impossibility of any general rising in Ireland until after a landing.

On his return journey to Hamburg Fitzgerald had,

unluckily, for a travelling companion, during the greater part of the journey, a foreign lady who had been once the mistress of an old friend and official colleague of Mr Pitt, and who was still in the habit of corresponding with her former protector. Wholly ignorant of these circumstances, Lord Edward, with the habitual frankness of his nature, not only expressed freely his opinions on all political subjects, but afforded some clues, it is said, to the secret of his present journey, which his fellow traveller was, of course, not slow in transmitting to her official friend.[1]

No premonition of this discovery clouded his enjoyment of what seems to have been a thoroughly agreeable interlude. He wrote a letter to his 'dearest mother' immediately he had arrived back with his family in Hamburg:

I had a very pleasant tour, am in rapture with Switzerland. I left my friend in Switzerland taking another tour. There never were two persons who more thoroughly admired Switzerland than we did. We saw it with the true Rousseau enthusiasm . . . he is as fond of Rousseau as I am, so you may conceive of how we enjoyed our journey. He entered completely into my way of travelling, which was walking most of the way, getting into a Boat where we could, taking our dinner in some pretty spot, and swimming when we could. In fact we agreed in every thing . . . I returned in a Diligence and the journey was troublesome enough as to body, but as to that you know I don't mind . . . I was an outside passenger the whole way, which though I got a little wet now and then, made the journey pleasant enough. I shall see you now in three weeks. God how happy I shall be to kiss my dearest Boy, how I miss its Dear Face . . .[2]

There is much that is disingenuous about this letter. For example, in Basle the pair had had discussions with Barthélemy about such

---

* Had he not died young in 1797, Lazare Hoche might have won glory as great as Napoleon's. He was perhaps equally gifted and ambitious, and the conquest of Ireland might well have provided him with a strategic success in the revolutionary wars as dazzling as that which Italy provided for his rival.

matters as organizing mutiny among Irish sailors.[3] It was far from Rousseau all the way. Then, again, even if the news that O'Connor was 'taking another tour' might not be decoded by his mother, it would arouse suspicions were his mail intercepted. All the same, the account of the journey reads very much in character. It is as though the soupçon of intrigue and adventure, half-confessed, gives spice to a truthful account of an idyllic holiday tour.

Reunited with Pamela and his family in Hamburg, Fitzgerald soon wrote another fond letter to his mother. At the end of August they were to leave Hamburg, and he was looking forward to a family holiday in the Malvern Hills:

> I . . . look forward with pleasure to the time we shall spend together, and I shall have double satisfaction, as my Pam has had her share of pleasure with her friends here. She is quite reasonable (as ~~usual~~ she always is) and will bear the parting very well; and so is Me Genlis . . .[4]

The one tiny, telling correction illustrates Edward's loyalty to his wife. There is no doubt that Pam might have been an embarrassment on many occasions, with her French airs and accent, her bizarreries of dress. But Edward crossed out the word 'usual', changing it to 'she always is'. What memories of Dublin sniping against Pam, real or imaginary, may lie there! Whatever else may be said of Lord Edward Fitzgerald, he had, and inspired in others, a touching, simple and constant loyalty. He was a rebel; he could never have been an informer.

Fitzgerald would have been amazed had he known that in July, as he was making his way back from Switzerland, his brother the Duke of Leinster was being suggested in some quarters as a candidate to become King of Ireland if, after a successful invasion, the tide set in favour of a monarchy. And Tone, when told of the rumour by General Clarke in Paris, was certainly taken aback and exclaimed, 'No: that everybody loved and liked the Duke, because he was a good man, and always resided and spent his fortune in Ireland, but that he by no means possessed that kind of character and talents, which might elevate him to that station'. The General followed this up by saying, 'Maybe, after all, you will choose one of your own leaders; who knows but it may be *yourself*?' Tone was even more baffled.[5]

He was amazed, with the most disarming ingenuousness, by his now being received into the highest military and political circles. He never quite became used to it: 'This was a grand day; I dined with the President of the Executive of France, beyond all comparison the most illustrious station in Europe.'[6] The greatest day, perhaps, came when:

> the door opened and a very handsome well-made fellow, in a brown coat and nankeen pantaloons, entered and said, *'vous êtes le citoyen Smith?'* I thought he was a *chef de bureau*, and replied, *'Oui, citoyen, je m'appelle Smith'* He said, *'vous appelez aussi, je crois, Wolfe Tone'*. I replied, *'Oui, citoyen, c'est mon veritable nom.'* 'Eh bien,' replied he, *'je suis le général Hoche'.*[7]

Here was a man with whom Tone felt an instant affinity. Not that Hoche was altogether open with him. He teased him with questions about O'Connor, without revealing that he had met him. Tone became prey to the disease of suspicion. There were days of hope, and weeks of dashed hope. He spent interminable time in writing memoranda about geography, victuals and the spirit of rebellion in Ireland. But there was some compensation when, at last, his appointment as an officer in the Army of the Republic came through:

> Put on my regimentals for the first time, am pleased as a little boy in his first breeches; foolish enough, but not unpleasant. Walked about Paris to show myself; huzza! *Citoyen Wolfe Tone, Chef de Brigade* . . . I think now I have got on regimentals, I begin to write like a very pretty gentleman.[8]

At long last, in mid-September, word came that Tone should leave Paris to join the headquarters of the Army of the West at Rennes; his pistols and sabre ready, he travelled without stopping for ten hours through the 120 miles of country still alive with royalist rebels. He enjoyed the officers' life. But when could the expedition, with its 15,000 troops and 42,000 stand of arms, put to sail? Hoche furiously tried to invigorate a sluggish and uncooperative Marine, which had set its sights on other ventures.

In his off-duty hours Tone enjoyed long conversations with the gallant, ancient Colonel Shee, an Irishman determined to join the expedition despite his gout. Shee's duties were not altogether clear. Perhaps he might have helped on local negotiations once the expedition had landed. At any rate they talked much of such matters as the ill usage of the late, guillotined Duke of Orleans. In *his* off-duty hours

Hoche conducted himself in a manner that Tone may secretly have envied, but could not approve:

> There is a charming little aristocrat, with whom [General Hoche] is perfectly well, although all her relations are *chouans*. In all the hurry of our expedition, he contrived to steal off, and spend two days and nights with her. Mr Shee and I were in a mortal fright at his absence, for, knowing where he was gone, and on what business, we apprehended some of the *chouans* might waylay and assassinate him. As they attempted it in the middle of Rennes, they might well execute it in a byroad, and if anything happened to Hoche, there is an end to our business. It is very indiscreet in him, but God forbid I should be the one to accuse him, for I have been buffeted myself so often by the foul fiend, that it would be rather indecent in me to censure another. (Sings.) 'Tis women that seduces all mankind'. I do not think, however (but God knows), that under the present circumstances I would have gone a-catterawauling for two days among the *chouans*.[9]

In early December they at last embarked, and rode at anchor in the roads of Brest. The Marine still displayed a mood of nonchalant laxity. Once when Hoche pressed Vice-Admiral Bruix he did not answer, but continued to 'dandle one of his little children'. But Tone does capture in one scene the authentic note of hectic gaiety of those about to go to war. The jollity is very much in contrast with the bitter days and nights to come:

> The *Etat Major* (general staff) came aboard last night; we are seven in the great cabin, including a lady in boy's clothes, the wife of a commissionaire, one Ragoneau ... I must remark the infinite power of female society over our minds which I see every moment exemplified in the effect which the presence of Madame Ragoneau has on our manners; not that she has any claim to respect, for she is not very handsome, she has no talents, and (between friends) she was originally a *fiue de joye* at Paris. Yet we are all attentive and studious to please her; and I am glad, in short, she is aboard, as I am satisfied she humanises us not a little. General Watrin paid us a visit this evening, with the band of his regiment, and I went down into the great cabin, where all the officers mess, and where the music was playing. I was delighted with the effect it seemed to have on them. The cabin was ceiled with the firelocks intended for the expedition, the candlesticks were bayonets stuck in the table, the officers were in their jackets and *bonnets de police* – some playing cards, others singing to the music, others conversing – and all in the highest spirits – once again I was delighted in the scene. At length Watrin and his band went off, and, as it was a beautiful moonlit

night, the effect of the music on the water, diminishing as they receded from our vessel, was delicious. We are still at anchor – bad! bad![10]

Far, far worse was to come. No sooner had they left harbour on 16 December than the 74-gun *Seduisant* foundered in treacherous narrows, with the loss of over 500 men. Then the ship carrying General Hoche (and his plans) was separated in thick fog from the rest of the fleet which, bereft and bewildered, made its way to Cape Clear, off which it beat for some three days. Finally, when the fleet arrived at the mouth of Bantry Bay they were met by a wild, screaming easterly gale and snowstorms. It became impossible to land. Brave councils of war were held among the substitute commanders, with Tone, to the end, advocating almost any landing, with any resources:

> it is altogether an enterprise truly *unique*; we have not one guinea; we have not a tent; we have not a horse to draw our four pieces of artillery; the General marches on foot; we leave all our baggage behind us; we have nothing but the arms in our hands.[11]

For their part, the British were by no means unprepared for the French, – though they would have been locally outnumbered. Already on 1 December a lucid dispatch had been forwarded by Brigadier-General Eyre Coote (in command of the camp at Bandon, and later in his career to be called 'more eccentric than mad') to the Chief Secretary Pelham, surveying all the possible bays of the south-west and identifying Bantry Bay as the likeliest spot for an invasion, should the French 'meditate a descent upon this part of Ireland – its extent, its width is so great as to contain an Immense Fleet . . . its length of habour is so great that an Enemy may land twenty miles nearer to Cork than any other point'. And on Christmas morning at 4 a.m. a naval officer, Lieutenant George Pulling, wrote a very clear report (despite the hour) from Mr White's house in Bantry:

> Being off Castle Haven on Friday evening and finding that many accounts are circulating that a fleet of French ships are beating up Bantry Bay but without any reason being assigned by which I could determine them to be the enemy I took horse in the morning and came here about three in the afternoon when I found the fleet to consist of sixteen sail – twelve ships – two brigs and two luggers – their being at the distance of at least eight leagues prevented my being able to ascertain with any degree of certainty

their force – they are certainly large ships and some of them men of war, but to say more at present can only be conjecture – I watched them till dark when they were working up towards Bantry, two with Topgallant sails, but neither with Mainsail – it is my intention as soon as it shall be day to go as near them as prudence will allow me – when that is attained I will immediately send you an account of my observations.[12]

In any event, beside the eternal blizzard, nothing else was of account. As Tone managed to write in his journal:

Last night (December 28) it blew a perfect hurricane. At one this morning, a dreadful sea took the ship in the quarter, and stove the quarter-gallery and one of the dead-lights in the great cabin, which was instantly filled with water to the depth of three feet . . . I had just fallen asleep when awakened by the shock . . . hearing the water distinctly rolling in the cabin beneath me, and seeing two or three of the officers mount in their shirts, as wet as if they had risen from the bottom of the sea, I con-cluded instantly that the ship had struck and was filling with water, and that she would sink directly . . . As I knew all notion of saving my life was vain, in such a stormy sea, I took my part instantly, and lay down in my hammock, expecting every instant to go to the bottom.[13]

The next day the remnants were scattered to the unrelenting gales. Seven ships including Tone's, out of the forty-three that had left Brest a fortnight earlier, straggled back to Brest on New Year's Day. Here was unredeemed failure. Had Tone's and Hoche's force not been overcome by the violence of the winter wind and waves, the history of the revolutionary wars, and of Ireland, might have taken a different turning. The fate of the United Irish movement was, in hindsight, sealed by the invasion that never landed at Bantry Bay.[14]

Throughout those long summer months when, in France, Tone had been urging on 'the invasion that never was', one personal anxiety weighed heavily on his mind. On his way to Brest he had heard that some of his dearest friends – Russell, above all – had been swooped on and arrested in Belfast, one autumn morning. For once, his gaiety deserted him:

This morning before we set out [from Morlaix] General Hardy sent for me, and showed me an English paper that he had just borrowed . . . by this unfortunate article, I see that what I have long expected, with the greatest anxiety, is come to pass. My friends Russell and Sam Neilson were arrested for High Treason on September 16. The persons who arrested them were the Marquis of Downshire, the Earl of Westmeath, and Lord Londonderry, together with *that most shameless of all – John Pollock* [my italics]. It is impossible to conceive the effect this heavy misfortune has upon my mind. If we are not in Ireland time enough to extricate them, they are gone; for the Government will move heaven, earth and hell and to ensure their condemnation. Good God! If Russell and Neilson fall, where shall I find two such men to replace them? My poor friend Russell, with whom I have spent the happiest hours of my life, and whom I love with the affection of a brother! a man who would, I know, sacrifice his life for me or my family, if it were necessary . . . My heart smites me now for the levity with which I have spoken of my poor Russell in these memorandums, under the name of P.P. Well, that levity exists no longer . . . God, I hope, has not so totally deserted me, but I may arrive in time to deliver my friends.[15]

Pollock, that arch-paymaster of informers, that 'master of vulpine elegance' who had tried to insinuate himself into intimacy with Drennan in order to recruit him into his web, was now Crown Solicitor. He had become the prime mover in the dramatic steps the Government was taking to stamp out the growing, radical militancy in the North. The United Irishmen's *Northern Star* reported, with lumpish irony at the end of its column:

This morning presented a very unusual appearance in this town. A large body of cavalry appeared in arms – the whole garrison was turned out – the artillery paraded – and there was every show of war. Several great people came to town. Detached guards were stationed in every part of the town, and several of the inhabitants were arrested . . . it is to be observed that the foreman compositor of the *Northern Star* was taken into custody, and a number of papers seized without any warrant to that effect . . . Mr Russell surrendered himself, in the same manner as Mr Neilson had done. There cannot, on the whole, be a stronger contrast between the discreet and excellent temper and conduct of the inhabitants of this peaceable and prosperous town, and that of the above mentioned Attorney and Lords. How long shall it be thought prudent to submit to this rough-riding of Lordlings and Attorneys!!! About half past three, the armed procession with their prisoners, left town. We have not time to give a description of it – suffice it to say, that Mr Pollock the Attorney, conducted himself with as much firmness as the *patriotic* Lord Castlereagh, the *disinterested* Lord Downshire etc., etc. In short, they did that by *nightly scouting* and *martial attack* which no human creature was disposed to resist – and which the meanest Constable in town could have done as well as they![16]

'Firmness' because Pollock was notorious for his slipperiness. And 'shameless' (without irony) because the fees he demanded in taxing court costs sometimes exceeded the amount of the costs themselves[17] – not that Tone was likely to have known about this particular peccadillo. Pollock enjoyed a number of offices, on top of that of Crown Solicitor, many of them simultaneous, many of them sinecures, all of them enjoying 'pecuniary stimuli'. Perhaps some payments made to him for his expert, secret management of McNally and other informers may have been concealed under the heads of some of these sinecures.[18] But they seemed a conspicuous example of a type of abuse hateful to reformers.

As a buyer of intelligence and paymaster of informers, Pollock was governed by motives similar to those he was well acquainted with, principally greed. Then there was the love of intrigue, secrecy, and deviousness for its own sake. *Open* dissemination of news, on the other hand, was another matter altogether, and not to be encouraged. On the same September day that Russell and others were arrested on the information of Pollock and others, the military entered and ransacked the offices of the Belfast *Northern Star*, even though on this occasion they seem to have delayed its publication by only a few hours.

Whatever one may think of this and other raids by the military of this time, there is a great deal of evidence that they did succeed in quashing an outright rebellion in the North, before the non-invasion of Bantry Bay. From the rebels' point of view, it was another failure; for the informers, another triumph.

Hearing of these Belfast arrests, Martha McTier wrote immediately to her brother urging him to visit the prisoners on their arrival in Dublin. She had always had an interest in Russell – no passionate friendship like Tone's, more of an affectionate and bewildered curiosity ('I am much interested in this seemingly unfortunate young man Russell. He seems very poor, is very agreeable, very handsome and well informed'). Now she wrote, 'Russell I feel for, as if for a younger, rasher brother,' though adding her disapproval of some of his recent sentiments:

> It is probable you will soon see these men. 'I was in prison and ye came unto me.' *You* were there also, and do not let anything prevent you doing

a humane and friendly action . . . they are taken up for high treason. I hope there will be no irons.

Was Drennan irked by the admonitory tone of his sister's letter, with its innuendo that he might, to an undue degree, exercise his customary care for his personal safety? At any rate, he replied immediately, with a trace of huffiness, to assure her that he had:

> thought it his duty to follow the golden rule of doing as you should wish that others should do to you, and remembering well that I thought my friends very long in paying me a visit after my night's imprisonment, I called at Newgate and enquired for the under-gaoler . . .[19]

He was refused admission, leaving a message that he had called. He added that he had known little or nothing of Russell for two years. He sounds a little relieved. There is no record of his calling again.

Rumours of imminent invasion often surfaced in the letters between Drennan and his sister during the pre-Bantry days; one keeps thinking how different it might all have been had the expedition of Hoche and Tone chosen to land – and succeeded – in the insurrectionary North, rather than the relatively trouble-free West. Drennan himself believed that the Government were turning the alarms to their own advantage; the fear of invasion would be 'an excellent pretext for putting the country into a sort of barrack and garrisoning it with Englishmen, preparatory, perhaps, to a forced union'.[20]

Once again, ambivalence towards the Catholics is easy to read between the lines of Drennan's letters. Generally, principle overcame prejudice. He never lost sight of the necessity of the unity of the sects, and in theory held firm to the end. (Before he died he directed that his coffin should be borne by six Catholics and six Protestants.) But he admitted to avoiding open commitment:

> I was talking yesterday with a Catholic of some consequence, and he was expressing a desire that I should enter into a small society they are instituting . . . I declined it, not on the plea of my patriotism being less ardent than ever, but on my being more anxious about personal independence.[21]

In the small change of life he found much that was distressing about the behaviour of his fellow citizens. He had written a fiercely teetotal ode 'The worm of the still',* and, to his eyes at least, Catholics drank more than Dissenters. One late summer's day Drennan, taking a holiday in Bray, some fifteen miles south of Dublin, wrote a sorrowful account of his dinner to his sister:

> You could scarcely credit the quantity of ale and whisky that passed by me in the course of two hours; never was such a drunkard house, and I firmly believe that Sunday in the Catholic part of this country is much the most sinful day of the week . . . I counted more than thirty who had certainly spent the earnings of 8 days before. The abolition of Sunday would be a blessing here, and Ireland must continue as she is, while her lower orders are kept in a state of intoxication . . . Will anything of a reforming cast remove the habits of this people, high and low, with the one half wine the chief good, and with the other whisky?[22]

But it was the dangers of the eternal differences that divided Irishmen which occupied the forefront of Drennan's mind, especially as the popular conflicts between the Catholic Defenders and the nascent Orange societies grew more and more bitter during 1796. An Association of 2,000 loyalists was formed to counter United Irish republicanism. Drennan wrote:

> What is this but the rallying of each party under the standard of war? If the parties get nearly equal and balanced, it will be civil war; if unequal, it will be rebellion in the weaker . . . the disaffection of the Catholics is said to be great . . . one of the wealthiest of them in a conversation about Defenders exclaimed, 'Defenders! Defender and Catholic is the same'.

Then, amidst a number of reports of intimidation there was his indignation at the assassination attempts which 'sully the honour of the north, and are really dreadfully ominous of the future'. He could not have been pleased to hear about activities of the new cells of United Irishmen, such as their anonymous threats to burn down homes unless support was sworn to them. 'They are now proselytising by terror' reads one report of the Under-Secretary Edward

---

* I have found what the Learn'd seemed so puzzled to tell
The true shape of Devil, and where is his Hell.
Into serpents of old, crept the Author of Ill
But Satan works now, as a Worm of the Still.
Of all his migrations, this last he likes best.
(*Glendalloch*, 'The Worm of the Still')

Cooke at this time.[23] Drennan reported that, in polite Dublin society, where his views and past were well known, barbed asides were made against him. In November:

> I went, with some ladies, to see some of the town sights, and as we went through the Castle Yard, Colonel Barber met us and asked his sister (one of the party) if she chose to see the Armoury. We went through it all and saw 25,000 stand of arms, beautifully disposed, with artillery, etc., etc., in busy preparation. Mrs A., mentioning the next day in a laughing way, that I was one of the visitors, the lady I mentioned wished with all her heart that they had put me into one of the seven-pounders and shot me off by way of trial. Such are the tender mercies of our judges' ladies . . .[24]

Rowan would have been surprised had he known that his name was quite so prominent in the bizarre initiation rites of Defenders. One of their oaths was to follow Sir Edward Bellew, James Cole, Napper Tandy and Hamilton Rowan – to serve France and Ireland. They were to have no King – they said 'We will recover our estates, sweep clean the Protestants, and leave none alive'. This oath may have fuelled the fury of Lord Clonmell: in one summing-up the Chief Justice referred to Defenders swearing to 'follow that fugitive traitor Hamilton Rowan', contrasting him with 'the sound of the name of one who is respectable to my ear, Sir Edward Bellew'. And again: 'there is existing, and has been for some time, a horrid system of murder and treason, the seeds of which were sown by such men as Rowan and Tandy, who have fled from their country'.[25]

All the same, the elevation of Rowan into a monstrous bogey, a legendary figure in whose name oaths were sworn, a millennial King of Ireland, is easy to understand in the light of his enormous size and strength. It helps to be a giant to create a myth.

In practice, the exiled Rowan had no connections with the Defenders, and would certainly not have approved of their murder and rapine. He was struggling to keep afloat in Wilmington, and went to some trouble to disassociate himself from politics of all kinds:

> Finding that the violence of party in Philadelphia, and what appeared to me the imprudent interference of some of my countrymen in their politics, which it was almost impossible to avoid, I rejoiced in my determination of quitting that great and flourishing town and went to board

and lodge for the winter at the house of a farmer . . . about four miles from Wilmington.[26]

He seems to have walked the four miles to and from Wilmington every day. For money he kept himself afloat (just) by brewing spruce and birch beer, which he delivered in person to his customers.

> I expected that, during the frost, the walk back and forward would be pleasant; but my disappointment was great, when I found that the early sun rendered the roads worse than in the most rainy weather; and on returning home in the evening, until the moon rose it was totally dark, for in those latitudes there is little or no twilight.[27]

His walks were prodigious; one neighbour observed a typically eccentric habit: 'He was famous for his "endurance hikes". Setting out on rainy mornings Mr Rowan would lie prone in the first pool to soak himself before the downpour wetted him.'[28]

Mrs Rowan was shocked to hear of the lowliness of his occupations, although her husband stoutly insisted that 'I will not live in abject dependence while I can clean boots in an alley'. She redoubled her efforts to see that some money reached him (not so easy to lay hands on money belonging to a fugitive traitor).[29] Meanwhile he began to enter into negotiations to become a calico dyer. A small factory about half a mile from the town had gone bankrupt. His first steps on taking possession were as eccentric as might have been expected. A small hut or 'cottage of rough boards', about ten foot square, had been left on the factory grounds:

> This [hut] I removed to a romantic spot on the grounds of the Brandywine, and I built around it a piazza towards the river, and thither I removed myself and my dog Charles; while I gave the dwelling-house [part of the factory premises] to Aldred . . . a dyer in the town, an Englishman from Manchester; who undertook the management of the shop and men . . . in less than a year it was calculated it would be productive.[30]

He arranged some advertising. As he explained to his wife, he was 'no longer a gentleman, but a printer and dyer of calicoes'. He attempted a sort of jingle in the leaflet which he circulated:

> 'It *was* Hamilton Rowan, Esq.
> Now it is Calico Printer and Dyer.'

Rowan's letters sometimes drew replies from his wife which could not have cheered his exile:

Every captain of a ship that comes from Philadelphia or Wilmington fills this country with accounts of your drawing beer, flour, &c. through the street, which gives fresh food for scandal against poor me. My own heart, and those who know me, acquit me from the crime of want of affection for you . . . What could, what should have obliged you to run from your house to the factory in a snow-storm, with your bed on a barrow? We are both suffering; but why should we make for ourselves unnecessary troubles? The truth is, a friend of yours has written to me from America, to say you are grown very thin, and that your health is indifferent . . . I am sensible that to give the body exercise is in a degree the means of lessening the sufferings of the mind; but then it must not be fatigued; for though that may procure rest for a night, lowness of spirits will succeed it in the morning. For myself, I have it not in my power, living as I do in town, to take much exercise. I am never happy, and seldom quite well . . .[31]

14

Northern violence

The spirit burning but unbent,
May writhe, rebel – the weak alone repent!
                          Byron, *Corsair*, Canto 2

When, in the previous summer, Tone had been made a General in the French army, he had sent for Matilda and her children, in the hope that they might settle – perhaps in a village near Le Havre – until they should all return, in victory, to Ireland. In January 1797 they landed safely in Hamburg and sent word to Madgett in Paris. But this did not arrive at once. There were long winter days in which Tone nursed his loneliness in cold lodgings. His disappointment over the failure of the expedition, his concern for his future, if any, in the French army, and above all his worries for the safety and health of his family, slightly affected the verve of his journal:

> The transports of joy I felt at the news of her arrival were most dreadfully corrected by the account she gave me of her health, which threw me into the most terrible alarms. I wrote to her instantly, to remain at Hamburg until further orders, and by no means to think of exposing herself, in her present weak state, and our dear little babies, to a journey from Hamburg, in this dreadful season, a great part of the road being through a wild country, where there is no better accommodation for travelling than open wagons.[1]

Even more agonizing were the last-minute delays. His wife was in the same continent. But she was far from well. Tone was only about a fortnight's ride from Hamburg. Yet he felt unable to absent himself from his military duties unless given a specific mission.

His tedium was briefly relieved when, in March, he met Paine, said to be at his best in a café at about ten at night, with a bottle of brandy before him. Tone records: 'He drinks like a fish – a misfortune I have known to befall other celebrated patriots.'

With sublime author's vanity, Paine attributed Burke's poor state of mind at the time to the publication of his own *Rights of Man*, rather than to Burke's heart being broken by the death of his son Richard. Tone commented:

> I am sure the *Rights of Man* have tormented Burke exceedingly; but I have seen myself the workings of a father's grief on his spirit, and I could not be deceived. *Paine has no children!* – Oh! my little babies! If I was to lose my Will, or my little Fantom! Poor little souls, I doat on them, and on their darling mother . . .[2]

Endless weeks later, having been showered with compliments on his valuable services, Tone left for Hoche's new headquarters at Cologne. Much of his melancholy was dissipated by travels, about which he wrote wonderfully – especially when he stopped reproaching himself for his failure to concentrate on his great aim in life, namely the severing of the hated English connection:

> Yesterday [in Cologne] I entered a church alone, for I visit all the churches . . . as I was gazing about, I perceived the corner of a green silk curtain behind a thick iron lattice lifted up, and someone behind it. I drew near, in order to discover who it might be, and it proved to be a nun, young I am sure, and I believe handsome, for I saw only her mouth and chin, but a more beautiful mouth I never saw. We continued gazing on one another in this manner for five minutes, when a villainous overgrown friar entering to say his mass, put her to the rout. Poor soul, I pitied her from the very bottom of my heart, and laying aside all grosser considerations, should have battered down the gates of the convent, and rescued her from her prison.[3]

One is reminded of Rowan's *coup de foudre* in the Azores.

Tone found country scenes delicious, too. His hatred of England is momentarily lifted when he considers the landscapes and gardens of Holland through which he was passing, now that he was free to travel on from Cologne to meet Matilda on the frontiers of Hanover:

> The features of a Dutch landscape are an immense tract of meadows (till the view is lost in the distance), intersected either by deep and wide

ditches or by fences of wicker made as neat as basket-work; large plant-ations of willows; small brick farm-houses, covered with red tiles, and in excellent order; here and there a château of a Seigneur, surrounded by a garden in the true Dutch taste . . . It is true it has not the picturesque beauty of an English garden but . . . I like it well enough in miniature. In a Dutch garden all is in straight lines and right angles; in an English, all is sinuosity. The Dutch garden is that of a mathematician, the English that of a poet. No question the English is far superior . . . But I am writing an essay about gardening, about which I know nothing.[4]

He is good on trifling, picaresque adventures, with a fondness for casting himself in the duel role of observer and main protagonist in any particularly affecting or dramatic scene. He tells of an incident on a *trakschuyt*, or broad-bottomed barge, in whose crowded cabin he made his way across parts of Holland – 'a most inconvenient scene for a battle, for it is impossible to stand upright therein, and we were, besides, stowed away in bulk like so many herrings'. Tone had been short-changed by a young Jew, and had also had another passenger thrown into his lap. After a scuffle:

> opposite me was placed a fat Dutchman, with his mistress, I believe; so, to divert myself, and support the honour of the Republic, I determined to act the Celadon with Mademoiselle, who did not know one word of French. That did not prevent me from making great way in her good graces, and Hans, who perceived he was losing ground fast, very wisely determined to renounce the contest, to which he found himself unequal, pulled down his cap over his eyes, and composed himself to sleep. I laid myself down, without ceremony, in the lap of Mademoiselle, and in five minutes was as fast as a church.[5]

But the war seldom left his thoughts, especially its theatrical side; he was still captivated by uniforms, parades, the distant sound of bugles:

> found myself [in the Hague] at last in a wood, intersected by a noble avenue, on the right side of which was a Dutch regiment (the uniform blue, faced white) at exercise, and on the left, a battalion of French. The Dutch . . . exercise with more precision than our [French] troops; they are taller and stouter men, better dressed and kept, their arms and accoutre-ments in better order . . . But I discovered in the French something of a fire and animation that spoke that ardent and impetuous courage which is their chief characteristic, and which the others totally wanted . . . It was very amusing to me to observe the *fierté* of our soldiers, as they marched

by the others; there was a saucy air of civil superiority, which made me laugh excessively, both then and ever since. The physiognomy of the French is sharp, quick and penetrating; that of the Dutch, round, honest, and unmeaning; the step, air and manner of the former are free and assured; they are the true stuff whereof to make soldiers. There are, however, some important points to be considered. You must leave the French grenadier permission to wear a very large cravat, if it be the fashion, tied just as he likes. His hat is likewise his absolute property . . . he must try it on in every possible shape and form, and wear it absolutely in that position which best becomes, as he conceives, the cast of his figure. When satisfied in these important, indeed indispensable points, he is ready for every thing, and Caesar himself is not so brave as these *petits maîtres*.[6]

He was coming close to a crossing of the Zuyderzee and the longed-for reunion with his wife and babies:

May 6 . . . walked out every day to the canal and two or three times a day to meet the boats coming from Lieuschans, whence she will arrive: No love! No love! I never was so unhappy in all my life.

May 7. At last, this day, in the evening, as I was taking my usual walk along the canal, I had the unspeakable satisfaction to see my dearest love, and our little babies, my sister, and her husband, all arrive safe and well; it is impossible to describe the pleasure I felt. Here is an end to my journals now, for some time at least . . . [which] I have continued pretty regularly for the amusement of my dearest love.[7]

During these early months of 1797, Tone dwelt less than usual on his hopes and fears for Ireland; sometimes it seemed *nearly* enough to be a General in the French Army and be reunited with his family. And then came the news of the mutiny of the British Navy at the Nore and of the Austrian Empire's overtures of peace. The latter would enable France to concentrate entirely on the defeat of England, and a new, promised expedition to free Ireland.

One piece of news from Ireland had, however, particularly distressed Tone before he set out on his travels. The press was full of tales of violence in the North, of insurrection about to burst. His journal for 18 February reads:

I see in the English papers, that Government is arresting all the world in Ireland. Arthur O'Connor, who it seems is canvassing for County Antrim, is taken up; but, I believe, only for a libel. It seems he was walking with Lord Edward Fitzgerald when he was arrested. It is not for nothing that these two young gentlemen were walking together. I would give a great deal for an hour's conversation with O'Connor. I see he has thrown himself, body and soul, into the revolution of his country. Well, if we succeed, he will obtain, and deserves, one of the first stations in the Government. He is a noble fellow, that is the truth of it.[8]

Fitzgerald was now taking an active part in helping to set up the military plans of the United Irishmen; and the 'twin of his soul', preparing to contest Antrim in the General Election due later in 1797, had published in January an inflammatory address to the electors, typical of the self-styled 'King of Connaught' in the *Northern Star*:

> Never will I seek your confidence by supporting a war that has been undertaken for the destruction of liberty abroad and for the preservation of a system of corruption at home . . . If to promote the UNION OF IRISH-MEN be treason, and to place the liberties of my country on its TRUE REPUBLICAN BASIS be treason, then I do glory in being a traitor – it is a treason I will seal with my blood, and that I hope to have engraved on my tomb.[9]

Although it might have been wiser for the Government to ignore such a farrago, O'Connor may well have been expecting his subsequent arrest. (Indeed, the provocation may have been deliberate.) No charge was laid against him, but he had to stay in remand for six months in solitary confinement in the Birmingham Tower of Dublin Castle. Here he was frequently visited by Fitzgerald's 'somewhat amorous' sister Lucy, together with Pamela. They communicated with the prisoner by waving handkerchiefs and hiding mawkish letters in books (his even more mawkish than theirs):

> Ten thousand thanks to my ever dearest Pam for her little purse and to the dear good-hearted Lucy for her Royal Unction.* I saw my dear beloved friend from my grated prison: alas! she looked pale, she grieves for her friend. Do not then, dear friends, add to his misery by letting it prey upon your warm generous hearts . . . the dear song, and the old dance, the conversation, the humble meal and the native punch, accompanied by social friendship – shall we ever pass those days again?[10]

---

* This must be Lucy's present, referred to again later in the letter: 'what a work I shall have to get Lucy's ointment (according to directions) to the root of my thick hair'.

The weeks in prison must indeed have contrasted bleakly with the evenings during the winter just passed. Three typical entries of Lucy's diaries catch the vanished scenes of aristocratic enjoyment:

Nov. 27. Lady Ed. and I left Carton and came to Kildare, where we found Mr O'Connor and Edward. Nothing can be more comfortable than this little habitation. Mr O'Connor read us the play of *Julius Caesar*. [Not all of it, one hopes.]

Nov. 30. The Apothecary dined with us, as he is a great democrat. We danced in the evening and had quite a ball; we made up seven couple calling in servants and maids.

Dec. 13. We had a dance in the evening. Our company was Cummins and the butcher's daughters. I danced with Arthur. We danced a great many jigs. Ed. is a great hand at them.[11]

It may be too easy to smile at the casualness of Fitzgerald's commitment to republicanism and revolution. He *was* serious, after his fashion. On the other hand, it was true that all the Fitzgeralds continued to move in Ascendancy circles, despite their revolutionary reputation. Pamela went up to Dublin for a ball at Lady Clare's where 'she had her hair turn'd close up, was reckon'd democratic, and was not danced with'. And Edward continued to write fond, idyllic letters to his mother. But again, when in 1797 (probably due in part to the kind services of John Fitzgibbon, Lord Clare) Fitzgerald was offered a safe exit from Ireland, he did not take it up. He had a sense of high duty, and he was loyal to his cause. He was still regarded by his French contacts as a man with whom they could deal in any second invasion.

One could say that he had courage and recklessness, idealism and folly, in equal proportions. The art, however, of balancing propaganda and secrecy does not come easily to rebels. The amateur, aristocratic and well-connected ones, like Fitzgerald and O'Connor, were much less adept at it than the working-class and peasant Defenders, working underground. Fitzgerald, especially, should not at any time have been looked on as a reliable conspirator.

In the North, insurrection was more than ever in the air this spring, after Bantry. Writing to her brother about O'Connor's virulent pieces in the *Northern Star* to the electors of Antrim, Martha McTier mentioned that Fitzgerald and O'Connor were behaving in evasive and conspiratorial ways. Was O'Connor *really* writing a book? Was Fitzgerald *really* intending to stand for Down? She looked on all this as a 'mere blind'. Somehow these inflammatory messages to the electors of Antrim were connected to plans for a new French invasion. She writes to Drennan only one month after Bantry:

> Do you think that O'Connor would ever have written that paper but from a desire to be taken up, or, rather, an impatience to bring on some work which the disappointment of the French retarded? He is now said to be mad. *But there is too much method.* I heard several government people say if the French had boldly landed, even without their artillery, they would have been successful. This may be a step of that nature. It is not a rash paper that is written in a hurry . . .[12]

Drennan himself was piqued, in these days when open revolution was so much talked about, and when the North was under proclamation (a form of martial law), that sometimes he was regarded as a 'frigid neutralist'. Was he not the framer of the original Irish Test? Was he not one of the patriarchs of the present popular societies? Should he be expected to take the oath again, in its new form? In a more prudent mood he said he was 'the quietest man in Ireland':[13]

> The students to a boy have taken up arms . . . every one you speak with is now enlisted and attested, and receives pay . . . I do not like the notion of being egged on by the initiated to serve as an instrument in the work, for I am not so persuaded yet of its virtue, its real patriotism, or its practicality . . . as to say, like the Spartans when the Athenians disputed with them the precedence on the field of battle 'place us where you think proper, there we shall endeavour to behave like brave men'.[14]

Still, he was shocked by the violence which was everywhere erupting. Windows never before bolted were now barred; rents were left unpaid; United Irish sedition was uncovered among the Monaghan militia; disaffected soldiers were shot. When Drennan heard of a whole regiment or more being made to witness the executions, he rebuked his sister: 'I should have wished you had given me some account . . . it must certainly have made a deep impression on the spectators . . . I hear the Highlanders refused to be employed and said "Let Irish kill Irish."'[15]

Drennan tried to reassure Martha about the militia's running amok and wrecking the presses of the *Northern Star*, although to judge by the tenor of her letters, she seems to have remained admirably calm throughout most of the disturbances. True, she observed that 'murders and assassination are dreadful subjects, but common here', and that 'nothing appears to me firm or trusted'; but she also wrote: 'I can walk from one end [of the town] to another without a servant at 9 o'clock . . . a stranger entering the town would be struck by the sounds of innocence, for the children are eternally crying 'ba-ee ma-ee' after every yeoman, while the mothers run after them crying if they do not behave themselves they will be put on board the Fleet.'[16] Like a good diarist, she also observed interesting trivia: in mid-March she had commented on a girl who caught cold when, 'in the present rage for slim persons', she went to a ball wearing *one* thin petticoat. And she kept her sense of humour:

> Lady Skeffington has a favourite parrot, on whose education the servants having bestowed some pains, and General Lake noticing him, he squalled out, *Are you* up?',* on which her ladyship, sorrowing, remarked that the people had made him a United Irishman while he was at her country house.[17]

In the spring of 1797, it was understandable that mothers in Belfast should keep their children close for fear they might be taken up into tenders, and spend the rest of their orphaned lives in Botany Bay. There was indeed one informer who made the unattractive boast that he 'was the cause of confining 227 innocent men to either the cell of a Bastille or the hold of a tender'.[18] His name was John Edward Newell.

There may have been a few informers who justified their activities on the grounds that United Irish advocacy of open rebellion, and of reliance on French aid, was sure to bring disaster to the country. Thus, their treachery was the lesser evil. Their motives, at least in their own eyes, were not wholly self-serving. It is just possible to believe McNally was one of these. Newell was clearly not.

In 1797 Newell was around twenty-five years old, and teaching art

---

* 'Up' signified that someone had been secretly sworn in as a United Irishman. Lake, the commanding General in the North, had been instructed by the Castle to put down agitators and disperse seditious assemblies, heedless of the civil authorities. Though his reputation was bloody, Martha McTier once called him 'a good man'. He does not seem to have shot the parrot.

in Belfast. He had moved from Dublin, where he had been an unsuccessful glazier, in his own words 'greatly addicted to private spouting'.[19] Now he became a painter of miniatures ('a business I had never dared to try before'), was sworn in as a United Irishman, and soon boasted to acquaintances that he knew all the secret plans of the organization. Not surprisingly, the authorities soon noticed him. Given the choice between being punished for his unconcealed seditious activities and accepting a free pardon in exchange for information, he seems not to have hesitated.

Newell is glimpsed in a letter which the forthright Belfast lady, Mary Ann McCracken,* wrote on 13 April to her United Irish brother Henry Joy McCracken, who was then in prison in Dublin. The High Constable had raided a house:

> Two boxes were broke open . . . it is said there were some letters from Mr Russell in [one], and in the other there were five guineas which they also carried off with them, it is supposed Newell the painter was the informer . . . [also last night a family was] knocked up and as soon as the door was opened up the whole party rushed upstairs . . . they were conducted by a little man dressed as a cavalry officer with a handkerchief tied across his mouth who everyone of the family instantly recognised to be Newell . . . [her other brother] William was taken up, he was in a tavern when that same little villain Newell came in disguised as he was last night and pointed him out.[20]

In such unnerving night-time prowling the masked or hooded Newell accompanied bands of soldiers about the streets of Belfast, arresting United Irishmen on suspicion.[21]

He was in a good position to identify men. He confessed that in earlier days he was a member of a secret assassination committee.[22] The Government was grateful for his confirming some of their suspicions about such bodies – however suspect his credibility. He had also been a member of one of the military committees that had recently been set up, which he criticized because in practice they had 'done little but consider plans for discipline'. In Belfast itself, however, an idea spread that discipline was not necessary – that men

---

* Mary Ann was very redoubtable indeed. Her devoted brother was one of the most active leaders in the Rebellion. She worked for the renaissance of Irish harp music, established with her sister a successful muslin business, and worked for the Belfast Poor House for a quarter of a century (see Mary McNeill, *The Life and Times of Mary Ann McCracken: A Belfast Panorama*, Dublin, 1960).

needed only to give one fire and rush out with the bayonet. Fitzgerald, who was now assuming greater responsibility for the newly organized military preparations, would not have approved. Although it is easy to criticize his political judgements, he was on surer ground when it came to order and discipline in army matters, and was listened to by virtue of his experience.[23]

Attention was beginning to be paid to rank. For example, in 1797 Newell reported that green cockades were widely used to distinguish officers from those whom they commanded in United Irish military bodies. The former wore the cockade adorned with a harp and cap of liberty (in place of a crown), with the motto 'Liberty or Death'.[24]

The United Irish were spending more time in attempting to suborn militiamen and soldiery. They may well have heard tales of Duckett and others suborning the English Navy (the Mutiny at the Nore broke out in May that year). In any case, Newell certainly informed that several soldiers of whom he knew, including some Englishmen, had been promised farms if they joined the revolutionary movement.[25]

Described as swaggering, boastful, officious and dissolute, he seems nevertheless to have been lucky, to have enjoyed a good pension, and not to have been visited in this world for his manifold sins (at least, not until his very last moments). His slim and self-laudatory autobiography contains no regrets; so his is hardly a cautionary tale. He is the subject of one revolutionary ballad, however. But it is less than complimentary:

> Allied to friends and foes, but false to all,
> He gained their confidence to work their fall.
> He sold his land and spent the gold in vice,
> Renewed his means, for blood still had its price.[26]

The reference to 'vice', I imagine, refers to the admission in his autobiography that, when living high at government expense later in his life in Dublin and licentious as always, he had contracted 'that worst of maladies, the fashionable disorder acquired by improper connections'.[27]

In 1797 bankruptcy and high financial alarms were in the news. In February the Bank of England instructed the Irish administration to suspend cash payments. General Lake, and others, worried that they would not even have a 'half-crown to pay informers' like Newell. As Professor McDowell observes, this did not mean that the Government was unable to keep the war going, successfully, with paper money.[28]

In Wilmington, Rowan soon came to find the going hard in the calico business. His partner had proved to be unreliable and crooked, and his Manchester experience was of no use. Rowan's marketing idea that he could succeed by buying muslin of 'only slightly inferior quality' and printing it with pirated patterns, did not work. Predictably and without too much difficulty, his large competitors foiled him. They threatened their retail customers that, if they did business with Rowan, their supplies would be stopped.

Within a year, Rowan had placed his last advertisement – to sell his business:

> Any person inclined to sacrifice his property by carrying on this manu-
> factory in America, may have the whole for one-half of the sum they cost,
> and immediate possession given.[29]

This advertisement says more for his honesty than his business acumen, confession of failure not being among the rules of advertising. All told, the sale left Rowan 500 dollars out of pocket.

Back in Ireland Mrs Rowan was fiercer, more practical. She may have been a virago: just as well. Her fight to save his estate was ceaseless. Now the property of a fugitive outlaw, it might well have been confiscated *in toto* but for her assiduous frequenting of the upper reaches of the Ascendancy. She gave endless undertakings about her husband's abandonment of revolutionary principles, his quiet, unmeddlesome life on the banks of the Brandywine. This was a task made no easier by all those well-documented rumours of his imminent return to Ireland – on the ships of a French invasion fleet, as a future King of Ireland, as the head of a rising of Defenders and so on.

She addressed many requests to Lord Clare, the Lord Chancellor, whose personal kindness was as marked as his judicial severity; in the end, after many years, it was his championing of her cause that won Rowan's return and pardon, indeed his complete restoration.

One expedition in pursuit of her family's welfare took her to England, a full account of which she sent to her husband. An incident immediately after her arrival at a hotel in Chester gives a good idea of her mettle, her absolute assurance of social standing, the inadvisability of tackling her, the quality of her indignation. It was

Sunday, immediately after breakfast, and she had spread out a table with papers that included mention of the Lord Chancellor:

Judge of my surprise when the man of the house came and said [the Mayor] was below and wished to see me. Without any hesitation, however, I desired he might be shown up. In he came, a poor old man, with white gloves, (he is a plumber by trade) who seemed much more embarrassed than I; two other men were along with him; one of whom, almost the only one who spoke and had the manners of a gentleman, after making some apology, requested to see my papers. I replied, I really did not understand what he meant. He said, he wished to examine my trunks and boxes to see if I had treasonable papers in them . . . I answered that I believed it was the first time it had ever been thought I was capable of assisting in carrying on a treasonable correspondence; nor had I been treated by the government of any country, as if they looked on me to be a person of that description.

It did not take much sagacity to find out that this was a business undertaking by the corporation of Chester, of their own wise heads; for the spokesman now declared that 'it was a business Mr Mayor had been very reluctant to undertake'; to which the poor Mayor continually replied 'very reluctant indeed'.

More haughty rebuttals followed. Her husband had NOT been at Bantry Bay. The date of his last letter from America was such-and-such. To 'the best of her belief' she would take her oath that he still was there. Then she came out with the name of General Johnson, the Commander-in-Chief in Chester, the first man in the town, and a gentleman. If he were sent for, he could, if he wished, see every paper she had:

This asking to see the General seemed still more to increase my consequence with the Chester citizens. [I insisted that] it was certainly worth their while to wait until General Johnson came, but if they would not do this I insisted upon their locking up all my boxes and taking their keys with them . . . Down they sat, looking very foolish . . . very soon after the General came in . . . a very old, venerable looking man, and the very first word I said to him, I perceived he was, unfortunately, uncommonly deaf.[30]

But all was soon sorted out. The venerable General expressed great concern, and the next morning called to see if there was any service at Chester he could do for her; he was going for a ride, but would not leave town without letting her know.

Formidable lady! My impression is that she thought of Hamilton

Rowan (as many wives do of their husbands) as an impossible, over-grown child – even more out of control now that he was so distant. One remembers her scolding about his running from house to factory in a snow-storm, with his bed on a barrow: 'You seem to think that the climate of America does not agree with you. I am rather inclined to think that your present mode of life would not agree with you anywhere.'[31]

15

Verging to rebellion

Confusion now hath made his masterpiece!
Most sacrilegious murder hath broke ope
The Lord's anointed temple, and stole thence
The life o' the building!

Macbeth, Act 2, scene 3

Lord Edward's 'dangerous little wife' was unlike Mrs Rowan in every way. The former seems on occasion to have been a mischievous, insurrectionary co-adjutor: colluding in the many letters which went to and from emissaries in Hamburg and France. Indeed, it was said that most correspondence was carried on by women (through Pamela and Lady Lucy Fitzgerald in London and Dublin, and Pamela's kinswoman Mme Mathiesson in Hamburg). Things of great consequence were 'conveyed by ladies in personal communication'. It sounds as though she, like her husband and his sister, relished the spice of cloaked danger, false names, conpiracy.

Fitzgerald himself had become high in the military counsels of the United Irishmen. So had O'Connor, when he was finally released from prison in July, the charge of high treason having been dropped (to the Lord-Lieutenant's frustration) through doubts of securing a conviction. The Northern Committee of which both United Irishmen were members was keener than Dublin to press ahead with revolution, without waiting for another French landing and despite the scarcity of arms other than pikes of ash wood stored in innumerable lofts. Implausible figures were tossed about: an army of 30,000 would take the North, O'Connor would come with 20,000 men from

225

the South. Then they would be strong enough to take Dublin: the city once taken, 'the game was theirs'. When the Dubliners prudently demurred, there were fearful rows. The Northerners accused the rest of cowardice, of being lukewarm in the cause, declaring that they would no longer sit in committee with them.

Towards the end of the year, however, the Northerners proposed a plan which smacks of the foolhardiness of Fitzgerald, and of the unscrupulous adventurism of O'Connor. It involved a bogus disruption of Christmas Mass, by an armed body ready to invade churches under the false colours of Orangemen. A Castle letter from Under-Secretary Cooke tells of some trustworthy information brought in just before Christmas:

> I learn from my Friend that Lord Edward Fitzgerald received some Days since orders from Paris to urge an Insurrection here with Speed in order to draw troops from England. In consequence of it there was a meeting of the Head Committee, where he and O'Connor urged immediate Measures of Vigour. They proposed arming a body of 500 men with short swords; that this Body should repair to the Masses' Houses at Midnight Mass on Xmas morning. That by false attacks they should persuade the Papists and raise a Cry that the Orangemen were murdering the Catholics, that having raised the uproar they should begin their attack on the Castle. Many priests were anxious for this Plan. But Emmet and Chambers opposed, and in consequence the Bishops who were against outrage put off their Mass till seven o'clock in the morning. The moderate Party are against Insurrection till the French land. My Lord Lieutenant has sent for the Speakers [of both Houses] and one or two more . . . our Friend received this Intelligence from John Tandy, son to Napper* who was alarmed beyond Expression at the Scheme.[1]

These were days when Edward Fitzgerald was very nearly 'taken up'. But indecision won the day. The Lord-Lieutenant's 'mature reflection' was to avoid grasping the nettle, in favour of keeping the lines of information open, despite warnings from the ubiquitous spymaster Pollock. Camden wrote:

> The account which I had given in writing fell far short of the verbal communication made to me by Pollock, upon which I sent an Express to

---

* Napper himself was one of the many Irishmen in Paris claiming authority to negotiate on behalf of the United Irishmen. He was detested by Tone. The informer Samuel Turner reported that 'Napper Tandy is looked upon as a madman and struts about the streets in the national uniform calling himself a major'.

the Speaker and to the Attorney General to come to town. I am very glad however I sent for them as I had a great deal of general conversation upon the state of this Kingdom and was glad to hear their opinion of the policy of taking steps to seize those whom we know to be Heads of the Rebels. The Fact which Cooke mentioned to produce an Insurrection on Xmas Eve is undoubted – I was in some degree doubtful in my own mind whether it might not be expedient to prevent the possibility of a similar event by confining O'Connor and Lord Edward – but their opinion agreed with my more mature reflexion that under all the circumstances of our chances of further information – and under the impression of the dis-advantage of taking up Persons without bringing them to Trial, it would be inexpedient to take up the Ringleaders of the Conspiracy at present . . . unless I receive more decided information I propose no particular or active Steps (of the nature I thought might have been necessary) . . .[2]

Perhaps it may not have been bad tactics to leave Fitzgerald and O'Connor at large. They rendered themselves conspicuous, and it was easy to keep an eye on them. On the other hand, Fitzgerald commanded a romantic following, particularly among the ordinary people. He had good military experience (even if his plans sound naïve and he was certainly better at commanding small bodies of men than at developing a serious strategy). On balance, the Lord-Lieutenant probably showed good sense in letting him be, and ensuring that his mail was read and spymasters were briefed.

Eyebrows, though, must have been raised at the blasphemy of a nobleman apparently ready to violate a Christmas Mass. On 19 December Fitzgerald wrote a long, typically affectionate letter to his mother in England:

I have nothing new to tell my dear Mother from this place. Wretched bad it is. Things take such a violent Turn . . . The Country has got into a crit-ical situation, and by all I hear is likely to remain so, for I see no sign of a change of those men who have brought to this state. But I won't talk of Politicks for they only torment one. One sees the Mischief, but not the remedy . . .[3]

Much of the information about the Northerners' reckless schemes for immediate risings, captures of ill-guarded arms depots in Athlone and so on, came from a new recruit to the army of inform-ers. Samuel Turner was a Protestant, Trinity-educated barrister, elected to the executive committee of the United Irishmen. While still loyal to the United Irish cause, Turner had travelled to Hamburg in June, carrying messages of encouragement to Reinhard about the readiness of the North to start the insurrection *before* the arrival of any French aid. (It is worth remarking that Fitzgerald was also 'conveying to him the most satisfactory assurances that the disaffected in Ireland were strong, numerous, well-disposed and united . . . and endeavoured to persuade [the Directory] – what the French appear with reason always to have doubted – that the militia and yeomanry of Ireland were friendly to their cause'.[4]

Whether Turner himself believed in some of O'Connor's and Fitzgerald's wilder schemes is not clear; but he certainly enjoyed the confidence of those with whom he dealt. At one point, claiming to speak for respectable Protestants, he wrote to Talleyrand asking him to guarantee that, when invasion came, the French Directory would help to secure property against historic Catholic claims: this shows the way that his mind was turning.

For Turner came to fear that the plans for rebellion had got out of hand, and would lead to the ruin of Ireland. His decision to change sides does not seem to have sprung from financial greed. Rather, it was a terrible distrust of the Catholics – once again this reveals how hard it was, on the ground, to come anywhere near to the will o'the wisp of the 'unity of the sects'.

Turner's rashness was of a very different order to the theatrical high spirits of Fitzgerald. It arose from a hot temper. Once, in the Crown inn at Newry, happening to meet the ferocious Lord Carhampton (said to be the most brutal of the pacificators of the North), he refused to take off his green scarf. A violent storm blew up. Amazingly, Turner forced an apology from the General.

He did not present such a bold front when he disclosed himself at Lord Downshire's house in London on a bleak October evening in 1797. Here is the Marquis's account of a spy (literally) coming in from the cold. It is written in a neat, spiky hand, and was sent round at once to the Home Secretary, the Duke of Portland, who forwarded it, in a dispatch with a number of other documents, to the Viceroy in Dublin:

> 8 October. Late at night a person came to my house much muffled up and insisted on seeing me on material business – after my going down *the Person* introduced himself by the name of Richardson* and desired to have

* This was his *nom d'espion*; his real name was, of course, Samuel Turner. Downshire always refers to him as '*the Person*'.

a private interview; which after some words had passed between us in the Hall and after recognising his features, but not then recollecting his name, I [asked him to come upstairs] . . . Immediately upon his coming into my room he unmuffled himself, and told his name and his business in the following words:

'That I must know that he had been actively employed for some time in the society of United Irishmen – that his intentions originally were perfectly pure, in endeavouring to bring about a reform in parliament, and amending the constitution of his country and for which purpose he had taken many very desperate steps and had connected himself with many violent and desperate people – that he now discovered that the object of the papists was the ruin and destruction of the country and the establishment of a Tyranny far worse than what was complained of by the Reformers – that Proscriptions, and Seizures of Property, Murders, Assassinations &c. &c. were the certain consequences to be expected from their machinations – that he was shocked at being led into steps in order to accomplish such measures and plans, and in order to counteract them and atone for his misconduct, he had come to England to make every discovery in his power and to prevent such mischief befalling his Country and therefore come to me and as he knew my sentiments and the active part I had taken, and if I had not been in town he would have gone to the Duke of Portland or to Mr Pitt.

'That he threw himself upon me for protection, and the only condition he would make, was that he should never be called upon to appear in a Court of Justice for the purpose of prosecuting any persons that might be taken up in consequences of his discoveries or information.'

I consented to this condition and encouraged *the Person* as much as I could to persevere in his last resolution and proposed to enter upon the important business which he had stated the next day (the night being then far advanced) and I desired him to come to my home at 12 next day.

He objected to come to my house from the apprehension of being known and said if any suspicion of him should be raised he should certainly be *taken off*, and therefore feared to come in the daytime to my house – this seemed so proper and reasonable that having the command of a friend's house (then vacant) in my neighbourhood, I proposed his coming in a hackney coach to the door (which should be left open) and into which he might pass unseen – this plan was agreed to and accordingly *the Person* came at the appointed time, when and at subsequent meetings in the same place I took down the following detail from his own mouth – he since took a lodging in a bye street near Golden Square where I met him two or three times.[5]

Turner then revealed how the General Executive Committee of the United Irishmen had planned to prevent the execution of the traitors in County Down the previous April, and how they had hoped to bribe or buy off witnesses. He gave a few brief sketches of the 'principal and active leaders' of the General Executive Committee, including of course O'Connor and Fitzgerald (and indeed himself). Most names were predictable, apart from 'Corey, a red-faced priest' and one or two others.

Turner's revelations of the violence of the split between the Northerners and the Dubliners may have been particularly useful to the Castle. But their value was limited by the agreement not to use him as a witness in court, which meant that it was impractical to prosecute O'Connor and Fitzgerald for high treason. For a second time the former thus slipped between their fingers.[6]

In the same bundle of official papers Samuel Turner made a reference to Rowan which would have pleased Mrs Rowan. She had become the almost daily suppliant of the Lord Chancellor, who endured her with great patience, and a wry amusement and admiration. The note ran:

> Hamilton Rowan was very much pressed to come over to France, but he determined to remain in America being quite sick of politics, having been thrown into jail on his first landing in France (after he fled from Ireland) and kept here six months till Robespierre's reign was at an end when he was liberated and went to America.[7]

This was not entirely accurate; but at least it may have reassured the Castle that he had no plans to return as King of Ireland.

Less welcome to Mrs Rowan's ears must have been the news of virulent yellow fever in Philadelphia. During the pestilence, Rowan continued to wheel flour from the mills in a small hand-barrow. He needed the flour because, his appetite for invention unassuaged, he had now begun to try to develop a bleaching liquid

> from a receipt of Thomas Cooper, late of Manchester . . . a mixture of a certain quantity of vitriolic acid, salt, and sulphur, which occasioned a vapour like that which has been recommended for its antiseptic qualities; and this, possibly, saved me from the contagion.[8]

By November 1797 the fever had claimed over 4,000 deaths. The population of Philadelphia dropped by a third, many fleeing the city.

There were bankruptcies, auction sales of the effects of the dead, distress and desolation everywhere. There were also brave and hardy survivors, including one man whose family name can still be seen in every high street in England. Rowan gives Mr Barclay a testimonial fit for a banker:

I do not find that anyone will lose by Mr Barclay, who, in my opinion, is as worthy a man as ever walked; and indeed is much respected, though blamed for overdrawing his credit at the bank, of which he was president.[9]

As the epidemic spent itself, Rowan allowed himself an excursion to pay his respects to the British Minister, on a visit to General Washington. (This sounds bold for one who was still an outlaw.) Rather to his own surprise, as well as to his wife's, he managed to be respectably turned out:

I am very seldom seen in any other garb than such as you have not often seen me in — short hair, no powder, and long beard; but this day [5 November] I was remarkably spruce in the Quaker coat you sent me, pomatumed [*sic*] and perfumed like any muscadin or musk-rat, which, by-the-bye, is a devilish mischievous beast in this country, and generally killed where he is found.[10]

He failed, however, to meet either Washington or the Minister. (One is reminded, years ago in Paris, of his being too sick to talk with Robespierre.) This was a pity. When he did succeed in meeting famous men, he would give light and vivid sketches. He called on the legendary hero of Polish nationhood, Kosciuszko, who for six hours with 4,000 men had once beaten off a Russian army of almost four times as many men:

in Philadelphia [I paid] two morning visits to Kosciuszko; he cannot rise from his chair, which I suppose is the reason that he bows very low, too low, I think; it hurt me, for one of the persons who was introduced to him while I was there, I knew to be a knavish scoundrel. He sits in an arm chair, his head bound up with a broad black ribbon, dark curling hair, sparkling eye, *nez retroussé*, his coat what we call Hussar, his legs bandaged, and the left one on a stool.[11]

However virtuous his withdrawal from politics, he could hardly be expected to abandon his admiration for *all* revolutionaries, at least for those who fought for their country's independence.

Indignation still ran high in him, too, whenever he saw abuse and injustice of any sort; whether she liked it or not Mrs Rowan had to read such expressions of anger as:

> The members of the society for the abolition of slavery have not the least objection to buying an Irishman or Dutchman, and will . . . get him indented at about the eighth part of the wages they would have to pay a *country born*. But they who are thus purchased generally do themselves justice, and run away before half their time is up.
>
> . . . swarms of Irish are expected here by the spring vessels, and the brisk trade for *Irish slaves* here is to make up for the low price of flax-seed![12]

A man of Rowan's natural generosity of spirit would be more likely to sympathize with those who kicked against the pricks of slavery than many of his contemporaries. His feelings show again in this account (which dates from the autumn of 1799, when he was still in America):

> In this ride I had again, as I constantly have, occasion to love and respect the lower order of men, when uncontaminated by too much intercourse with their superiors. I lost one of my gloves, and having searched back the road for it in vain I continued. Overtaking a negro, I threw him the other, saying that 'I had lost the fellow on the hill somewhere; that perhaps he might find it, and never was he possessed of such a pair in his life'. The fellow smiled. 'No master, you not lost it: here it is' . . . and gave both back to me. And this man was a slave, whose portion was stripes and *black dog* – his appellation from a whey-faced Christian.[13]

Drennan expressed his indignation in ways more measured and *worthy* than Rowan. It was as though the shades of his father and of Edinburgh Academy were watching over him, encouraging merit and virtue. But usually he addressed himself more to the general than to the particular, the individual. Thus, Drennan might not have given his gloves to a black slave met by chance on a road, but we have seen how he joined a campaign of abstinence from sugar in protest against plantation-owners' use of slavery.

On the other hand, of all the Irish causes that engaged radicals in 1797, none roused the pity and indignation of Drennan more than the 'judicial murder' of William Orr that autumn. Orr was a young Presbyterian farmer of Antrim, well liked, well connected, of considerable property and of an excellent reputation.

Under the Insurrection Act, it was now a capital crime to administer seditious oaths, such as those of the United Irish and Defenders. When Orr was arrested and held on a charge that he had 'sworn in' two soldiers, he spent a long year in prison waiting to be brought to court (as was all too common). He was eventually found guilty in a trial presided over by Lord Yelverton, a judge with a reputation for clemency who was said to have cried as he passed sentence. This sanctimoniousness caused Drennan to remark, 'I hate those Yelvertonian tears'.

The Crown should have found it easy to secure Orr's conviction. The jury had been packed. But before the sentence of death was delivered, it was revealed that the jurors, who had spent a whole night in their deliberations, had enjoyed two bottles of 'very strong whiskey', smuggled though the bars of the courtroom window. 'Enjoyed' may be the wrong word. One juror complained of having been extremely sick, and incapable of coherent thought. Another one complained that he had been intimidated, his agreement bought by asking for a recommendation of mercy to go forward. Despite the affidavits, it was ruled that the sentence could still be passed.

As Lecky observes, the case is not so easy. Was it right, was it decent to hang a prisoner when two jurors swore that some of their number were intoxicated when they delivered their verdict, and one juror swore he had been coerced by violence? But then again:

> [Might this be] a case such as frequently occurs in Ireland, of a treasonable conspiracy which had failed to procure an acquittal . . . and which was now making a last desperate effort to save the life of a popular and important member, and by doing so to inflict a damaging defeat on the administration of justice?[14]

Yelverton had another judge to assist him. In the end, they decided that since the evidence was so clear, and Orr's guilt so patent, there was no reason not to let the verdict stand, and to pass sentence. But that was not the end of it. Now an affidavit was produced showing that one of the soldier witnesses for the prosecution had confessed that he had once murdered and twice 'sworn away the life' of two men. True, this referred to another case. But the jury (who had found it hard enough to come to a verdict as it was) would surely have found his evidence dangerously tainted, even if the other soldier's evidence was unimpeachable.

There were two postponements, and one attempted jail-break,

before the sentence was carried out. There were memorials written pleading against execution. There was confusion over whether Orr had or had not signed a confession in return for these memorials. Orr was executed, at last, on 14 October. He left behind a pregnant widow and six young children.

Whatever one's views of the justice of the case, there is no doubt of the swell of public opinion, the chorus of doubt whether it could have been right to execute a man after a trial so full of flaws. The phrase 'judicial murder' appeared in newspaper columns, and has been reiterated in history pages ever since. And REMEMBER ORR became a revolutionary rallying cry in the Rebellion of the following year.

Drennan's verses commemorating the event express the popular theme of martyrdom, but they were well this side of sedition. A recent thesis has shown how carefully they combine austere Scots Presbyterianism – an earnest appeal to 'virtue', 'merit', 'truth' – with a seven-syllable scansion borrowed from a Gaelic tradition. Some interpreters today like to see it very much as a United Irish composition, dedicated to the appeal for the unity of the sects, with a muted threat like a roll of distant thunder.[15]

THE WAKE OF WILLIAM ORR

There our brother worthy lies;
Wake him not with woman's cries;
Mourn the way that manhood ought –
Sit in silent trance or thought.

Write his merits on your mind;
Morals pure and manners kind;
In his head, as on a hill,
Virtue placed her citadel.

Why cut off in palmy youth?
Truth he spoke, and acted truth.
'Countrymen, UNITE', he cried,
And died for what our Saviour died.

God of peace and God of Love!
Let it not Thy vengeance move –
Let it not Thy lightnings draw –
A nation guillotined by law.

Hapless Nation, rent and torn,
Thou wert early taught to mourn;
Warfare of six hundred years!
Epochs marked with blood and tears!

Hunted thro' thy native grounds,
Or flung reward to human hounds,
Each one pulled and tore his share,
Heedless of thy deep despair.

Hapless Nation! hapless land!
Heap of uncementing sand!
Crumbled by a foreign weight:
And by worse, domestic hate.

God of mercy! God of peace!
Make this mad confusion cease;
O'er the mental chaos move,
Through it SPEAK the light of love.

Monstrous and unhappy sight!
Brothers' blood will not unite;
Holy oil and holy water
Mix, and fill the world with slaughter.

Who is she, with aspect wild?
The widow'd mother with her child –
Child new stirring in the womb!
Husband waiting for the tomb!

Angel of this sacred place,
Calm her soul and whisper peace –
Cord, or axe, or guillotine,
Make the sentence – not the sin.

Here we watch our brother's sleep:
Watch with us, but do not weep:
Watch with us thro' dead of night –
But expect the morning light.[16]

Thanks in part to Drennan, now 'the Protestants had their martyr'.[17] And REMEMBER ORR became the two last words, literally, that many of the United Irishmen in the terrible year to come would have heard or uttered.

Throughout the late summer, Tone waited and waited for the sailing of a second expedition to Ireland. He was cooped up aboard the 74-gun *Vrijheid*, at anchor in the channels of the Texel. This is the Frisian island off the north-west coast of the Netherlands, agriculturally famous for their wool and cheese, militarily famous for the sea battle in which Admiral van Tromp was killed nearly 150 years earlier: hardly an auspicious precedent for Tone.

Victim once more of contrary winds, he reflected on the contrast between the grandness of his visions and the pettiness of time passing:

> There never was and never will be such an expedition as ours; if it succeeds; it is not merely to determine which of two despots shall sit upon a throne, or whether an island shall belong to this or that state; it is to change the destiny of Europe – to open the sea to the commerce of the world; to found a new empire, to demolish an ancient one; to subvert a tyranny of six hundred years. And all this hangs today on the wind! Well, 'tis but in vain for soldiers to complain' (for the 595th time).[18]

Alternative plans were considered, some of them sounding very wild – for example, sending the fleet round the North of Scotland, or landing on the east coast of England and marching to set up the flag of rebellion in Hyde Park.

When not brooding, he occupied his time by reading Voltaire. He also had consolation from the company of the newly appointed Dutch General Daendels, who hoped to restore some lustre to his country's name. There were musical evenings, too, with the Admiral: 'It is terrible to be locked up by the wind as we are now ... Admiral Dewinter and I endeavour to pass away the time, playing the flute, which he does very well; we have some good duets, and that is some relief.'[19]

Once he received a visit by emissaries from Ireland, who were travelling via Hamburg on their way to bring news and requests to the Directory in Paris. They brought him the distressing news of divisions in the movement between the North and South, between the daredevil schemes of Fitzgerald and the caution of Keogh. Tone notes in his *Memoirs*:

> there seems to have been a great want of spirit in leaders in Dublin ... the people have been urgent more than once to begin, and, at one time, eight hundred of the garrison offered to give up the barracks of Dublin, if the leaders would only give the signal; the militia were almost to a man gained over ... with eight hundred of the garrison, and the barracks to begin with, in an hour they would have had the whole capital, and by seizing the persons of half a dozen individuals, paralysed the Government and, in my

opinion, accomplished the whole revolution by a single proclamation . . . Keogh, I know, is not fit for a *coup de main*.[20]

The most awful happening of these months, however, was the death of Hoche, who had been Tone's champion, protector and friend, and the keenest advocate (after Tone himself) of a French liberation of Ireland. He was the one General, ambitious and decisive, who might have become a serious rival of Napoleon. He was only twenty-nine, and, in command of the Army of the East, would have probably led the fresh expedition, had he not stood down for the Dutchman Daendels. Tone visited him at his headquarters near Bonn in September, *en route* to consultations with the Directory in Paris. By then, Hoche was already hollow-cheeked from tuberculosis. He was carried from room to room by four grenadiers; and, for all the reassurances Tone was given, his death two days later probably put paid to any serious French plan to use Ireland as a major tool for the conquest of England.

The next day Tone, beckoned by the brief, desirable oblivion of sex, resisted the temptation. He confides to his journal:

I had promised a very pretty woman at dinner, 'whose name I know not, but whose person I reverence' to meet her to-night at a grand ball given by the Municipality; but I will deceive her like a false traitor, and go to my innocent bed; yet she is very pretty for all that and speaks very pretty German French, and I am sure has not one grain of cruelty in her composition, and besides, *à la guerre, comme à la guerre* – but then, I must set off tomorrow, and so, 'Oh, cruel fate! that gave thee to the Moor!' Besides, I have just received a delightful letter from my dearest love, written three month ago, which has put me out of conceit with all women but herself, so, as before, I will go to my virtuous bed.[21]

In December Tone at last conferred with Napoleon. It was on the 21st, at a house in the rue Chantereine:

He lives in the greatest simplicity; his house is small, but neat, and all the furniture and ornaments in the most classical taste. He is about five feet six inches high, slender and well made, but stoops considerably; he looks at least ten years older than he is, owing to the great fatigues he underwent in his immortal campaign of Italy. His face is that of a profound thinker, but bears no mark of that great enthusiasm and unceasing activity by which he has been so much distinguished. It is rather, to my mind, the countenance of a mathematician than of a general. He has a fine eye, and a great firmness about his mouth; he speaks low and hollow. So much for his manner and figure. We had not much discourse with him; and what little there was, was between him and Lewins* . . . [who] *insensed* him a good deal on Irish affairs, of which he appears singularly uninformed; for example, he seems convinced that our population is not more than two millions – which is nonsense. Buonaparte listened, but said very little. When all this was finished . . . turning to me, he asked whether I was not an Adjutant General . . . [and] asked me where I had learned to speak French? To which I replied, that I had learned the little I knew since my arrival in France, about twenty months ago. He then desired us to return next evening but one, at the same hour, and so we parted. As to my French, I am ignorant whether it was the purity or the barbarism of my diction which drew his attention . . . His manner is cold, and he speaks very little; it is not, however, so dry as that of Hoche, but seems rather to proceed from languor than anything else. He is perfectly civil, however, to us.[22]

Tone was disappointed with himself at having seen the greatest man in Europe three times, and having so little to record about him:

I am sure I wrote ten times as much about my first interview with [the Foreign Minister] Charles de la Croix, but then I was a greenhorn; I am now a little used to see great men, and great statesman, and great generals, and that has, in some degree broke down my admiration. Yet, after all, it is a droll thing that I should become acquainted with Buonaparte. This time twelve months, I arrived in Brest, from my expedition to Bantry Bay. Well, the third time, they say, is the charm. My next chance, I hope, will be with the *Armée d'Angleterre – Allons! Vive la République!* I make no memorandums now at all, which is grievous; but I have nothing to write.[23]

---

* Edward Lewins was appointed as the official plenipotentiary of the United Irishmen to France in February 1797. Tone does not seem to have taken it amiss. They knew each other from Tone's old days on the Catholic Committee. He sounds the caricature of an eighteenth-century attorney: dry, pedantic, with sunken eyes, prominent eyebrows and protuberant chin. Reinhard was unimpressed (see Marianne Elliott, *Wolfe Tone*, p. 343).

16

Prelude to the '98

Perhaps those, who, trembling most, maintain a dignity in their fate, are the bravest: resolution on reflection is real courage.

Horace Walpole, *Memoirs of the Reign of King George III*

This is the year when the heavens fell in. But the skies, at its opening, gave little hint of the deluge to follow. In January Tone had a last meeting with Napoleon, handing him 'a whole sheaf of papers relative to Ireland', including his two memorials of 1795, 'a great part of which stands good yet'. The principal one argued simply that Ireland was still a British colony, and that the colonists – 450,000 Protestants of the established Church, comprising one-tenth of the population – were determined to maintain the British connection. Until a few years earlier the Dissenters of the North were thought to be alongside them. Now, inspired by the ideals of the French Revolution, the example of the American War of Independence and the propaganda of the United Irishmen, the Dissenters were at one with the Catholic peasantry. Presbyterian rationalism and Catholic nationalism were uniting to bring about the Irish revolution:

It would be a great and splendid act of generosity and justice . . . to rescue a whole nation from a slavery under which they have groaned for six hundred years . . . it is to the glory of France to establish one more free Republic in Europe . . . it is to her interest to cut off one half of the resources of England.[1]

'*Mais vous êtes brave*', Napoleon said at the end of the meeting. Tone replied that, when the occasion presented itself, that would appear. '*Eh bien*', said Napoleon, '*cela suffit.*'[2]

By late spring Tone was back at Le Havre, as ever preparing for invasion. He found himself within two cannon shots of a squadron of English frigates; as they passed the battery about a dozen shells were exchanged:

> It was a fine sight, and I should have enjoyed it more, had it not been for certain speculations on futurity and transmigration of souls . . . I defy any man to know whether he is brave or not, until he is tried, and I am very far from boasting of myself on that score; but the fact is that . . . as I thought to begin the cannonade, though I cannot say with truth that I was perfectly easy, yet neither did I feel at all disconcerted . . . the crowd and the bustle, the noise, and especially the conviction that the eyes of the cannoniers were fixed on my *chapeau galonnée*, settled me at once; it is the etiquette in such cases, that the General (i.e. himself) stands conspicuous on the parapet, while the cannoniers are covered by the *épaulement*, which is truly amusing for him that commands. Nevertheless, I have no doubt it is easier to behave well on the parapet, exposed to all the fire, than in the battery, where the danger is much less . . . [but] it was six in the evening before the English stood off; and on the faith of an honest man, I cannot truly say I was sorry when I saw them decidedly turn their backs. Huzza! *Vive la République*![3]

The trials of bravery grew through all that year.

Tone did not, however, read any account of the outbreak of the Rebellion, and of the arrest and death of Lord Edward Fitzgerald, until 11 June, in the French papers. Tone suffered a violent spasm in the stomach, which confined him all day. It is the only time in all his *Memoirs* we hear of his being thus prostrated:

> I knew Fitzgerald very little, but I honour and venerate his character, which he has uniformly sustained, and, in this last instance, illustrated. What miserable wretches by his side are the gentry of Ireland! I would rather be Fitzgerald, as he is now, wounded in his dungeon, than Pitt at the head of the British Empire. What a noble fellow! Of the first family in Ireland, with an easy fortune, a beautiful wife, a family of lovely children, and the certainty of a splendid appointment under Government if he would condescend to support their measures, he has devoted himself wholly to the emancipation of his country, and sacrificed everything to it, even to his blood . . . I dread everything for him, and my only consolation is in speculations of revenge. If the blood of this brave young man be

shed by the hands of his enemies, it is no ordinary vengeance which will content the People, whenever the day of retribution arrives.[4]

Premonitions of the fate of his own family of 'lovely children' must have filled Tone's mind, as he wrote these words.

A week later, his thoughts again turned to vengeance after he had read the papers:

As I suspected, the brave and unfortunate Fitzgerald was meditating an attack on the capital, which was to have taken place a few days after he was arrested. He is since dead in prison; his career is finished gloriously for himself, and, whatever the event, his memory will live for ever in the heart of every honest Irishman. He was a gallant fellow . . . for us, who remain as yet, and may perhaps soon follow him, the only way to lament his death is to revenge it.[5]

This was two days before Tone's thirty-fifth birthday. He had not been at all reassured by all that he had heard on his last visit to Paris. Finally he was told on 20 June that, since England enjoyed such superiority at sea, and it was thus impractical to escape from any ports in the fine weather, the Directory had decided to postpone the expedition again. For the first time Tone confessed to have lost his temper. Here was Ireland in full revolt, but abandoned to its own meagre resources. The tide in Ireland's fortunes was ebbing fast.

When the expedition finally set sail in the autumn, it was too late.

The same paper in which Tone read the news of the arrest and death of Fitzgerald also carried a distressing paragraph about Arthur O'Connor's misadventure at Margate.

Impatient with the timidity of the Committee of United Irishman in Dublin (as shown in their refusal to adopt such daring plans as the bogus Orange disruption of the Christmas Mass), O'Connor had decided to make a foray to Paris. The Directory must be kept up to date with the Irish situation.* Had he succeeded in crossing the channel to France, he would probably have joined Tandy, 'strutting in Paris', and further queered the pitch for Tone and Lewins, who

---

* The 'somewhat amorous' Lady Lucy Fitzgerald saw him in London on January 8. His departure from Ireland may have had other causes . . . (see Frank MacDermot, 'Arthur O'Connor', *Irish Historical Studies*, xv).

were already suffering from the internecine quarrels of self-proclaimed Irish revolutionary emissaries.

But thanks to the information of Samuel Turner and others, O'Connor was swooped upon by Bow Street runners in Margate. He was conspicuous by his amazing welter of boxes, trunks and portmanteaus, but fortunately carried no incriminating documents, apart from a code in his razor-case. (The more damaging ones had been disposed of in the lavatory, just in time.)[6]

O'Connor, his megalomania at full stretch, persuaded a splendid queue of the great to troop into the witness-box to testify to the excellence of his character, and the nobility of his errand. He was, he said, going to France to help recover Lady Fitzgerald's property there. Fox, Lord Suffolk, Sheridan, the Duke of Norfolk, Grattan, Lord John Russell, Lord Oxford, all appeared. This is a typical exchange:

> *Counsel:* During the whole course of your acquaintance, have you had reason to suppose him a man well or ill affected to his country?
> *Fox:* I have always thought Mr O'Connor to be perfectly well affected to his country; I have always considered him to be a very enlightened man, attached to the principles and the constitution of this country, upon which the present family sit upon the throne, and to which we owe all our liberties.[7]

The judge was intimidated, the jury impressed. Not having wished to prejudice their sources of information, the Government failed to secure his conviction for high treason.* He was as lucky as he was plausible. He had, incidentally, behaved most disgracefully at the trial. Attempting to exculpate himself, he had incriminated another defendant, to the point where the judge rebuked him, 'Mr O'Connor, do you not see how much this is to the prejudice of the other prisoner?'

Drennan was among those who had been 'earnestly entreated' to testify on his behalf, although he had not met O'Connor more than half a dozen times. His agreement reflects his integrity: it was the right, the virtuous thing to do. But the tone of his letters suggests, too, that he was not altogether displeased to be asked to give evi-

---

* After his acquittal he was re-arrested, sent to Ireland and held in prison (for the most part in Scotland, with other United Irish leaders) until 1803.

dence for O'Connor, despite the expense of the visit to Margate. He was flattered; he would be in the company of great men; he would travel with Grattan. And it sounds as if he did indeed enjoy his visit to England in April:

> Mr Grattan was in company and during the whole excursion he was civil, kind and courteous . . . How many beautiful country seats did we pass, built for the pleasure of the travellers rather than the possessors! How many comfortable cottages did we see, more certainly filled with happiness; such lovely verdure in the fields, such neatness, and even elegance in their little gardens, in the kitchens of their inns, in the dress of their servant maids who in general officiate as waiters; such excellent roads . . . such hearty and seemingly happy horses, such a smooth celerity of pleasant conveyance is not to be found but in England . . .[8]

The letters also contain Drennanesque passages of moral approval and disapproval. The smell of the Liverpool docks reminded him of the iniquities of the slave trade; other towns were so agreeably clean to him that cleanliness 'really appears to me if not the mother, at least the nurse of all the virtues'. There was much to edify him. He allowed himself a visit to Drury Lane, however, when temptation appeared to him (though in the very mildest, least reprobate of forms):

> In the evening I accompanied [Mr Grattan] to the gallery of the opera . . . a very fine orchestra, over which we nodded at each other, not so much with delight as with the astonishing influence of sleep; sometimes, indeed, aroused by the display of female dancing, which, in spite of the Bishop of Durham, is divine . . .[9]

There is something Pooter-like about the outcome of the expedition, too. In the end, he never appeared in court. After spending three days in London (as his attendance at the trial proved unnecessary, and he was not even called), he found that it had been intended that he should testify only to the 'really trivial circumstance' that on the few times they had met, O'Connor had spoken of his eagerness for peace, and that all countries should be left to work out their own freedom: that is to say, that he had *not* talked revolution. Drennan recounts this without any expressions of the irritation he must surely have felt for his wasted and expensive journey.

Drennan returned just as the news of the proclamation of County Dublin was about to come into force. Rebellion was imminent. Yet the playhouses still played and the promenades took place; for the time being there was little apparent alteration in the tenor of life.

At one point in the pre-Rebellion days of March Drennan had written to his sister about a seeming oversight. Nearly all the National Committee of United Irishmen had been taken up: 'Seven whom I know and consider as friends are now in prison.' The few who were still at large included Lord Edward Fitzgerald. Yet Drennan himself was left alone, unmolested.

For many years outside the counsels of the Society, Drennan kept up only social links. But his political opinions, though seldom if ever expressed in public, had not greatly changed. He did not think that the Government had by their arrests broken the back of the United Irishmen:

> The Chancellor may imagine he has taken off the heads of the union, but it is a perfect asparagus bed and bears cutting ... The people here look on me as a solitary ninepin, standing by chance when the other eight are bowled down; but some more deeply infer that something serious must be committed by the rest when I am suffered to go at large, as if all the arrests had been made by a precise line of discrimination.[10]

Relief seemed to have eliminated *almost* every trace of pique at being passed over.

When Drennan thought of his United Irish friends and ex-colleagues, his mind often turned to Rowan. Here, too, he seems to have felt just a little nettled. Rowan may not have been in any way a turncoat, but it was known that he was lying very low in Philadelphia. And known, too, that Mrs Rowan was constantly pleading on his behalf with the Government. Drennan once wrote to Martha McTier:

> The Chancellor rode up the other day to Mrs Rowan's carriage, congratulated her on the behaviour of Mr R. for some time past, so opposite to that of his former political companions, and assured her that at the conclusion of the *war* such conduct must facilitate his return to his country, his wife and his property. Their son here is a complete convert to maternal opinion and the leniency of Government, and is eager to serve in army or navy against the common enemy.[11]

Rowan himself was, however, not so entirely innocent of political activity as he made out to his wife, or as his wife made out to the Lord Chancellor. He remained quick to be stirred by injustices, a glutton for causes. At least his crusades were now American-based. At about this time the United States went through a phase of believing it was time to close their doors, just a little, to the uncontrolled flood of immigrants from the Old World. They introduced an Aliens Act. For a while it looked as though this might be very uncomfortable for Rowan. It required those who did not take out citizenship to leave the country within fifteen days. He felt that, for others as well as himself, this was a penal statute. 'Penal' was a fighting word for any Irishman. He appeared before a large assembly on a platform in Philadelphia, and was taken aback at hearing the last speaker say: '*Now let us give three cheers for the persecuted patriot, Hamilton Rowan, and KICK THE TREATY TO HELL.*' With that he threw a copy into the crowd.

This was a passport, Rowan feared, to unwelcome notoriety, however much he may have brought it on himself. An item appeared in the Baltimore newspapers, talking of 'this Rowan who is known to have escaped from the hands of justice and to have fled from France . . . apostle of those abominable principles which have deluged Europe with blood . . . known to have joined the democratic, Jacobin, anti-federal faction here from the moment of his landing'. A paper called *Peter Porcupine's Gazette* made the most of it.

Now the ominous words, reminiscent of his duelling days, began to crop up. A letter to the editor of the *Gazette* ended with the words, 'I request you to explain', and a demand for an interview. Why, he asked, had the *Gazette*, which was no doubt widely read in Europe, presumed to break in on the peace of his family? He had studiously avoided mingling in the politics of the United States. Offending neither the Government nor individuals, he had expected to live unmolested.

His friends persuaded him in the end that the editor was too much like a blackguard to be treated like a gentleman. Universal contempt was the proper answer. A duel was averted; but it was a narrow squeak.

Less dangerous pastimes would have caused Mrs Rowan less anxiety. Her husband was quite prepared to write to her about the familiar aquatic misadventures, in a way that perhaps brought back rueful memories of France. They at least would not prejudice his eventual pardon. In the summer, he tells how,

The night before last I passed in my batteau on the Delaware. I was fool enough to trust a fine day, and as I used to do with you at Epinay, forgot how to turn about until the tide turned; but with the evening came on one of those sudden changes of weather, that among others, make this country detestable and detested. The swell prevented me from benefiting by the tide; I ran on shore, as one would call it; but the rivers have no shore, they are bounded by marsh, *alias* mud, and there was no getting on dry land; and in my batteau full of water, with my oars etc., lashed to the seat, I spent the night, and this being the fourth day after it, I have been as well as I have been this year, so you see . . . have still a bit of iron in my constitution, though the steel may be ground off.[12]

Such 'unnecessary troubles' certainly brought a rebuke from his wife; but they were harmless enough, and no doubt tallied with her general opinion of her husband's antics. In his history Lecky calls Mrs Rowan 'a woman of very superior intellect and character': somehow a rather daunting tribute.

Rowan might well have realized (almost as well as his wife) that the Irish Government would read his letters; and that there would be displeasure in Dublin over that 'KICK THE TREATY TO HELL'. But by 1798 a host of far greater worries and uncertainties occupied the Castle. The trouble did not lie in any shortage of informers: Dublin swarmed with them. They sent in long, detailed reports about imminent revolution, making correct assessment all but impossible, differences about times and places bewildering, and agreements on the magnitude of the danger the only common factor.

There was, as ever, the shrewd and insinuating McNally. Apart from his contributions to intelligence, his comic opera *Robin Hood* was being staged that spring in Dublin. On the night Lord Edward Fitzgerald was eventually arrested, the audience included a party taken by the Viceroy Lord Camden.

There was Tone's own brother-in-law, Thomas Reynolds, who had long lived idly, in comfort and dissipation. He had become a friend of Fitzgerald's, and the Duke of Leinster had given him an advantageous lease of a castle in County Kildare. He had more or less drifted into the Society of United Irishmen, becoming the Treasurer of the Leinster Directory. This was a singularly bad appointment, since he was hopeless with the care of money, almost to the point of bankruptcy.

Early in the year, Reynolds, by his own account, had become

alarmed at the vast and bloody designs of his fellow conspirators, including the proposal to assassinate eighty prominent men. In terror he turned for advice and help to his chief creditor; and the two hatched a profitable plot between them (although Reynolds virtuously insisted that his only motive was to save his country from the horrors of a civil war). In any case, it was on his information that the 'asparagus bed' was cropped. What made Reynolds's information particularly useful was his agreement to testify, in open court, against those whom he betrayed – the refusal of other informers to do so had greatly reduced their value.

Now came a most important turning point. Oliver Bond and a dozen or so of the other members of the Leinster Committee were successfully swooped upon on 12 March. The consequent lack of firm direction of the Rebellion, though it did not reduce the carnage, put paid to any chance of its success.

Only three of the Committee escaped arrest. The principal of these, Edward Fitzgerald, remained at large for another two months; Reynolds seems to have had enough conscience to tip off his friend and benefactor.

Thus it was that, as preparations for rebellion ought to have been reaching their climax, the most important of the United Irish directorates was a rump of fewer than a handful of members. And what members! Fitzgerald was the rashest of men. Sam Neilson, lately released from prison, a principal founder of the Belfast Society, former proprietor of the closed-down *Northern Star*, had once been a man of substance, but was by now a hopeless alcoholic. And Francis Magan, a new and untried recruit to the United Irishmen, a young, briefless Catholic barrister, was, in addition, an informer.

The most conspicuous service Magan performed for the Government was the discovery of Fitzgerald on the night of 19 May. He 'set' Fitzgerald, as game dogs set their quarry.

It was in some ways extraordinary that the Government had not discovered and arrested Fitzgerald before. They knew enough about his comings and goings. So why had they let him be? In part, as we have seen, the Lord-Lieutenant doubted they would be able to bring him successfully to trial, since informers other than Reynolds refused to testify. In part, too, Fitzgerald had formidable connections. Perhaps it was also because the Government could not take him wholly seriously as a leader. In any case, until a very late hour it took few steps to reel him in.

All the same, the time came in the spring when his complicity, so long almost condoned, and the glamour of his name so openly attached to the revolutionary cause, made his arrest imperative. It is very doubtful that he would have made a competent leader, but certain that he would have made a popular one.

Magan was so good at diverting suspicion from himself that, on the same night as Fitzgerald was arrested, he was elected a member of the head Committee of the United Irishmen. He had all the airs of a patriot, voting against the proposed Union at a meeting of the Bar, after the Rebellion, in September. He took an active interest in the campaign for Catholic emancipation, earning the confidence of its leaders while, as always, continuing (for a price) to supply information to the Government.

During the two-month interlude between the arrests at Oliver Bond's house and his capture in mid-May – between Reynolds's betrayal and Magan's setting – Fitzgerald led a vagabond life in a number of Dublin lodgings, using a variety of disguises. That might be called prudent, although prudence was out of character. And he played his parts with such gusto and high spirits that it is hard to think of him as in any kind of timorous hiding. His biographer Thomas Moore describes a few of his escapades, with relish at his bravado:

> The name he went by, while at the house of [one] widow lady, was Jameson* . . . he had, however, not been more than two or three days in the house, when one of those slight accidents, which seem to defy all caution, made the secret known to all the family. A pair of his boots having been left outside his door to be cleaned, the man-servant to whom they had been given for that purpose told his mistress that he 'knew who the gentleman upstairs was – but that she need not fear, for he would die to save him'. He then showed her Lord Edward's name written, at full length in one of the boots. Thinking it possible that, after such a discovery, her guest might deem it dangerous to remain, Mrs ** mentioned it to him. But his fears were not easily awakened: – 'What a noble fellow!' he exclaimed. 'I should like to have some talk with him'. In the hope that it might be an incitement to the man's fidelity, the lady told him of his lordship's wish; but he answered 'no, – I will not look at him – for, if they should take me up, I can then, you know, swear that I never saw him.'[13]

---

* Presumably because he was indeed one of the seventeen sons of James, Duke of Leinster.

This mixture of unselfconscious arrogance and charm is not uncommon in those brought up in great houses and cosseted by servants. Lord Edward stayed in his first, unsuspected safe house for a month, making few efforts to hide. He did not allow despondency to set in:

> as it was feared that to one accustomed so much to exercise confinement might prove injurious, he used to walk out, most nights, along the banks of the canal, accompanied generally by a child, who became a great favourite of his, and whom it was his amusement sometimes to frighten by jumping in the boats that were half sunk in the reservoir or basin of the canal. So light-hearted, indeed, and imprudent was he at times that [his landlady] Mrs ** . . . used often to hear him at a considerable distance, laughing with his young companion, and more than once went out to meet them, and try to impress upon him the necessity of more caution.
> Another subject of merriment between him and his young play-fellow arose from a large bed of orange lilies which grew at the bottom of the garden, and which they had conspired to root up, some day, when Mrs ** should be away from home.[14]

Was this a horticultural repudiation of the 'unity of the sects'?

There were also occasions of resourceful cross-dressing. Once, a guard of soldiers with fixed bayonets had passed by on the other side of the canal. A police office had been seen looking up determinedly at the house:

> The maid . . . made him instantly put on a lady's night-dress and get into bed; then, darkening the room, as for a person indisposed, she placed a table with medicine bottles upon it, beside the bed. In this situation he remained for two hours – but neither policemen nor soldiers again made their appearance; and the scene served but as a subject of mirth for the evening's conversation.[15]

Another transvestite episode of these weeks also entered family legend, though it had almost ended in tears:

> As it was now more than a month since he had seen any of his family, insisting that Mr Murphy [his new landlord] should dress him in women's clothes he went, attended by his host, in that disguise, to Denzel street [where Pamela was lodged]. The surprise, however, had nearly proved fatal to Lady Fitzgerald. Some friend being with her at the moment, the servant came to say that there was a lady in the parlour waiting to see her; and, on Lady Edward discovering who it was, and that he meant to remain

till next night, her alarm at his danger, and her anxiety about his return, brought on a premature confinement, and her second daughter, Lucy, was born.[16]

Despite such antics, Fitzgerald does not seem to have neglected all military duties. He drew up plans for the armies of the three counties of Dublin, Wicklow and Kildare to join forces a few miles to the west of Dublin, immediately before the rising. He examined and reviewed the signals which should open the Rebellion. He read the coded letter from France which brought the dusty news that there was no hope of a preliminary landing of a force of 5,000 men. (Fitzgerald had never believed in waiting for the French, anyway.) He had impromptu discussions with other leaders. But although he was still in nominal command of the Leinster Directory, it is hard to see how, in these Scarlet Pimpernel days, he could have been very effective.

Once he went out, again in disguise, to reconnoitre the routes which it was hoped the armies of the Rebellion might take. He nearly came to grief:

> It appears that he rode, attended by Neilson, to reconnoitre the line of advance, on the Kildare side, to Dublin, – the route marked out on one of the papers found upon him when he was arrested – and it was on this occasion that he was, for some time, stopped and questioned, by the patrol at Palmerston. Being well disguised, and representing himself to be a doctor on his way to a dying patient, his companion and he were suffered to proceed on their way.[17]

Another report commented that his companion Neilson played the part of a drunk to perfection. It came naturally to him.

For a while, the Government would have been very happy to see Fitzgerald simply leave the country. His arrest would have caused a furore, and might have immediately triggered the uprising. The Lord Chancellor, fond as he was of members of his family, was especially keen he should escape. He told his stepfather, 'For God's sake get this young man out of the country: the ports shall be thrown open to him, and no hindrance whatever offered.'

In early May, however, rumours of massive gatherings of rebel troops, and of imminent assassinations in the heart of Dublin, turned the scales. Even as a figurehead, Fitzgerald was too dangerous to leave at large any longer. The sum of £1,000 was put on his head.

His last recorded moments of freedom were employed in the receiving of his revolutionary uniform, delivered to Murphy's house on the evening of Ascension Day. This gave those in the know a moment's alarm; the revolution was obviously about to begin. The uniform itself was described as 'a bottle green braided suit with crimson cape, cuffs, silk lace and a green and crimson cap of liberty 2 ft. long'. It was hidden under some goat skins in a nearby loft, in the hope that their 'offensiveness would be a security against search'.[18]

17

Rebels' ends

What is the worst of woes that wait on age?
What stamps the wrinkle deeper on the brow?
To view each loved one blotted from life's page,
And be alone on earth, as I am now.
                    Byron, *Childe Harold's Pilgrimage*, Canto 2

Lord Edward Fitzgerald was captured on 19 May, three days before the outbreak of open rebellion in Leinster. A posse burst in to his attic bedroom in the feather-merchant's house. Knives were drawn, shots were fired. It was a brief and bloody affair. An unfortunate Captain Ryan was left with his bowels spilling over the floor. Fitzgerald, who had defended himself with the pistols lent him by Reynolds, sustained only minor injury – or so it was thought at first. This disappointed him. It would have been better to have died in battle. Told that his wound was not dangerous, he said, 'I'm sorry for it'.[1]

He was taken through the streets in an open sedan chair, to the Castle. His rebel's bottle green uniform and his green and crimson cap of Liberty were taken separately after him. His wounds were dressed. Papers were found on him, one containing the proposed line of rebel attack on Dublin. He must certainly have realized that he would now be arraigned for high treason, and that the Government would have all the evidence they needed to secure his conviction. Then, carried on to Newgate, he was placed in a small cell, and was allowed no visitors at all, apart from a surgeon. Wildfire rumours of his arrest spread through the city: 'People were perceived in small parties, conversing with that seriousness of countenance and energy of gesticulation, which strongly indicated the agitation of their minds.'[2] One or two rescue efforts were made, all too late.

Now, as his recovery was still very much hoped for, began day after day of passionate attempts by his family to visit him, to condole Pamela ('only break it to her gently'), to influence the Lord-Lieutenant, to appeal to the Home Secretary, the Duke of Portland, to beseech the Prince of Wales and the King himself for mercy. One of his uncles wrote:

> My sister, at the King's feet, imploring a pardon on condition of exile, *may* do more than all the politicians, lawyers or exertions in the whole world; let her try it *instantly*, and never quit him until obtained: stop at no forms or refusals. Human nature must give way . . .[3]

Slowly, the forlorn hope of pardon gave way to the wait for death. Spasms brought on by septicaemia grew more agonizing. Towards the last, that sternest of judges, the Lord Chancellor Lord Clare, took it on himself to disregard the Lord-Lieutenant's weak inflexibility about visitors, and to exercise the quality of mercy. In his own carriage he escorted Fitzgerald's aunt Louisa Conolly and his much-loved brother Henry to his prison deathbed (his adoring mother was still on her way from England). Louisa's affecting account of the dying moments of the favourite son of all the family allows one to see something of the love which he inspired in others, and of his simplicity:

> I first approached his bed; he looked at me, knew me, kissed me, and said (what will never depart from my ears), 'it is heaven to me to see you!' and, shortly after, turning to the other side of his bed, he said, 'I can't see you'. I went round, and he soon after kissed my hand, and smiled at me, which I shall never forget, though I saw death in his face at the time. I then told him that Henry was come. He said nothing that marked surprise at his being in Ireland, but expressed joy at hearing it, and said, 'Where is he, dear fellow?'
>
> Henry then took my place, and the two dear brothers frequently embraced each other, to the melting a heart of stone; and yet God enabled both Henry and myself to remain quite composed. As every one left the room, we told him we only were with him. He said, 'That is very pleasant.' However, he remained silent, and I then brought in the subject of Lady Edward [Pamela had been dispatched to England, out of trouble], and told him that I had not left her until I saw her on board; and Henry told

him of having met her on the road well. He said, 'And the children too? – she is a charming woman:' and then became silent again. That expression about Lady Edward proved to me, that his senses were much lulled, and that he did not feel his situation to be what it was; but, thank God! they were enough alive to receive pleasure from seeing his brother and me. Dear Henry, in particular, he looked at continually with an expression of pleasure.

When we left him, we told him, that as he appeared inclined to sleep, we would wish him a good night, and return in the morning. He said, 'do, do;' but did not express any uneasiness at our leaving him.[4]

Two and a half hours later, he died. It was 4 June, and the Rebellion was in full swing.

It is hard to disagree with the verdict of Lecky, writing at the end of the last century:

> There is not, indeed, the smallest reason to believe that Fitzgerald had any of the qualities of a great man, or was in the least likely to have led his country to any high or honourable destiny. But he was a well-known public man. He was a Protestant. He was a member of a great aristocratic family, and if he had appeared at the head of a rebellion, it is extremely probable that the Northern rebels would have risen at his call, though they remained almost passive when they found the rebellion headed by fanatical priests and by obscure country gentlemen of whom they had never heard. In that case the sea of blood which in the next few months deluged a few counties would have probably overspread the whole island. From this great calamity Ireland was saved by the arrest of May 19.[5]

Equally, on a personal level, it is hard to disagree with the temperate reflections of his uncle the Duke of Richmond, in a letter to Lord Edward's mother:

> Goodwood, June 19 1798
> whatever faults he might have, he had a warm and affectionate heart . . . it might be better for [Pam] to leave a country where she meets with so little justice from the generality of mankind and to settle with her friends abroad. I cannot think it proper to judge the simplicity of his idealism too harshly, however terrible the consequences were to himself and others. Most will find it in their hearts to forgive, even if not to applaud, a man so gallant, generous and simple.[6]

Everybody who came in touch with Lord Edward Fitzgerald does seem to have liked him from the heart. Charm, courage, simplicity, openness, mingled with warmth and affection, are attractive virtues: dangerously so. True, Drennan's sister Martha McTier had no good words to say about him. But then she was *very* unimpressionable.

The reported death of the 'noble fellow' Fitzgerald, and the failure of the North to break into co-ordinated rebellion, produced in Tone an unusual lowness of spirits. He was also coming to realize that Napoleon was not, after all, going to mount any major expedition to Ireland. There would be forays, yes, but nothing of the scale to bring true Tone's dream of independence: no great military campaign. The East was now in Napoleon's eye: Egypt or even the great prize of India. Hints of despair and the chill hand of mortality were beginning to enter Tone's journal.

The force which in late summer sailed to Ireland under General Humbert did cheer him a little. Over a thousand officers and men landed at Killala, thirty miles west of Sligo, and fought some successful engagements, briefly occupying a large part of County Mayo. Not a very large force, to be sure, in a country in which some hundred times as many British troops were deployed. From the French point of view, it was little more than a diversion. And how sluggishly the recently 'pacified' Ulster seemed to rise! Tone remembered the 'rascal Digges's' observation of eight years earlier, that one Southerner, when roused, was worth twenty Northerners. Indeed, the rebellion which blazed through the South-East that summer, without any French aid, might have confirmed his judgement. The news of the bloody battles in Wexford came to Tone only in confused forms, and the uncertainty filled him with anguish.

At last, in mid-September, Tone sailed from Brest, in an expedition comprising one ship of the line, the *Hoche*, together with eight frigates and a schooner. It had no chance. It was meant as a reinforcement of General Humbert's expedition – which however, had by now been repulsed. Its destination, Lough Swilly, was known to the English. It had to fight a ferocious sea battle (the one type of engagement Tone feared). It was buffeted by fearsome storms. Tone's *Hoche* nearly sank beneath him before it was captured. Sir John Borlase Warren, (who, three years earlier had stopped Rowan's boat in mid-Atlantic) commanded the English force: his victory was complete.

After yet more storms, the remnants of the French were at last brought ashore in small boats on 3 November. They had been at sea for six terrible weeks. Tone disembarked, and saw on the beach an old acquaintance from Trinity College days prominent among those waiting to receive the survivors. This was Sir George Hill, a local magistrate, a Colonel of the militia, and a fierce conservative. Sir George reported to the Castle on the day of the landing:

> This morning some hundreds of the prisoners are just landed. The first man who stepped out of the boat habited as an officer was T.W. Tone; he recognised and addressed me instantly with as much sangfroid as you would expect from his character.[7]

Despite the ambivalence of his position, Tone does seem really to have hoped that he would be treated as a French Officer rather than an Irish renegade; that his rank and uniform would procure him some such crumb of consolation. Indeed, this became a major pre-occupation for the remaining days of his life. Insults and indignities offered to him were, he insisted with all the pride at his command, insults to the honour of France.

Unsurprisingly, this was not a view shared by the Lord-Lieutenant and his staff. A secretary wrote, in reply to his indignant letter:

> Theobald Wolfe Tone is known only to His Excellency as a traitor, who sought to return to Ireland in order to attempt by armed force what he failed to do by intrigue, who has never ceased to promote rebellion and discord, and who at last is about to receive the punishment due for crimes he has been guilty of committing against his King and country.[8]

For all his high protests, Tone was conveyed in irons to Dublin to stand trial. He insisted on changing into full-dress uniform for the last stage of his journey, just as later, in court, he also dressed in full ceremonial French uniform. Presumably salvaged from the wreck of the *Hoche*, this consisted of:

> A large and fiercely cocked hat, with broad gold lace, and the tricoloured cockade, a blue uniform coat, with gold and embroidered collar, and two large gold epaulets, blue pantaloons with gold laced garters at the knees, and short boots bound at the top with gold lace.[9]

He pleaded guilty to the charges laid against him. He was allowed to address the court with an apologia for his life, during which he reiterated that:

The connexion of England I have ever considered the bane of Ireland, and have done everything in my power to break it, and to raise three million of my countrymen to the rank of citizens.[10]

Here he was stopped by the President of the Court, but allowed to proceed for a while, as he claimed that he had never had recourse to any other than 'open and manly war':

In the glorious race of patriotism, I have pursued the path chalked out by Washington in America, and Kosciuszko in Poland. Like the latter, I have failed to emancipate my country; and, unlike both, I have forfeited my life – I have done my duty, and I have no doubt the Court will do theirs.[11]

He asked only 'for the death of a soldier, and to be shot by a file of grenadiers'. This was denied him. He was told that he must suffer the same fate with other traitors who were taken in war against their King and country.

It was so grievous for him to be refused a soldier's death – so contrary to his wish that a firing squad should provide the last act of his tragedy – that he determined on a measure he abominated: suicide. He cut his windpipe, it was said with a pen-knife, in his wretched cell.

The wound was not immediately fatal. Tone had, *in extremis*, not lost his gift for self-mockery: he muttered, 'I find, then, I am but a bad anatomist'. Nine days of excruciating pain followed, with his head propped in one position. He died on the morning of Monday, 19 November 1798.

Innumerable judgements have been passed on Tone's life and death. I imagine he would have been pleased by those that paid tribute to his gaiety, courage, love of country and sense of honour. Whether or not a man who esteemed the military virtues would have been pleased by later republicans purloining his name for some of their *chouanneries* is another matter altogether.

The measured, high Victorian tribute of Lecky still reads well, I think, though Tone might have smiled at its high-minded lack of homour, and, ruefully, at its comment on Irish independence:

It would be a manifest exaggeration to call him a great man, but he had many of the qualities of mind and character by which, under favourable conditions, greatness has been achieved, and he rises far above the dreary level of commonplace which Irish conspiracy in general presents. The tawdry and exaggerated rhetoric; the petty vanities and jealousies; the weak sentimentalism; the utter incapacity for proportioning means to ends, and for grasping the stern realities of things, which so commonly disfigure the lives and conduct even of the more honest members of his class, were wholly alien to his nature. His judgement of men and things was keen, lucid, and masculine, and he was alike prompt in decision and brave in action. Coming to France without any advantage of birth, property, position or antecedents, and without even a knowledge of the language, he gained a real influence over French councils, and he displayed the qualities that won the confidence and respect of such men as Carnot and Hoche, Clarke and Grouchy, Daendels and De Winter. His journals clearly show how time, and experience, and larger scenes of action, had matured and strengthened both his intellect and character. The old levity had passed away. The constant fits of drunkenness that disfigured his early life no longer occur. The spirit of a mere adventurer had become much less apparent. A strong and serious devotion to an unselfish cause had unquestionably grown up within him, and if he had become very unscrupulous about attaining his end, he at least was prepared to sacrifice to it, not only his life, but all personal vanity, pretensions, and ambition. If his dream of an independent Ireland now seems a very mad one, it is but justice to him to remember how different was then the position of Ireland, both in relation to England, and in relation to the Continent.[12]

Drennan recorded Tone's entry into Dublin without any great emotion:

1798   November 8, Dublin. I hear that Tone came into the city this day under a strong military guard, dressed in rich French regimentals, and the carriage passed the Four Courts just as the lawyers were coming out. It is said he looked well and unembarrassed.[13]

A few days after the trial and Tone's death, and with equal dispassion, he wrote another letter about his old colleague and rival. It occurred to him, with some gratification, that his own part in the founding of the Society would not, in due course, go unrecorded:

W. Sinclair . . . was present at Tone's trial, whose behaviour was, he [thought], perfectly like a gentleman and a brave man . . . They are making biographical sketches of the leaders and instigators in the Irish Rebellion of '98, and it is done by a tolerable hand for a hireling.[14]

But although Drennan was pleased with the thought that he might be 'honoured with a niche', his *amour propre* was offended by a reference made to himself as 'an unpractising physician of Newry', and he sent a solemn, injured note to the author:

> [You are] incorrect in stating that I was an unpractising physician in Newry. I had considerable practice for seven years in that place, and in this city, although inconsiderable, it is sufficient (and were it smaller it should be sufficient) in spite of petty and unprovoked malignity, to preserve me, unconscious either of neglect or disappointment in the proud possession of honest and honourable independence, the best blessing for myself, and my first and last prayer for my country.[15]

By the end of the year, many people's thoughts, including Drennan's, were beginning to switch from reminiscences of the Rebellion and its 30,000 dead. They were concentrating on Pitt's proposal for the Union. Pamphlets rained down, and Drennan joined in the flurry: he was vehemently against the 'terrible and eternal termination . . . [of] the individuality of Ireland in the duplicity of an Union'.[16] Long gone, however, were the days when he would enter on any activity which smelt of conspiracy. He thanked God that if there were plots, he was unacquainted with them. He talked of renewing his engagement, so desultorily pursued, with the wealthy Miss Swanwick of Wem in Shropshire. He was becoming thoroughly respectable.

Within a few years he was able to leave Dublin, settle in Belfast, and give up practising medicine in order to spend all his time in literary pursuits. He was also thinking earnestly about the proper books for his two little sons to read; in an early will, he left an emphatic direction to his sister:

> soon after putting the best of the books in their hands (the *New Testament*) you will buy for them the second best book in the world, which I think is Plutarch's *Lives* – [the] book that first blew my infant spark of reason into a glow of enthusiasm, which will burn even in my ashes . . . which I used to read when a very child on the rocks near Craigavad, while the Carrickfergus bell in distant toll was wafted over the lough, and the seals plunged into the smooth water . . .[17]

But young Tom Drennan, his elder son, died before he could have properly studied his Plutarch, when he was twelve years old. The Doctor himself lived on to a good age, writing regularly to his sister until the end of his life, helping to found the Belfast Academical Institution, co-editing the *Belfast Magazine*, publishing his lyrics in a slim work entitled *Fugitive Pieces*, and translating Sophocles' *Electra*.

Full of years, he died at Belfast on 5 February 1820, and his coffin was carried to the grave, as he had requested, by six Protestants and six Catholics. Yet it is clear that William Drennan, by birth a son of the manse and by education a child of the Scottish Enlightenment, was much more deeply influenced by the political imperative of the 'unity of the sects', than by any liking or sympathy with Catholics and Catholicism. He was governed by Scottish Enlightenment ideas of worthiness, of *virtus*, of abstinence. He seldom took off the coat of seriousness, certainly never dressed in the clothes of ribaldry. Tone and he had little in common.

On the other hand, it is too easy to underrate him, saying in conformity with present-day tastes that one prefers the high spirits, the sense of theatre, the self-mockery and whistling despair of Wolfe Tone. Drennan's piety (in the Latin sense) was something he had inherited from his father, and passed on to his surviving son. It was a noble tradition. Nor was Drennan just made up of the sterner qualities. The curtain is *sometimes* drawn aside. William, who edited *Glendalloch*, remembered that: 'Naturally grave, his smile, perhaps from its rarity, was very sweet. In company, which he relished, he was extremely agreeable, and even sportive, and to good female society always partial.'[18]

When Rowan first heard news of the failure of Humbert's 1798 campaign in County Mayo he was shocked. A letter he wrote to a Reverend George Potts in Franklin County, Pennsylvania, shows his bewilderment, even dismay. It suggests that on occasion and to suitable correspondents (other than Mrs Rowan) his old revolutionary fire could be kindled:

> The affairs of Ireland are a riddle to me. That an insurrection so partial and so ill-supported should have taken place! That a force should land, which established itself with some éclat, should remain for 15 days, and neither become an army, nor encourage any risings in the north or elsewhere . . . wounds as much as it astonishes me. If the people do not wish a revolution, if they have not suffered enough, no art or force of man can or ought to drive them so. If they hug their chains let them lie upon their necks until they are sufficiently galled and they will then wince.[19]

When he wrote this letter he did not know of the death of Tone. He had first believed that no Irishman had been aboard General Humbert's ships. He could not have heard of the failure of the

Lough Swilly reinforcement that had been much too small, and had arrived much too late. And, like Tone, he might not have been told of the success of General Lake's brutal pacification of the previous months.

At last his wife's solicitations and assertions of his good behaviour, and the good offices of Lord Clare, won for Rowan the assent of the English Government that he could return across the Atlantic without fear of molestation, and live anywhere in Europe he chose. In midsummer in 1800, after five weary and unprofitable years in exile, he sailed back from Philadelphia together with his dog Sally, his opossum, a red parrot and a sack of birdseed. He was bound for Hamburg.

This was a perverse choice. It was a hive of revolutionary exiles of every sort, an 'emporium of mischief'. He was put under surveillance, together with such fellow exiles as Lady Pamela Fitzgerald, who was staying with her cousins, and he met with a lukewarm reception from the British Resident. But at least he was soon with his family.

They moved to Altona, where life was cheaper. Because he was still attainted of treason, he could not touch any income from his great properties, might still lose them in their entirety, if he could not annul his sentence. In the end, he was obliged to 'sue humbly' for pardon, and was allowed to return to Ireland, his outlawry reversed in the same court that had pronounced it. 'In a few manly words which did not compromise his principles, [he] publicly thanked the King for the clemency shown to him and his family during his exile.' He could not much have relished this act of obeisance, made on his knees.

Popular acclaims and celebrations, however, followed his return. When, after his father's death, he returned to their family estates at Killileagh (where his descendants still have their castle today) he was moved by the tremendous reception he received:

Hundreds of horsemen preceded the procession; Mr Hamilton Rowan's servants came first in his post chaise; then the hero of the scene, mounted in an exceedingly high phaeton; then his barouche with his wife and children drawn by four elegant bays . . . ropes were fastened to the carriage and all the family were drawn triumphantly into the town – except Mrs Hamilton Rowan who very sensibly observed that she would not be drawn by human creatures who could debase themselves to the rank of beasts.[20]

It delighted him to hear, within a few years, that Nelson had written a letter to his old friend the Marquis of Abercorn, in high praise of Rowan's son, Captain Rowan Hamilton, RN. It pleased him (and, one presumes, Mrs Rowan) to be well received in the Castle drawing-rooms by the Lord-Lieutenant, where he and his family were seen 'in dresses singularly splendid'.[21]

Yet in no way did he cease to concern himself with those less fortunate than he now was. He reduced his rents. He listened to the grievances of the Dublin lamplighters. He championed ribbon-weavers and silk-manufacturers.

He continued to interest himself in mechanical experiments. (One thinks of his youthful passion for timepieces.) He installed chemical laboratories in each of his three Irish homes, studied printing and lithography, and proposed schemes for making Killileagh into a prosperous centre of the linen production.

Altogether he was not idle in his middle and old age. Nor did he lose his quickness of temper. When he was nearly seventy-four years old he took umbrage at words 'wantonly handled' in the House of Commons (he was referred to as 'a convicted traitor' and as helping the designs of 'this abominable [Catholic] association'). He set out to London, ready to ask for an explanation. It took all the tact of an officer whom Rowan described as 'a polite young man in the Guards, cool, clear and temperate, who acted in the most gentlemanlike manner', to avert a duel.

Hamilton Rowan died on All Souls' Day, 1834, in the sad year following the death of his wife and elder son, and is buried in the vaults of St Mary's Church, Dublin. The memory of the atrocities of the revolution in Paris never left him, nor did his indignation at the injustices he saw around him. He had nevertheless become respectable, and wary of politics. I suppose his wife could be said to have won. She might not, however, be pleased if she knew that he is still honoured by Nationalists as a rebel – for all his reformation.

Only one of the informers mentioned in these pages met an appropriate end. Most continued to live in not too great discomfort – apart, that is, from any visitation by ghosts betrayed – on the pensions the Government paid them, and 'verged to eternity' in their beds.

There were indeed schemes to assassinate John Cockayne, the sad lawyer, envoy of Pitt, who had compassed the death of the Reverend

William Jackson (and indirectly led to the exiles of Hamilton Rowan and Wolfe Tone). But Cockayne survived. Like some other informers, his unquiet conscience seems to have led him to make appearances long after acquaintances had supposed him dead. A lawyer, Charles Phillips, tells us of one such apparition:

> Somewhere about the year 1822, after I had been some short time at the English Bar, a tall and venerable figure entered my chambers with a brief, which he presented with much courtesy. There was something, however, unusual in his manner. He lingered and hesitated, and seemed as if doubtful of what to do. At last it was all explained. 'To tell you the truth, sir,' said he, 'I have ventured to make this brief the medium of an introduction to you. Some occurrences took place in Dublin many years ago, with which I was mixed up; and as you may have heard of them, perhaps you would permit me to give my explanation – my name is Cockayne!' I felt for the moment as if stunned. The man had for long been a matter of history to me. I had thought him in the grave. Yet there he stood, the survivor of his victim and his patron, still living on the wages that had purchased life! I had hardly nerve enough to say to him 'Sir, when I tell you I was the intimate friend of Mr Curran, and often spoke with him on the wretched Jackson's fate, you must see the futility of any explanation.' He uttered not a syllable, and left the room.[22]

Thomas Collins, whose precise and laconic reports to the Castle tell us who attended and what was said at almost every meeting of the original Dublin Society of United Irishmen, was (as mentioned earlier) given a post as a naval officer in Dominica, largest of the Windward Islands. During the mid-1790s there had been terrible outbreaks of yellow fever on the island, so the prospect might not have been altogether pleasing. In the early 1800s there were tussles with the French; perhaps Collins was able to steer well clear of these. Towards the end of his life he would have had to serve under the governorship of George Ainslie who was said to have subdued the maroons on the island 'with such thoroughness that it was called cruelty'. Some of this might have sounded familiar to Collins. Still, his pension was £600 a year, which he drew until his death in 1814.

Thomas Attwood Digges continues to be suspected as the rogue American adventurer responsible for sneaking to the Government the private covering letter from Tone to Thomas Russell in 1791, which had revealed that Tone's aim on behalf of the United Irishmen was not primarily Catholic emancipation and parliamentary reform, but the total separation of Ireland from England. It would have been a valuable piece of evidence had Tone ever been tried for high treason. Digges does not, however, seem to have been rewarded for his betrayal.

> He was 80 when 'growing afflictions' forced him to retreat into a variety of cheap hotels in Washington – the Washington Hotel, Tennison's Hotel, Strothers Hotel, and Mansion Hotel. From Strothers Hotel he wrote on December 19 1819 that he had come from his 'tatterd & comfortless home only yesterday with a hope that in a warm room (which I keep in it for going & comeing purposes) to attain some amelioration in spasm complaints in my ankle, joints & Rheumatics in my Shoulders & neck joint, afflictingly bad at times although internally in good health.' At Strothers Hotel he died, Thursday, December 6, 1821.[23]

William Duckett, that sedulous seducer of British seamen, continued to admire the achievements of the French Revolution through the first two decades of the 1800s, even although he seems to have been shunned by fellow Irish exiles in Paris. They may well have still suspected him as an informer, as Tone did. For a long time, he insisted that a core of leaders could be found in counties round Dublin among '98 'men who had kept their pikes for another day'.

On the whole, however, respectability claimed him in middle age. By 1820 he was teaching English literature and Classics in Paris. He also published odes on Princess Charlotte's death and on Greek and South American independence. He was an accomplished classicist with a wonderful memory; undimmed up to the point of quoting Horace on his deathbed in 1841: that is, almost half a century after Tone had first eyed him with suspicion in the antechamber of Carnot.

Old spies never die. Twenty-one years after the Rebellion, Leonard McNally had a last trick to play. A Venezuelan General visited Dublin in order to raise money and troops for Simon Bolivar. The Castle, it seems, did not mind seeing revolutionary militants fighting for the independence of another, faraway country and put no obstacles in the General's way. 'A military passion seized on the popular mind. For many weeks, the streets of Dublin, gay with plumage, reminded one of Paris during the Napoleonic fever.'[24]

McNally's contribution to the cause of Venezuelan independence was characteristically ambiguous. Was it a feigned tribute to a popular hero, another piece of enjoyable deceit? A real if half-felt tribute to a champion of freedom? In any case, he presented the Irish legion, successfully raised by the General, with the badge of the United Irishmen, the very same one which he claimed to have been taken from the remains of Edward Fitzgerald when he lay dead in Newgate.

How had McNally got hold of the heroic relic, if, indeed, it was genuine? Perhaps it was blood-money for his services to the Castle.

McNally was, on his deathbed, received into the Church of Rome, though even here, ambiguities accompanied him. His son reproached his stepmother for admitting the priest into the house with the words, 'Can't you let him go to the devil his own way?'

Francis Magan, who had so successfully 'set' Lord Edward Fitzgerald, does seem to have had a conscience, a rare and disturbing possession for an informer. He became a recluse. Although a miser, dying worth the considerable sum of £14,000, he repaid in late life a debt of £1,000 incurred by his father, long after the creditor had given up hope for repayment. There are two glimpses of his sad old age. One comes from a fellow lawyer, who as a Commissioner for enclosing commons was brought into close relations with him:

> Magan in later years was sufficiently gentleman like in appearance; tall, yet rather of plain and even coarse exterior; perhaps a little moody and reserved at times, and *something may have been pressing on him of which he said little.*[25]

And this is how the most celebrated Irish spy-writer of the late nineteenth century, W.J. Fitzpatrick, describes Magan's latter days:

> The few surviving friends of Mr Magan describe him as a prim and somewhat unsociable being, though moving in good society. He looked wise, but never showed much wisdom, and it was more than once whispered of him 'Still waters run deep' . . . for the last twenty years of his life he rarely went out. He never married, and lived a recluse at 20 Usher's Island . . . he did not like to meet old friends. The neighbours wondered, speculated and

pried, but Magan's windows and doings could not be seen through. From this dingy retreat, festooned with cobwebs, Mr Magan, almost choked in a stiff white cravat, would, as we have said, occasionally emerge, and pick his steps to the courts in which he held office . . . In 1843 Mr Magan died [with his secret undiscovered]. He was generally regarded as an honourable man, and an eminent Queen's counsel stood beside his death-bed.[26]

The painter of miniatures Edward Newell, who was of such assistance to General Lake, was one of the few informers to come to a sticky end, but probably for reasons of sexual rather than political double-dealing. He tried to abscond to America with the wife of a friend. Induced to board a boat taking him to the ship bound for America, he was said to have been thrown into the sea. There was also a local tale that his bones were found on the beach at Ballyholme, ten miles from Belfast.[27]

After selling the information which led so precipitously to the break-up of the Dublin directory of United Irishmen on the eve of the Rebellion, Thomas Reynolds felt it unsafe to continue to live in Ireland. The English Government did not renege on its promises to take care of him. On top of a pension of £1,000 a year, he was told he might settle in any part of England he liked, and be given letters that would introduce him and his family 'to the particular attention of the gentry of the place'. But he led such an extravagant life in Cumberland and Monmouthshire that he had to plead for a paid post, and was eventually appointed packet agent at Lisbon. After the end of the Peninsular War the rewards became miserable. Early in 1817 he accepted the post of British consul in Iceland on condition that he need not reside there. The Government was growing tired of Reynolds. After Castlereagh's death in 1822 he was told they wished to have as little to do with him and his family as possible. He retired permanently to Paris, where 'he loved to parade his pompous person in the Champs-Elysées. He is said to have undergone a religious conversion in 1831.'[28]

Of all the spies and informers, Samuel Turner fits most closely into the picture of a model modern spy. He was flamboyant, deceptively so. He did not deceive only for gold. He assumed not one but many different aliases (for example, Richardson, Furnes). His disguises sound elaborate. He was impudent and brave; it must have taken nerve to demand a rise in his pension from £300 to £500 from Sir Arthur Wellesley in 1807; the future Duke of Wellington hated the trade of informers but was persuaded that Samuel Turner had 'strong claims to the favour of the Government for the loyalty and zeal with which he conducted himself during the Rebellion in Ireland'.

He was evidently good at his job. When, throughout the Rebellion and for five years or so afterwards, he stayed in Hamburg, that hive of spies, as a representative of the United Irishmen, he passed on extremely reliable information on the activities of his colleagues. He died a suitably mysterious death, in a duel on the Isle of Man. Had his honour, perhaps, been impugned?[29]

Postscript – and the worst of times

None of my chosen four progenitors of the United Irishmen could have foreseen the bloody aftermaths of those distant meetings in the autumn days of 1791 – when Drennan had composed the solemn Tests and oaths, Tone sat in conclaves deep into the night with Russell and Digges in the Franklin Tavern – and, later, when Rowan in Dublin distributed the seditious Address, and in Paris Fitzgerald effectively cashiered himself, renounced his title and embraced the cause of revolution.

As described in the previous chapter, Fitzgerald died in Newgate Prison of a septic wound, and Tone cut his own throat. They are still honoured by many Irishmen today with the tribute accorded to martyrs. But most other founding fathers of the early United Irishmen were out of action during the terrible days of the Rebellion, which Lecky, writing a hundred years later, talked of as unfolding 'a scene of horror . . . hardly surpassed in the modern history of Europe'. (Eclipsed now, alas.) The head had always been far too erratically in control of the body: a besetting cause of failure over the years.

Drennan was in semi-revolutionary retirement; although still true to the old ideals of reform and emancipation, his wings had been scorched by the trial in 1794 that might possibly have led to his death. And Rowan was to sit out the Rebellion in exile in Philadelphia, in the company of Quakers, occasionally lost in the marshes in his boat.

It was not only the 30,000 dead and numberless destitute who provide the tally of losses. Equally sad, in the long, Irish perspective of history, was the death of the illusion of the 'unity of the sects', which had been the rock – or rather, sand – on which the foundations of the United Irish movement had been built.

There was always an element of wilful delusion about this ideal. The optimism of the well-educated middle classes of Dublin and Belfast had managed to set to one side the ignorance and superstition of the vast body of the Catholic peasants: to look upon them as of no real political account. (Thomas Russell was the great exception, who walked everywhere, visiting the cabins of the poor, and listening.) There was also more than an element of hoodwinking in the proclaimed 'unity'. Many of the leaders, above all Tone himself, used the ideal, as they used that of parliamentary reform, to present the respectable face of the movement. But the deeper wellspring of the motives of many was the desire to remove the 'hated English connection'.

Above all, the ideal simply did not begin to stand up to the test of the Rebellion itself, which was an outpouring of riot, murder and mayhem, and culminated, in most of its practical manifestations, in a sectarian bloodbath.

The months of rebellion themselves have more recently been chronicled in *The Year of Liberty* by Thomas Pakenham (one of whose ancestors, Captain Thomas Pakenham, was Lieutenant-General of the Ordnance during these times). I have drawn on his accounts of one or two incidents during the bloodstained months from June to October; but have not begun to attempt to reconsider or rewrite any of its history.

The eventual hopelessness of the Rebellion stemmed from its lack of professional leadership, efficient timing, and of any sustained attempt at co-ordination. Intervals between the major risings gave the Castle enough space to draw breath. Had the initial plan worked (that is, to signal the start of the rising to the waiting rebels of the North, South, East and West, by a simultaneous stoppage of the mail coaches leaving Dublin), it would have been a different matter. This was a brilliant idea, equivalent to the destruction, today, of the entire communications network of the country. But it misfired. Only one of the five mail coaches was stopped in the appointed place. How agreeably Tone would have been surprised, if events had turned out otherwise, and he had read in the French press of concerted risings throughout the country, together with the imminent arrival in Ireland of the promised invasion by even a modest contingent of French! But nothing like that was to be.

On the other hand, if anything could be said to have made a rebel victory possible, it would have been the indecision of Lord-Lieutenant Camden and the Castle. They feared that if they denuded the capital of troops, and sent them to the scenes of insurrection outside the capital, Dublin itself would then rise. On the other hand, if they kept the troops nearby to guard the capital, how would the country ever be pacified? This dilemma was the more insoluble because of the unknown quality of the Irish militia and yeomanry. The Castle had been furious about the incautious announcement of General Abercromby, the sacked Commander-in-Chief who had written off the Irish army in words ever since quoted in every history. When Cornwallis, whose campaigns in the American War and in India had proved his calm generalship, took over in late June, both as Lord-Lieutenant and Commander-in-Chief, the improvement in terms of discipline, decisiveness and (where appropriate) leniency, was immediate.

On the whole, the Government had perceived Dublin itself to be the scene of the greatest threat, even although, after the capture of Fitzgerald and the general indecision and splits of the Dublin United Irish Directory, the rebels were left as aimless groups awaiting a call that never came.

One thing the Government was never short of was information. The faithful McNally continued to report reliably what was said at private meetings, dinners and conferences with clients. He talked of the wildfire spread of the revolutionary movement among Dublin's middle classes: merchants, traders, bank-clerks, servants. This was more frightening than familiar news of peasant uprisings.

The insurrection, however, broke out in full force in Leinster, on 23 May. It came no nearer to Dublin than that. It could never be called well organized, but it was massive, frenzied, and waged with incredible courage as well as incredible fury. It is easy to say it was doomed. Yet, for months after Cornwallis's arrival, a large area of the county of Wexford did experience something like the beginnings of a revolutionary state; the brief rebel Government was less ram-shackle than might have been expected. It exercised real power. Manifestos appeared on walls, local government by sub-committees sprang up, forms of rationing were introduced.

Then, in the late summer, almost the whole of County Mayo fell into the hands of a belated and inadequate French invasion. But through most of the year, the only hopes that sustained the rebels –

hope of the fall of Dublin above all – were themselves sustained only by rumour.

Here is an example of the spontaneous, bestial savagery in the early days of rebellion, when large parts of Kildare were engulfed. A massacre at Rathangan, about thirty-five miles west of Dublin, was terrifying in its wild surge of inhumanity:

> About three o'clock in the morning of May 26, a large party of rebels had entered Rathangan. No resistance was offered. Spenser [the kindly, old local agent of the Duke of Leinster] was surrounded in a house where he had barricaded himself. The window shutters were broken in by some of the workmen with the butts of their muskets. Spenser surrendered, and so did his first lieutenant, a retired English officer called Moore, who had taken refuge in the home of a quaker family. They were promised their lives if they gave up their arms to the rebels. And then, without threat or provocation, as it seemed, but simply on the blind impulse of the mob, the killing began. One by one, the Protestant men believed loyal to the Government were piked or shot: Spenser, whose mangled body was dis-played as a trophy in front of his door; Moore, whose wife had lain in labour in three days before; six of the others who had taken refuge with the Quaker, including a boy of fourteen; a carpenter and a shoemaker; in all nineteen men, unarmed and inoffensive, of that small town where Catholics and Protestants had seemed to live comfortably together, were now piked or shot or hacked to death . . . the loyalists who were Catholics were allowed to pass unharmed.

Mob frenzy, all restraint cast aside, took hold of men who had lived most of their lives with at least the outward appearance of common decency and fair consideration for others. And the frenzy was common on all sides, and liable to break out at any minute. Soon after the massacre just quoted, in one Wicklow town which had seemed quiet, twenty-eight Catholic suspects were taken from the town prison by a squad of loyalist yeomen and militia, paraded and simply shot in cold blood.

Frenzy eliminated scruples. But it did not preclude cunning. One account tells how Catholics played the Orange card to excite peasants to fresh rampages – reminiscent of Fitzgerald's plan for disrupting the Christmas Mass. Bogus tales were spread that every Orangeman had sworn to wade up to his knees in Catholic blood. Then Catholic farmers posed as groups of Orangemen; Catholics ran amok and indiscriminate murder of Protestants swept through the countryside (and this in a part of Ireland where, in fact,

Orangemen scarcely existed!) Such was the power of rumour in spreading pandemonium.

Perhaps it is the sheer press of numbers which is most difficult to conceive; even although, paradoxically, numbers lay near the heart of the failure of the Rebellion. Swarms of rebels, often leaderless, could often be dealt with by a few disciplined, steady troops able to outface and repel them. Panic, rout and slaughter were a consequence against which individual rebels' acts of defiance and heroism were, as a rule, powerless. The greater the numbers the more fatal the consequences. But steadiness was not a common feature of the conduct of most rebels.

After the town of Wexford had fallen in late May to the rebels:

[they were] in the most disorderly state, without the least appearance of discipline. They had no kind of uniform, but were most of them in the dress of labourers, white bands round their hats and green cockades being the only marks by which they were distinguished. They had a most fantastic appearance, many having decorated themselves with parts of the apparel of ladies, found in the houses they had plundered. Some wore ladies' hats and feathers, others, caps, bonnets and tippets. From the military they had routed they had collected some clothing which added to the motley show. Their arms consisted chiefly of pikes of enormous length, the handles of many being of sixteen or eighteen feet long. Some carried rusty muskets. They were accompanied by a number of women shouting and huzzaing for the croppies and crying, 'Who now dare say "Croppies, lie down?"'

Nearly everything was misconceived, desolate, sickening and familiar about the thousands of pikings, hangings, murders through the summer months of 1798. One small, final atrocity: a thug called Hunter Gowan marched into the town of Gorey with the amputated finger of one of his victims stuck on the point of his sword. This made a trophy used to stir punch at a party. Yet myths grew from the bloodstained earth, all the same. For years to come, the question was asked: 'Where were *you* in the '98?' Rare moments of humanity lightened the sky, too: occasions when Catholics hid Protestants in their houses or barns, and vice versa.

There were even some lighter moments. When Humbert's French invasion – the predecessor to the doomed, delayed expedition that left from Brest nearly two months later with Tone – arrived at Killala, the French were chivalrous to the excellent Bishop in whose house they encamped. They could not, however, resist making tart mockery of the Irish for whom they had brought a quantity of uniforms:

> The coxcombry of the young clowns in their new dress; the mixture of good humour and contempt in the countenances of the French, employed in making puppies of them; the haste of the undressed to be as fine as their neighbours, casting away their old clothes long before it came their turn to receive the new; above all, the merry activity of a handsome young fellow, a marine officer, whose business it was to consummate the vanity of the new recruits by decorating them with helmets beautifully edged with spotted brown paper to look like leopard's skin, a task which he performed standing on a powder barrel, and making the helmet fit any skull, even the largest, by thumping it down with his fists, careless whether it could ever be taken off again . . .

Such a ragamuffin episode comes as a relief – but is certainly a far cry from that bright dawn when it was bliss to be alive. I am reminded of the colourful hopes of the editor of the *Belfast Telegraph* in the autumn of seven years earlier:

> The French Revolution acted as a spell on the minds of Irishmen . . . their sympathy was roused to a state of excitement almost painful, and that longed to find relief and indulgence, in re-enacting such spirit-stirring scenes . . . they dedicated that day to the commemoration of the greatest event in human annals. Twenty-six millions of our fellow-creatures (nearly one-sixth of the inhabitants of Europe) breaking their chains, and throwing off almost in an instant the degrading yoke of slavery, is a scene so new, so interesting, and sublime . . .
>
> The Volunteer societies, horse, foot, and artillery, with a dense multitude of spectators, assembled at the Exchange, and thence paraded the principal streets in all the pomp and pride of military array . . . such was the demonstration of public feeling in the liberal and enlightened town of Belfast, the Athens of Ireland . . .

As civilized Europeans, educated in the classics, heirs to the ideals of the Scottish Enlightenment, Wolfe Tone, William Drennan, Hamilton Rowan and most of the other leaders of the United Irishmen, were unaware of the alternative history, myths and power of Catholic, peasant Ireland. Their splendid hopes were rooted in the examples of the American War and the fine words of the French Revolution. That was their tragedy. They seem to have attached only secondary importance to the everyday sufferings and dreams of most of their fellow countrymen. It is a familiar failing: one which persists, and helps to make so much of Irish history slip across the page and lose itself like so many blobs of mercury.

Epilogue

Was it for this the wild geese spread
The grey wing upon every tide;
For this that all that blood was shed,
For this Edward Fitzgerald died,
And Robert Emmet and Wolfe Tone,
All that delirium of the brave;
Romantic Ireland's dead and gone,
It's with O'Leary in the grave.
                    Yeats, *Responsibilities*: 'September, 1913'

Notes

1. INTRODUCTION AND SOME REFLECTIONS

1. Professor Herbert Butterfield, 'Eighteenth Century Ireland', in *Irish Historical Studies*, xv (1965), p. 381.
2. Elizabeth Bowen, *Bowen's Court, passim*.
3. A.W.P. Malcolmson, *John Foster: The Politics of the Anglo-Irish Ascendancy*, p. 14.
4. Theobold Wolfe Tone, *Memoirs*, i, p. 258.
5. William Beresford (ed.), *The Correspondence of the Rt Hon. John Beresford*, p. 169.
6. Tone, *Memoirs*, ii, p. 112.
7. 'Speech of Lord Moira on the present alarming and dreadful state of Ireland in the House of Lords', Wednesday 22 November 1797, p. 11.
8. F. Bickley (ed.), *The Diaries of Sylvester Douglas, Lord Glenbervie*, i, p. 35.
9. Ibid., p. 36.
10. *Parliamentary Register of the Debates of the House of Commons in Ireland*, xiii (Dublin, 1793), p. 159.
11. J.C. Beckett, *The Making of Modern Ireland, 1603–1923*, p. 211.
12. A.T.Q. Stewart, *A Deeper Silence: The Hidden Origins of the United Irish Movement*, p. 4.
13. Ibid., p. 53.
14. D.A. Chart (ed.), *The Drennan Letters*, p. 44.
15. Ibid., p. 53.
16. Public Record Office, H.O. 100/30/8/331.
17. James Kelly, 'Napper Tandy: Radical and Republican', in *Dublin and Dubliners*.
18. Miles Byrne, *Memoirs*, ii, p. 14.
19. Frank MacDermot in *Irish Historical Studies*, xv (1966) has written the best account of O'Connor's life.
20. Quoted in R.B. McDowell, *Ireland in the Age of Imperialism and Revolution, 1760–1801*, p. 459.

2. REBELS AND INFORMERS

1. Beckett, *The Making of Modern Ireland*, p. 204.
2. Quoted in Marianne Elliott, *Wolfe Tone* (passage omitted in the published

276

Memoirs), p. 11. (I have drawn on Elliott's biography especially heavily for Wolfe Tone's early life.)

3. Tone, *Memoirs*, i, p. 13.
4. Quoted in Frank MacDermot, *Theobald Wolfe Tone and his Times*, p. 13.
5. Tone, *Memoirs*, i, p. 26.
6. Ibid., p. 37.
7. Ibid., p. 38.
8. Theobald Wolfe Tone, *An Argument on Behalf of the Catholics of Ireland*, p. 7.
9. Quoted in McDowell, *Ireland in the Age of Imperialism*, p. 312.
10. Chart, *Drennan Letters*, p. 66.
11. Ibid., p. 34.
12. Lady Sydney Morgan, *The O'Briens and O'Flahertys: A National Tale*, quoted in Elliott, *Wolfe Tone*, p. 104.
13. Chart, *Drennan Letters*, p. 1.
14. William Drennan, *De venaesectione in febribus continuis*.
15. Chart, *Drennan Letters*, p. 30.
16. Ibid., p. 12.
17. Ibid., p. 55.
18. Ibid., p. 37.
19. Ibid., p. 50.
20. William Drennan, *Letters of Orellana: An Irish Helot*, p. 7.
21. Ibid., p. 12.
22. Ibid., p. 24.
23. Ibid., p. 38.
24. Chart, *Drennan Letters*, p. 14.
25. Ibid., p. 72.
26. Stewart establishes this attribution in *A Deeper Silence*, p. 159.
27. Ibid., p. 177; see also chapter 18, 'The Company and the Lodge'.
28. Chart, *Drennan Letters*, p. 51.
29. Ibid.
30. Ibid., p. 54.
31. W.H. Drummond (ed.), *Autobiography of Archibald Hamilton Rowan*, p. 15.
32. Ibid., p. 38.
33. Ibid., p. 28.
34. Ibid., p. 33.
35. Ibid., p. 35.
36. Ibid., p. 78.
37. Ibid., p. 83.
38. Ibid., p. 88.
39. Harold Nicolson, *A Desire to Please: A Story of Hamilton Rowan and the United Irishmen*, p. 38.
40. Sir Jonah Barrington, *Personal Sketches of his Own Times*. Sir Jonah is not any more reliable as a storyteller than as a judge – he was removed from the Admiralty Court for misappropriation of funds in 1830. (William Beresford, editor of his grandfather's *Correspondence* remarks drily in a footnote that he was 'the author of several works on Ireland, more remarkable for the miraculous than for correct and authentic information'. But the tale about Mary

Neil is repeated in Rowan's edited *Autobiography*; and reputable historians are happy often to quote from the judge's memoirs, even if with similar caveats.

41. Barrington, *Personal Sketches*, ii, pp. 115–20.
42. Drummond, *Autobiography*, p. 106.
43. Nicolson, *A Desire to Please*, p. 74.
44. J.E. Walsh, *Sketches of Ireland Sixty Years Ago*, pp. 152–3.
45. This account of Edward's and his brothers' education is based on Stella Tillyard's *Aristocrats: Caroline, Emily, Louisa and Sarah Lennox, 1740–1832*, pp. 247ff.
46. Ibid., p. 248.
47. Thomas Moore, *The Life and Death of Lord Edward Fitzgerald*, i, p. 241.
48. Ibid., p. 27.
49. Ibid., p. 24.
50. Ibid., p. 26.
51. Ibid., pp. 78–93.
52. Ibid., p. 92.
53. Ibid., p. 119.
54. Tillyard, *Aristocrats*, p. 330.
55. Moore, *Life and Death*, i, p. 40.
56. J. Beresford, *The Correspondence*, i, p. 148; see also Malcolmson, *John Foster*, p. 196n.
57. Quoted in Malcolmson, *John Foster*, p. 203, n.3.
58. Moore, *Life and Death*, i, pp. 163–4.
59. W.J. Fitzpatrick, *The Sham Squire; and the Informers of 1798*, p. 248.
60. Ibid., p. 250.
61. McDowell, *Ireland in the Age of Imperialism*, p. 386.
62. John Larkin, *The Trial of William Drennan, on a Trial for Sedition in the Year 1794*, p. 10.

3. FOUNDING OF THE SOCIETY

1. Tone, *Memoirs*, i, p. 67.
2. Ibid., ii, pp. 381ff.
3. Ibid., i, p. 64.
4. Beresford, *Correspondence*, ii, pp. 156–7.
5. Tone, *Memoirs*, ii, p. 384.
6. Ibid., ii, pp. 383–4.
7. Franklin, *Papers of Benjamin Franklin*, xxvii, p. 420.
8. Ibid., xxviii, p. 248.
9. Tone, *Memoirs*, ii, p. 382.
10. Ibid., ii, p. 380.
11. Quoted in Stewart, *A Deeper Silence*, p. 155.
12. Tone had drafted these resolutions earlier in the summer and sent them to Russell in Belfast. It had originally been intended that the Society's inaugural meeting, at which the resolutions would be declared, should coincide with Belfast's Bastille commemorations on 14 July.
13. Chart, *Drennan Letters*, p. 168.

14. Thomas O'Brien Hanley (ed.), *The John Carroll Papers*, ii, pp. 25–6.
15. Elliot, *Wolfe Tone*, p. 107.
16. Chart, *Drennan Letters*, p. 64.
17. R. Jacob, *The Rise of the United Irishmen*, p. 62 (quoted in Stewart, *A Deeper Silence*, p. 161).
18. Chart, *Drennan Letters*, p. 60.
19. Ibid., p. 66.
20. Ibid., pp. 68–9.
21. Drummond, *Autobiography*, p. 153 (Rowan's editor has conflated a number of descriptions).
22. W.E.H. Lecky, *A History of Ireland in the Eighteenth Century*, iii, p. 34.
23. Drummond, *Autobiography*, p. 148.
24. Chart, *Drennan Letters*, p. 124.
25. Debate on 20 February, in the *Parliamentary Register*, xii (1792), p. 202.
26. Debate on 18 April, in the *Parliamentary Register*, xii (1792), p. 305.
27. Chart, *Drennan Letters*, p. 86.
28. W.F. Rae, *Sheridan: A Biography*, i, p. 262; quoted in *DNB*.
29. R. Crompton Rhodes, *Harlequin Sheridan: The Man and the Legend*, p. 158.

4. TANDY'S NOSE

1. So described in *Sketches of Irish Political Characters*, p. 158.
2. Elliott, *Wolfe Tone*, p. 107.
3. R.B. McDowell, 'Proceedings of the Dublin Society of United Irishmen', in *Analecta Hibernica*, xvii, p. 17.
4. Barrington, *Personal Sketches*, i, p. 279.
5. Marianne Elliott in her *Wolfe Tone* recites many other details showing Matilda's 'punctilio and sense of order about listing things' (p. 165).
6. *Parliamentary Register*, viii (Dublin, 1793), p. 186.
7. Tone, *Memoirs*, i, p. 339.
8. McDowell, *Ireland in the Age of Imperialism*, p. 48.
9. Drummond, *Autobiography*, p. 169.
10. Ibid., p. 285.
11. Chart, *Drennan Letters*, p. 84.
12. Ibid., p. 80.
13. Ibid., p. 79.
14. Stewart, *A Deeper Silence*, p. 133.
15. Chart, *Drennan Letters*, p. 94.
16. Ibid., p. 80.
17. In this chapter I have drawn very heavily on two definitive articles by Professor R.B. McDowell, which also are models of *their* kind: 'The Personnel of the Dublin Society of United Irishmen, 1791–94', in *Irish Historical Studies*, ii, and 'Proceedings of the Dublin Society of United Irishmen', in *Analecta Hibernica*, xvii.
18. McDowell, 'Proceedings', p. 8.
19. William Drennan, *Glendalloch and Other Poems*, 2nd edn (Dublin, 1859).

20. McDowell, 'Proceedings', p. 12.
21. Public Record Office H.O. 100/52.
22. Moore, *Life and Death*, i, p. 167.
23. Ibid.

5. DINNER AT WHITE'S

1. Moore, *Life and Death*, i, p. 171.
2. Ibid., p. 174.
3. Ibid., pp. 172f.
4. Marianne Elliott, *Partners in Revolution*, p. 61.
5. Moore, *Life and Death*, i, p. 183–4.
6. Elliott, *Partners in Revolution*, p. 25.
7. Chart, *Drennan Letters*, p. 89.
8. Ibid.
9. Public Record Office, H.O. 100/37/177.
10. Chart, *Drennan Letters*, p. 94.
11. Beresford, *Correspondence*, ii, p. 156.
12. Chart, *Drennan Letters*, p. 108.
13. Ibid., p. 96.
14. McDowell, 'Proceedings', p. 32.
15. Ibid., p. 47.
16. Chart, *Drennan Letters*, pp. 96ff.
17. Ibid., p. 99.
18. Ibid., p. 101.
19. Fitzpatrick, *The Sham Squire*, p. 258.
20. McDowell, 'Proceedings', pp. 40–41.
21. Ibid., p. 42.
22. Ibid., p. 44.
23. Chart, *Drennan Letters*, p. 107.
24. Tone, *Memoirs*, ii, pp. 410ff.
25. Ibid., p. 414.
26. Ibid.
27. Ibid., p. 418.
28. Ibid., p. 419.
29. Ibid., p. 422.
30. Tone, *Memoirs*, ii, pp. 120–21.

6. INCREASING BOLDNESS

1. Tone, *Memoirs*, i, pp. 119ff.
2. See *Annual Register* (1793), and Elliott, *Wolfe Tone*, p. 201.
3. Tone, *Memoirs*, i, p. 122.
4. Ibid., p. 123.
5. Ibid., ii, p. 423.

6. *Parliamentary Register*, xiii (Dublin, 1793), pp. 81–3.
7. Fitzpatrick, *The Sham Squire*, p. 316.
8. Chart, *Drennan Letters*, p. 126.
9. Ibid., p. 138.
10. Ibid., p. 128–9.
11. Ibid., p. 133.
12. Ibid., p. 131.
13. Ibid., p. 135.
14. Ibid., p. 143.
15. *Parliamentary Register*, xiii, p. 153.
16. Chart, *Drennan Letters*, p. 150.
17. Ibid., p. 151.
18. Ibid., p. 117.
19. Ibid., p. 137.
20. Ibid., p. 140.
21. Ibid., p. 112.
22. Ibid., p. 160.
23. Ibid., pp. 124–5.
24. Drummond, *Autobiography*, p. 149.
25. Chart, *Drennan Letters*, p. 135; T.W. Moody, F.X. Martin and F.J. Byrne (eds), *A New History of Ireland*, iv, p. 327; Nancy J. Curtin, *The United Irishmen*, p. 58; Elliott, *Wolfe Tone*, p. 216; *Northern Star*, 20 February 1793.
26. Chart, *Drennan Letters*, p. 153.
27. McDowell, 'Proceedings', p. 67.
28. Chart, *Drennan Letters*, p. 131.
29. Ibid., p. 135.
30. McDowell, 'Proceedings', p. 67.
31. Ibid., p. 140.

7. FIGHTING TALK

1. Quoted in James Kelly, *That Damn'd Thing Called Honour*.
2. McDowell, 'Proceedings', p. 66.
3. Ibid., p. 87.
4. Chart, *Drennan Letters*, p. 173.
5. Drummond, *Autobiography*, p. 171.
6. Ibid., p. 172.
7. Ibid., p. 175.
8. McDowell, 'Proceedings', p. 94.
9. Ibid.
10. Drummond, *Autobiography*, p. 176, quoting from Henry Joy, *Historical Collections Relative to the Town of Belfast*, (1817).
11. Tone, *Memoirs*, ii, p. 273.
12. Public Record Office, H.O. 30/8/327/82–3, quoted in Elliott, *Wolfe Tone*, p. 226.
13. *Journals of the House of Lords*, p. 128.

14. Lecky, *History of Ireland*, iii, p. 221.
15. Tone, *Memoirs*, i, p. 154.
16. Moore, *Life and Death*, i, pp. 226–7.
17. Ibid., p. 231.
18. Ibid., pp. 231–2.
19. Quoted in Tillyard, *Aristocrats*, p. 361.
20. Chart, *Drennan Letters*, p. 173.
21. Drennan, *Glendalloch*, p. xiii.
22. Ibid., p. 175.
23. Chart, *Drennan Letters*, p. 377.
24. McDowell, 'Proceedings', p. 85.
25. Ibid., p. 86.
26. McDowell, 'The Personnel', p. 18.
27. McDowell, 'Proceedings', p. 104.
28. Yeats, quoted in Oliver MacDonagh, *States of Mind: A Study of Anglo-Irish Conflict, 1780–1980*, p. 13.
29. Fitzpatrick, *The Sham Squire*, pp. 286ff.

8. DISPERSAL OF THE DUBLIN SOCIETY

1. Revd William Jackson, *Sermons on Practical and Important Subjects*, pp. 174–5.
2. W. Curran, *The Life of John Philpot Curran*, p. 289.
3. Fitzpatrick, *The Sham Squire*, pp. 287–9.
4. William Sampson, *The Trial of the Rev. William Jackson for High Treason*, p. 33.
5. T.B. Howell, *Collection of State Trials*, xxv, p. 832.
6. Sampson, *The Trial*, p. 33.
7. Ibid., pp. 39, 43.
8. Howell, *State Trials*, xxv, p. 889.
9. Curran, *The Life*, pp. 281ff.
10. *Annual Register* (1794).
11. Drummond, *Autobiography*, p. 201.
12. Ibid., pp. 214ff (I have slightly abbreviated the passage).
13. Nicolson, *A Desire to Please*, p. 180.
14. Elliott, *Wolfe Tone*, p. 35.
15. Beresford, *Correspondence*, ii, pp. 28–9.
16. Tone, *Memoirs*, ii, pp. 163ff.
17. Elliott, *Wolfe Tone*, p. 390.
18. Beresford, *Correspondence*, ii, p. 34.
19. Nicolson, *A Desire to Please*, p. 121.
20. Moore, *Life and Death*, i, pp. 239–40.
21. Chart, *Drennan Letters*, p. 180.
22. Ibid., pp. 195–8.
23. Ibid., pp. 182–3.
24. Ibid., p. 191.
25. Ibid., pp. 192–3.

9. TRIALS AND INDIGNITIES

1. Chart, *Drennan Letters*, p. 199.
2. Larkin, *Trial of William Drennan*, pp. 121 ff.
3. Ibid., p. 11.
4. Ibid., pp. 138–9.
5. Ibid., p. 137.
6. Chart, *Drennan Letters*, p. 209.
7. Michael Durey in 'The Dublin Society of United Irishmen and the Politics of the Carey–Drennan Dispute' has partially rescued Carey's character; I have drawn on the article.
8. Ibid., p. 108.
9. 'Intended Defence' in Larkin, *Trial of William Drennan*, p. 138.
10. Chart, *Drennan Letters*, pp. 111, 195, 199, 200.
11. Durey, 'The Carey–Drennan dispute', p. 107.
12. McDowell, 'Proceedings', pp. 91–2.
13. I.S.P.O. 620/18, quoted in McDowell, *Age of Imperialism*.
14. Moore, *Life and Death*, i, p. 255.
15. Ibid., p. 245.
16. Lecky, *History of Ireland*, iii, p. 256.
17. Moore, *Life and Death*, i, p. 250.
18. Quoted in Elliott, *Wolfe Tone*, p. 256.
19. Quoted in Elliott, *Wolfe Tone*, p. 253.
20. Ibid., p. 250.
21. Drummond, *Autobiography*, pp. 225–6.
22. Ibid., p. 226.
23. Ibid., p. 232.
24. Ibid., p. 238.
25. Ibid., p. 237.
26. Ibid., p. 266.

10. TO THE NEW WORLD

1. Drummond, *Autobiography*, p. 247.
2. R. Wardle (ed.), *Collected Letters of Mary Wollstonecraft*, (1979), p. 141.
3. Drummond, *Autobiography*, p. 259.
4. Ibid., p. 267.
5. Ibid., p. 271.
6. Ibid., p. 273.
7. Ibid., p. 279.
8. Tone, *Memoirs*, i, p. 185.
9. Ibid., p. 186.
10. Ibid.
11. C.J. Woods (ed.), *Journals and Memoirs of Thomas Russell*, p. 82.
12. Ibid., p. 20.
13. Quoted by Marianne Elliott in her foreword to Woods, *Journals*, p. 8.

14. Tone, *Memoirs*, i, pp. 186–7.
15. Ibid., p. 189.
16. Chart, *Drennan Letters*, p. 221.
17. Ibid., p. 222.
18. Ibid., p. 224.
19. Ibid., p. 223.
20. Ibid., p. 220.
21. Brian Fitzgerald (ed.), *Correspondence of Emily, Duchess of Leinster, 1731–1814*, iii, p. 247.
22. Pelham Correspondence, B.Mus. Addit. Mss. 33,118, p. 257.
23. *Parliamentary Register* (1795), pp. 286ff.
24. R.B. McDowell (ed.), *The Correspondence of Edmund Burke, 1794–1796*, viii, pp. 215–6, 242–3, 245–6; quoted in Conor Cruise O'Brien, *The Great Melody*, p. 526.
25. Moore, *Life and Death*, i, p. 267.
26. Quoted in Lecky, *History of Ireland*, iii, p. 377 [Camden to Portland, May 1795].
27. Ibid. [Portland to Camden, 22 May; Camden to Portland, 26 May].
28. Ibid., pp. 382–3.
29. Ibid., p. 377.
30. Ibid., p. 380.

11. TUMULTUOUS RISING

1. Thomas Bartlett in 'Select Documents XXXVIII: Defenders and Defenderism in 1795', *Irish Historical Studies*, xxiv (1985), p. 373ff.
2. Ibid., p. 377.
3. *Walker's Hibernian Magazine: A Compendium of Entertaining Knowledge for 1795*, p. 434.
4. Tone, *Memoirs*, i, p. 193.
5. Elliott, *Wolfe Tone*, p. 275.
6. Ibid., p. 272.
7. Tone, *Memoirs*, p. 195.
8. This description, as well as many other details in this section, are drawn from Marianne Elliott, *Wolfe Tone*, p. 272.
9. Lecky, *History of Ireland*, iii, p. 497–8.
10. Tone, *Memoirs*, i, p. 198.
11. Ibid.
12. Drummond, *Autobiography*, p. 281.
13. Ibid., p. 282.
14. Ibid., pp. 286ff.
15. Ibid., pp. 289, 297.
16. Ibid., p. 283.
17. Ibid., p. 291.
18. Ibid.
19. Ibid., p. 290.
20. Stewart, *A Deeper Silence*, p. 133.

21. Maria Edgeworth, *Ormond*, p. 211.
22. Chart, *Drennan Letters*, p. 231.
23. Ibid.
24. Ibid., p. 230.
25. 'Erin', in Drennan, *Glendalloch*.
26. *Parliamentary Register*, xvi (1796), p. 12.
27. Ibid., p. 43.
28. Ibid., p. 49.
29. Ibid., pp. 120–21.
30. Ibid., p. 148.
31. Ibid., p. 45.
32. Ibid., p. 18.
33. Ibid., p. 52.

12. FRENCH CONNECTIONS

1. Gerald Campbell, *Edward and Pamela Fitzgerald*, p. 107.
2. Quoted in Lecky, *History of Ireland*, iii, pp. 502–3.
3. Lecky, *History of Ireland*, iii, pp. 503–4, quoting Reinhard to De La Croix, 18 Prairal, 1 messador, an iv.–6, 9 June, 1796. F.F.O.; Elliott's *Partners in Revolution*, p. 101.
4. Louisa Conolly's letter to Emily in B. Mus. Addit. Mss. 30,990.
5. Tone, *Memoirs*, i, pp. 255; 295.
6. Ibid., p. 299.
7. Ibid., p. 286.
8. Ibid., p. 274.
9. Ibid., p. 214.
10. Ibid., pp. 218, 219, 221.
11. Ibid., p. 418.
12. Ibid., pp. 247–8.
13. Ibid., p. 250.
14. 'Letter 1' of Junius Redivivus in the *Morning Chronicle*, 27 November 1794.
15. Tone, *Memoirs*, i, p. 269.
16. Elliott, *Wolfe Tone*, p. 232.
17. Drummond, *Autobiography*, p. 299.
18. Ibid., p. 292.
19. Ibid., p. 298.
20. Ibid., p. 293.
21. Ibid., p. 294.
22. Ibid., pp. 295 ff.
23. Pelham Papers, B. Mus. Addit. Mss. 33,102.
24. Chart, *Drennan Letters*, p. 233.
25. Ibid., p. 232.
26. Ibid., pp. 235–6.
27. Ibid., p. 233.
28. William Drennan, *Fugitive Pieces*, pp. 87–94.

13. FAILURE OF AN INVASION

1. Moore, *Life and Death*, i, pp. 280–81. Moore was writing some thirty-two years after the event; I have not been able to trace this tale further back, but Moore would have been reluctant to tell anything unfounded to the discredit of his man.
2. Campbell, *Edward and Pamela Fitzgerald*, p. 108.
3. Elliott, *Partners in Revolution*, p. 139.
4. Campbell, *Edward and Pamela Fitzgerald*, p. 108.
5. Tone, *Memoirs*, ii, pp. 27–8.
6. Ibid., p. 20.
7. Ibid., p. 15.
8. Ibid., pp. 48–9.
9. Ibid., pp. 112–13.
10. Ibid., pp. 127–8.
11. Ibid., pp. 143–4.
12. Pelham Papers, B. Mus. Addit. Mss. 33,102.
13. Tone, *Memoirs*, ii, p. 155.
14. Apart from Tone's own *Memoirs*, I have drawn on Elliott's *Partners in Revolution* and E.H.S. Jones's *An Invasion that Failed* for the account of the expedition.
15. Tone, *Memoirs*, ii, p. 83.
16. *Northern Star*, from Monday 12 September to Friday 16 September 1796.
17. Fitzpatrick, *The Sham Squire*, p. 257.
18. Larkin, *Trial of William Drennan*, p. 8; Fitzpatrick, *The Sham Squire*, p. 254.
19. Chart, *Drennan Letters*, p. 241.
20. Ibid., p. 239.
21. Ibid., p. 238–9.
22. Ibid., p. 238.
23. Nancy J. Curtin, *The United Irishmen*, p. 122.
24. Chart, *Drennan Letters*, p. 243.
25. Howell, *State Trials*, xxvi, p. 447.
26. Drummond, *Autobiography*, p. 306.
27. Ibid., p. 307.
28. Nicolson, *A Desire to Please*, p. 167.
29. Ibid., p. 166.
30. Drummond, *Autobiography*, pp. 307ff.
31. Ibid., p. 337.

14. NORTHERN VIOLENCE

1. Tone, *Memoirs*, ii, p. 159.
2. Ibid., pp. 172–3.
3. Ibid., pp. 183–4.
4. Ibid., pp. 187–8.
5. Ibid., pp. 191–2.

Notes

6. Ibid., pp. 198–9.
7. Ibid., pp. 208–9.
8. Ibid., p. 168.
9. *Northern Star*, January 1798, quoted in Curtin, *United Irishmen*, p. 210.
10. Campbell, *Edward and Pamela Fitzgerald*, p. 115.
11. Ibid., p. 111.
12. Chart, *Drennan Letters*, p. 249.
13. Ibid., p. 247.
14. Ibid., p. 248.
15. Ibid., p. 257.
16. Ibid., p. 253.
17. Ibid., p. 255.
18. Curtin, *United Irishmen*, p. 112.
19. Edward Newell, 'The Life of Newell', in *The Mercenary Informers of 1798*, p. 19.
20. Mary McNeill, *The Life and Times of Mary Ann McCracken*, pp. 118–9.
21. Curtin, *United Irishmen*, p. 113.
22. Ibid., p. 82.
23. Public Record Office, H.O. 100/69/202–5.
24. Ibid., p. 249.
25. In 'Secret Committee of the Irish House of Lords', 2–3 May 1797; quoted in Sir John T. Gilbert (ed.), *Documents Relating to Ireland, 1785–1804*; also in Curtin, *United Irishmen*, p. 167.
26. R.R. Madden, *Literary Remains of the United Irishmen of 1798*, p. 72.
27. McDowell, *Ireland in the Age of Imperialism*, p. 533.
28. Ibid., p. 499.
29. Drummond, *Autobiography*, p. 313.
30. Ibid., pp. 302–5.
31. Ibid., p. 337.

15. VERGING TO REBELLION

1. B. Mus. Addit. Mss. 33,307 [Edward Cooke to Pelham].
2. B. Mus. Addit. Mss. 33,312 [Lord Camden to Pelham].
3. Campbell, *Edward and Pamela Fitzgerald*, p. 138.
4. Castlereagh, *Memoirs and Correspondence*, p. 271.
5. Public Record Office, H.O. 100/70/339.
6. Ibid., H.O. 100/70/339–48.
7. Ibid., H.O. 100/70/339.
8. Drummond, *Autobiography*, p. 317.
9. Ibid.
10. Ibid., p. 317–8.
11. Ibid., p. 320.
12. Ibid., p. 318.
13. Ibid., pp. 345–6.
14. Lecky, *History of Ireland*, iv, p. 107.

287

15. P.G. Curley, 'William Drennan and the young Samuel Ferguson: Liberty, Patriotism and Senses of Patriotism in Ulster Poetry between 1778 and 1848'.
16. Drennan, *Fugitive Pieces*.
17. A.T.Q. Stewart, *The Summer Soldiers: The 1798 Rebellion in Antrim and Down*, p. 31.
18. Tone, *Memoirs*, ii, p. 233.
19. Ibid., p. 232.
20. Ibid., p. 240.
21. Ibid., p. 262.
22. Ibid., pp. 268–9.
23. Ibid., p. 270.

16. PRELUDE TO THE '98

1. Tone, *Memoirs*, ii, pp. 428ff.
2. Ibid., p. 271.
3. Ibid., pp. 311–12.
4. Ibid., pp. 313–4.
5. Ibid., p. 319.
6. Howell, *State Trials*, xxvi, p. 1348.
7. Ibid., xxvii, p. 41.
8. Chart, *Drennan Letters*, p. 273.
9. Ibid., p. 274.
10. Ibid., p. 270.
11. Ibid.
12. Drummond, *Autobiography*, p. 323.
13. Moore, *Life and Death*, ii, p. 53.
14. Ibid., p. 54.
15. Ibid., p. 60.
16. Ibid., p. 69.
17. Ibid., p. 80.
18. Thomas Pakenham, *The Year of Liberty: The Story of the Great Irish Rebellion of 1798*, p. 93; Moore, *Life and Death*, ii, p. 84.

17. REBELS' ENDS

1. Moore, *Life and Death*, ii, p. 90.
2. R. Musgrave, *Memoirs of the Irish Rebellion of 1798*, p. 187.
3. Moore, *Life and Death*, ii, p. 104.
4. Ibid., pp. 136–7.
5. Lecky, *History of Ireland*, iv, p. 307.
6. Miscellaneous letters to Emily, B. Mus. Addit. Mss. 30,990.
7. SPOI, 620/51/239, quoted in Elliott, *Wolfe Tone*, p. 387.
8. Quoted in Elliott, *Wolfe Tone*, p. 389.
9. Howell, *State Trials*, xxvii, p. 616.
10. Ibid., p. 619.

11. Ibid., p. 621.
12. Lecky, *History of Ireland*, v, pp. 79–80.
13. Chart, *Drennan Letters*, p. 281.
14. Ibid., p. 281.
15. Ibid., p. 282.
16. William Drennan, 'Second Letter to the Rt Hon. William Pitt', p. 14.
17. Chart, *Drennan Letters*, p. 320.
18. Drennan, *Glendalloch*, p. xiv.
19. 'Irish Manuscripts in Philadelphia', *Analecta Hibernica*, xxxiii, pp. 215–16.
20. Quoted in Nicolson, *A Desire to Please*, p. 181.
21. Barrington, *Personal Sketches*, ii, p. 120.
22. Fitzpatrick, *The Sham Squire*, p. 287.
23. H. Elias and E.D. Finch, *Letters of Thomas Attwood Digges*, p. 626.
24. W.J. Fitzpatrick, *The Secret Service under Pitt*, p. 207.
25. *DNB*.
26. Fitzpatrick, *The Sham Squire*, p. 140.
27. R.R. Madden, *The United Irishmen, their Lives and Times*, 2nd series, i, p. 352.
28. *DNB* and Thomas Reynolds (ed.), *Life of Thomas Reynolds*.
29. Elliott, *Partners in Revolution*; Fitzpatrick, *Secret Service under Pitt*.

Bibliography

I have divided the bibliography into contemporary sources, i.e. published before 1820; and subsequent material.

CONTEMPORARY SOURCES

Annual Register (London, 1794–8).

Beauties of The Press: *With a Speech by Arthur O'Connor on the Catholic Question on May 4, 1795* (London, 1800).

Drennan, William, *Dissertatione de venaesectione in febribus continuis* (Edinburgh, 1778).

——, *Letters of Orellana: An Irish Helot* (Dublin, 1785).

——, *Essay on the Moral State of Ireland* (Dublin, 1797).

——, 'Second Letter to the Rt Hon. William Pitt' (Dublin, 1799).

——, *Fugitive Pieces* (Belfast, 1815).

——, *Glendalloch and Other Poems*, 2nd edn (Dublin, 1859).

Fitzgerald, Lord Edward, 'Letters to his Mother' 1796–8', B. Mus. Addit. Mss. 30,990.

Jackson, Revd William, *Sodom and Onan* (London, 1776; under pseudonym of Humphrey Nettle).

——, *Sermons on Practical and Important Subjects* (London, 1795).

[Belfast] *Northern Star* (1792–7).

Parliamentary Register of the Debates of the House of Commons of Ireland, xii–xvi (Dublin, 1793–6).

Proceedings against Simon Butler and Oliver Bond, House of Lords of Ireland (Dublin, 1793).

Pelham Papers [including Correspondence, etc.], edited by his son, B. Mus. Addit. Mss.

Public Record Office, H.O. 122/3 (Ireland, 1791–8).

Report from the Secret Committee of the House of Lords in Ireland (Dublin, 1793).

Report from the Committee of Secrecy of the House of Commons of Ireland (Dublin, 1798; 8145.d 49).

Sampson, William, *The Trial of the Rev. William Jackson for High Treason* (Dublin, 1795).

Tandy v. *Westmorland* ['Proceedings in certain Actions wherein James Napper
Tandy, Esq., was Plaintiff . . . Reported to the Society of United Irishmen of
the City of Dublin, 7 Dec. 1792] (Dublin, 1792).
Tone, Theobald Wolfe, *An Argument on Behalf of the Catholics of Ireland*, 5th edn
(Dublin, 1792).
——, *Memoirs*, ed. by his son, William Theobald Wolfe Tone (London, 1827).
—— et al., *Belmont Castle* (Dublin, 1790).
Walker's Hibernian Magazine: A Compendium of Entertaining Knowledge for 1795.

LATER PUBLISHED WORKS

Adams, J.R.R., *The Printed Word and the Common Man: Popular Culture in Ulster,
1700–1980* (Belfast, 1987).
Ball, F. Elrington, *The Judges in Ireland, 1221–1921* (London, 1926).
Barrington, Sir Jonah, *Personal Sketches of his Own Times*, 2 vols (London, 1827).
Bartlett, Thomas, 'An End to Moral Economy, the Irish Militia Disturbances of
1793', in *Past and Present*, xcix (1983).
——, 'Select Documents XXXVIII: Defenders and Defenderism in 1795', in *Irish
Historical Studies*, xxiv, 95 (1985).
Beckett, J.C., *The Making of Modern Ireland, 1603–1923* (London, 1981).
Beresford, J., *The Correspondence of the Rt Hon. John Beresford*, selected from his
original papers, and ed., with notes, by his grandson William, 2 vols (London,
1854).
Bickley, F. (ed.), *The Diaries of Sylvester Douglas, Lord Glenbervie* (London, 1928).
Birch, Revd Thomas Ledlie, *The Causes of the Rebellion in Ireland (1798)*, ed. Brendan
Clifford (Belfast, 1991).
Bowen, Elizabeth, *Bowen's Court*, 2nd edn (London, 1964).
Butterfield, Herbert, 'Eighteenth-century Ireland', in *Irish Historical Studies*, xv
(1965), p. 381.
Byrne, Miles, *Memoirs*, ed. by his widow, 2 vols (Dublin, 1907).
Campbell, Gerald, *Edward and Pamela Fitzgerald* (London, 1904).
Castlereagh, Robert, Lord, *Memoirs and Correspondence*, ed. by his brother, Charles
Vane, first Marquess of Londonderry, 12 vols (London, 1848).
Chart, D.A. (ed.), *The Drennan Letters* (HMSO, Belfast, 1931).
Corkery, Daniel, *The Hidden Ireland* (Dublin, 1956).
Cornwallis, Charles, *Correspondence of Charles, 1st Marquis Cornwallis*, ed. Charles
Ross, 3 vols (London, 1859).
Coughlin, R., *Napper Tandy* (Dublin, 1977).
Curley, P.G., 'William Drennan and the Young Samuel Ferguson: Liberty,
Patriotism and Senses of Patriotism in Ulster Poetry between 1778 and 1848'
(Queen's University of Belfast, 1987; Ph.D thesis).
Curran, William, *The Life of John Philpot Curran* (Edinburgh, 1822).
Curtin, Nancy J., 'Transformation of the Society of United Irishmen', in *Irish
Historical Studies*, xxiv, 95 (1985).
——, *The United Irishmen: Popular Politics in Ulster and Dublin, 1791–1798* (Oxford,
1994).

Daiches, David, Jones, Peter and Jones, Jean (eds), *A Hotbed of Genius: The Scottish Enlightenment* (Edinburgh, 1986).

De Latocnaye, J.L., trans. John Stevenson, *A Frenchman's Walk through Ireland, 1796–7* (Belfast, 1917).

Drummond, W.H. (ed.), *Autobiography of Archibald Hamilton Rowan, Esq.* (Dublin, 1840).

Dunlop, Robert, *Life of Henry Grattan* (London, 1889).

Durey, Michael, 'The Dublin Society of United Irishmen and the Politics of the Carey–Drennan Dispute, 1792–1794', in *The Historical Journal* (Cambridge, 1994).

Edgeworth, Maria, *Ormond* (1817; repr. Gloucester, 1990).

Ehrman, John, *The Younger Pitt*, 3 vols (London, 1984–96).

Elias, H. and Finch, E.D., *Letters of Thomas Attwood Digges, 1742–1821* (Columbia, 1982).

Elliott, Marianne, *Partners in Revolution* (London, 1982).

——, *Wolfe Tone, Prophet of Irish Independence* (London, 1989).

Falkiner, H.L., 'Lord Clare', in *Studies in Irish History and Biography* (London, 1902).

Fitzgerald, Brian (ed.), *Correspondence of Emily, Duchess of Leinster, 1731–1814*, 3 vols (Dublin, 1949–57).

Fitzpatrick, W.J., *The Sham Squire; and the Informers of 1798*, 3rd edn (Dublin, 1866).

——, *Ireland before the Union, with Revelations from the Unpublished Diary of Lord Clonmell* (Dublin, 1867).

——, *The Secret Service under Pitt*, 3rd edn (London, 1892).

Foster, R.F., *Modern Ireland* (London, 1988).

Franklin, Benjamin, *Papers of Benjamin Franklin*, 30 vols (Yale, 1959–93).

Furber, Holden, *Henry Dundas, First Viscount Melville* (Oxford, 1931).

Gilbert, Sir John T. (ed.), *Documents Relating to Ireland, 1795–1804* (Dublin, 1893).

Godwin, William, *Memoirs of the Author of A Vindication of the Rights of Women* (London, 1798).

Gough, Hugh and Dickson, David (eds), *Ireland and the French Revolution* (Dublin, 1990).

Hale, Leslie, *John Philpot Curran, his Life and Times* (London, 1958).

Hanley, Thomas O'Brien (ed.), *The John Carroll Papers*, 3 vols (Notre Dame, Ind., 1976).

Hardy, Francis, *Hardy's Life of the Earl of Charlemont*, 2nd edn, 2 vols (London, 1812).

Howell, T.B., *Collection of State Trials*, xxv–xxvii (London, 1818–20).

'Irish Manuscripts in Philadelphia', in *Analecta Hibermica*, xxxiii (Dublin, 1981).

Hutchison, W.R., *Tyrone Precinct* (Belfast, 1951).

Jacob, R., *The Rise of the United Irishmen* (Dublin, 1936).

Jones, E.H.S., *An Invasion that Failed* (Oxford, 1950).

Kavanagh, P.J., *Finding Connections* (London, 1990).

Kelly, James, *'That Damn'd Thing Called Honour': Duelling in Ireland, 1570–1860* (Cork, 1995).

——and Macgearailt, Uáitéar, 'Napper Tandy: Radical and Republican', in *Dublin and Dubliners* (Dublin, 1990).

Larkin, John, *The Trial of William Drennan, on a Trial for Sedition in the Year 1794* (Dublin, 1991).

Lecky, W.E.H., *A History of Ireland in the Eighteenth Century*, iii, iv (London, 1892; repr. 1909).

MacDermot, Frank, 'Arthur O'Donnor', in *Irish Historical Studies*, xv (1966).

——, *Theobald Wolfe Tone and his Times*, rev. edn (Tralee, 1969).

MacDonagh, Oliver, *States of Mind: A Study of Anglo-Irish Conflict, 1780–1980* (London, 1983).

MacDougall, Henry, *Sketches of Irish Political Characters of the Present Day* (Dublin, 1799).

McDowell, R.B., 'The Personnel of the Dublin Society of United Irishmen, 1791–94', in *Irish Historical Studies*, ii (1940–41), pp. 12–53.

——, 'Proceedings of the Dublin Society of United Irishmen', in *Analecta Hibernica*, xvii (Dublin, 1949).

——, *Ireland in the Age of Imperialism and Revolution, 1760–1801* (Oxford, 1979).

——(ed.), *The Correspondence of Edmund Burke, 1794–1796*, viii (Chicago, 1969).

——(ed.), *The Writings and Speeches of Edmund Burke*, IX: *Ireland* (Oxford, 1991).

McNally, Leonard, *Retaliation, A Farce* (London, 1782).

——, *Resolution of Volunteers Vindicated* (Dublin, 1782).

——, 'Fashionable Levities', in *Modern Theatre*, xi, selected by Mrs Inchbald (London, 1811).

McNeill, Mary, *The Life and Times of Mary Ann McCracken, 1770–1866: A Belfast Panorama* (Dublin, 1960).

——, *Little Tom Drennan* (Dublin, 1962).

MacNeven, W.J., *Pieces of Irish History* (New York, 1807).

MacNevin, T., *The Lives and Trials of A.H. Rowan etc.* (Dublin, 1846).

Madden, R.R., *The United Irishmen, their Lives and Times* (London, 1857–60).

——, *Ireland in '98: Sketches of the Principal Men of the Time*, ed. J. Bowes Daly (London, 1888).

——, *Literary Remains of the United Irishmen of 1798* (Dublin, 1887).

Malcolmson, A.W.P., *John Foster: The Politics of the Anglo-Irish Ascendancy* (Oxford, 1978).

Maxwell, C., *Dublin under the Georges* (London, 1936).

Moody, F.W. and Vaughan, W.E. (eds), *A New History of Ireland*, IV: *Eighteenth-century Ireland* (Oxford, 1986).

Moore, Thomas, *The Life and Death of Lord Edward Fitzgerald*, 3rd edn, 2 vols (London, 1832).

Morgan, Lady Sydney, *The O'Briens and the O'Flahertys: A National Tale*, 4 vols (Paris, 1828).

Musgrave, R., *Memoirs of the Irish Rebellion of 1798*, 4th edn, ed. S.W. Myers and D.E. McKnight (Fort Wayne, Ind., 1995).

Newell, Edward, 'The Life of Newell', written by himself, in *The Mercenary Informers of 1798* (London, 1846).

Nicolson, Harold, *A Desire to Please: A Story of Hamilton Rowan and the United Irishmen* (London, 1943).

O'Brien, Conor Cruise, *The Great Melody: A Thematic Biography and Commentated Anthology of Edmund Burke* (London, 1992).

O'Flanagan, J.R., *The Lives of the Lord Chancellors and Keepers of the Great Seal of Ireland*, 2 vols (London, 1870).

O'Higgins, Paul, *A Bibliography of Irish Trials and Other Legal Proceedings* (Abingdon, 1986).

Pakenham, Thomas, *The Year of Liberty: The Story of the Great Irish Rebellion of 1798* (London, 1969).

Phillips, Charles, *Curran and his Contemporaries* (London, 1856).

Rae, William Fraser, *Sheridan: A Biography*, 2 vols (London, 1896).

Reynolds, Thomas (ed.), *Life of Thomas Reynolds*, 2 vols, ed. by his son (London, 1839).

Rhodes, R. Crompton, *Harlequin Sheridan: The Man and the Legends* (Oxford, 1933).

Stewart, A.T.Q., 'A Stable Unseen Power: Dr William Drennan and the Origins of the United Irishmen', in *Essays Presented to Michael Roberts* (Belfast, 1976).

——, *A Deeper Silence: The Hidden Origins of the United Irish Movement* (London, 1993).

——, *The Summer Soldiers: The 1798 Rebellion in Antrim and Down* (Belfast, 1995).

Tillyard, Stella, *Aristocrats: Caroline, Emily, Louisa and Sarah Lennox, 1740–1832* (London, 1994).

Walsh, J.E., *Sketches of Ireland Sixty Years Ago* (Dublin, 1847).

Woods, C.J. (ed.), *Journals and Memoirs of Thomas Russell* (Dublin, 1991).

Index

Abercorn, John James Hamilton, 1st Marquis of, 261

Abercromby, General Sir Ralph, 8, 270

Adams, John Quincy, 157

Adet, Pierre, 173, 175, 177

agrarian unrest, 114–15

Ainslie, George Robert, 263

Aliens Act (USA, 1798), 245

Altona, 261

American War of Independence, 7, 9, 12–13, 30, 45, 54, 56–7, 239, 273

Anacreon (ship), 18

Anglo-Irish *see* Ascendancy (Anglo-Irish)

Annual Register, 80

Anti-Jacobin (journal): mocks Moira, 8n

Aristogeiton, 184

Ascendancy (Anglo-Irish): nature of, 3; fears of reform, 53; Rowan's hatred of, 61; Fitzgibbon idealizes, 66; Tone's antipathy to, 66, 113; and maintenance of English connection, 74; and moves for Catholic relief, 97; and social class, 146; and Fitzwilliam's Viceroyalty, 161

Auckland, William Eden, 1st Baron, 5

Austria: sues for peace (1797), 215

Avonmore, 1st Viscount *see* Yelverton, Barry

Azores, 35, 213

Ball, F. Elrington, 61n

Ballinasloe (Co. Galway), 92

Bank of England: suspends Irish cash payments, 221

Bantry Bay: attempted French landing (1796), 15, 51, 203–4, 206, 238

Barclay, Robert, 231

Barrington, Sir Jonah, 38, 48

Barthélemy, François, Marquis de, 186, 198–9

Bartlett, Thomas, 171n

Basle, 186, 198–9

Bath, William Pulteney, Earl of, 125n

Behn, Aphra: *Oronooko*, 30n

Belfast: republicanism in, 59–60; Tone meets Russell in, 158; unrest in, 219–20

Belfast Academical Institution, 259

Belfast First Volunteer Company, 12

Belfast Magazine, 259

Belfast Newsletter, 30

Belfast Society of United Irishmen, 57, 59, 91

Belfast Telegraph, 273

Bellew, Sir Edward, 209

Beresford family, 16, 148

Beresford, John: warns of Catholic antipathy to England, 5; and Fitzwilliam's Viceroyalty, 17, 132n, 161, 163; and English connection, 74; on Catholics and Dissenters, 84; and Tone's confession, 132, 134–5

Beresford, Marcus, 132, 135

Blake, William, 84

Blue Company of Volunteers (Belfast), 13

Bolivar, Simon, 264

Bond, Oliver, 104–5, 107, 120, 128, 247–8

Boruwlaski, Count (dwarf), 2n

Braughall, Thomas, 92

Bruce, Revd William, 53 & n

Bruix, Vice-Admiral Eustache, 202

Brunswick, Karl Wilhelm Friedrich, Duke of, 92

Buckingham, George Nugent-Temple-Grenville, 1st Marquis of, 163

Burke, Captain, 172

Burke, Edmund, 60, 148, 162, 165, 197, 213

Burke, Richard (Edmund's son): death, 213

Burrowes, Peter, 132–4, 150

Butler, Simon: chairs United Irishmen meetings, 41, 61, 65, 104; takes Drennan's 'Test', 58; Fitzgibbon attacks, 66; represents Tandy in

Index

A0001500050883